reading research

ANTHOLOGY
The Why? of Reading Instruction

CŎRE CONSORTIUM ON READING EXCELLENCE, INC.

ARENA PRESS *Novato · California*

ARENA PRESS
20 Commercial Boulevard
Novato, California 94949-6191
1-800-422-7249

CONSORTIUM ON READING EXCELLENCE, INC. (CORE)
1-888-249-6155

International Standard Book Number: 1-57128-121-5

8 7 6 5 4 3 2 1 0 9

1 0 9 8 7 6 5 4 3

 This icon indicates where a photograph or illustration was used in the original publication.

CREDITS

Project Manager: Linda Gutlohn
Book and Cover Design: Lucy Nielsen
Permissions Editor: Teresa McDermott
Special acknowledgment is given to Rick Brownell at Arena Press

ACKNOWLEDGMENTS

For each of the selections listed below, grateful acknowledgment is made for permission to adapt and/or reprint original or copyrighted material as follows:

American Association of School Administrators: "Reading the Right Way," by Bill Honig, in *The School Administrator* September 1997 issue. Copyright ©1997 by the American Association of School Administrators. Reprinted by permission of the publisher.

American Educational Research Association: Excerpted from "A Cognitive Theory of Orthographic Transitioning: Predictable Errors in How Spanish-Speaking Children Spell English Words," by Olatokunbo S. Fashola, Priscilla A. Drum et al., from *American Educational Research Journal*, Vol. 33, No. 4, Winter 1996 issue. Copyright ©1996 by the American Educational Research Association. Reprinted by permission of the publisher.

American Federation of Teachers: "The Role of Decoding in Learning to Read," by Isabel L. Beck and Connie Juel. Page layouts reprinted with permission from the Summer 1995 issue of *American Educator*, the quarterly journal of the American Federation of Teachers.

American Psychological Association: Excerpted from "Cross-Language Transfer of Phonological Awareness," by Aydin Y. Durgunoğlu, William E. Nagy, and Barbara J. Hancin-Bhatt, in *Journal of Educational Psychology*, Vol. 85, No. 3. Copyright ©1993 by the American Psychological Association. Reprinted by permission of the publisher.

The Baltimore Sun: "The Brain Reads Sound by Sound," by Kathy Lally and Debbie M. Price, from *Reading by 9: Part Two*. Copyright ©1997 by The Baltimore Sun. Reprinted by permission of the publisher.

International Reading Association: "Romance and Reality," by Keith Stanovich, in *The Reading Teacher*, Vol. 47, No. 4, December 1993/January 1994 issue. Copyright © 1993 by the International Reading Association. Reprinted by permission of Keith Stanovich and the International Reading Association. All rights reserved. "The Reader, the Text, and the Task: Learning Words in First Grade," by Francine Johnston, from *The Reading Teacher*, Vol. 51, No. 8, May 1998 issue. Copyright ©1998 by the International Reading Association. Reprinted by permission of Francine Johnston and the International Reading Association. All rights reserved. "The Role of Decoding in Learning to Read," by Isabel L. Beck and Connie Juel from *What Research Has to Say About Reading Instruction*, edited by S. Jay Samuels and Alan E. Farstrup. Copyright ©1992 by the International Reading Association. Reprinted by permission of Isabel L. Beck and the International Reading Association. All rights reserved. "Interactive Writing in a Primary Classroom," by Kathryn Button, Margaret J. Johnson and Paige Furgerson, in *The Reading Teacher*, Vol. 49, No. 6, March 1996 issue. Copyright ©1996 by the International Reading Association. Reprinted by permission of Kathryn Button and the International Reading Association. All rights reserved. "Vocabulary Teaching and Learning in a Seventh-Grade Literature-Based Classroom," by Janis M. Harmon, in *Journal of Adolescent & Adult Literacy*, Vol. 41, No. 7, April 1998 issue. Copyright ©1998 by the Interna-tional Reading Association. Reprinted by permission of Janis M. Harmon and the International Reading Association. All rights reserved. "Learning with Text in the Primary Grades," by Andrea M. Guillaume, from *The Reading Teacher*, Vol. 51, No. 6, March 1998 issue. Copyright © 1998 by the International Reading Association. Reprinted by permission of Andrea M. Guillaume and the International Reading Association. All rights reserved. "Engaging with Reading Through Interactive Read-Alouds," by Shelby J. Barrentine, in *The Reading Teacher*, Vol. 50, No. 1, September 1996 issue. Copyright ©1996 by the International Reading Association. Reprinted by permission of Shelby J. Barrentine and the International Reading Association. All rights reserved. "Research Foundations to Support Wide Reading," by Richard C. Anderson, excerpted from *Promoting Reading in Developing Countries*, edited by V. Greany. Copyright ©1996 by the International Reading Association. Reprinted by permission of Richard C. Anderson and the International Reading Association. All rights reserved. "Diverse Learners and the Tyranny of Time: Don't Fix Blame; Fix the Leaky Roof," by Edward J. Kameenui, from *The Reading Teacher*, vol. 46, no. 5, February 1993. Copyright ©1993 by the International Reading Association. Reprinted by permission of Edward J. Kameenui and the International Reading Association. All rights reserved.

(Continued on page 226)

CONTENTS

SECTION I

The Big Picture

 Reading the Right Way

 Statement of Dr. G. Reid Lyon

 Romance and Reality

 The Brain Reads Sound by Sound

Reading the Right Way

What research and best practices say about eliminating failure among beginning readers

T eaching children to read is the key to subsequent educational success and should be the most important priority of elementary school.

Yet in many inner-city, suburban and rural schools, large and growing numbers of children are reaching upper elementary levels unable to read and understand grade-appropriate material—as many as 70 to 80 percent in some inner-city schools and 30 percent in some suburban schools. The magnitude of this problem causes not only innumerable personal tragedies but also significantly drives instruction down and jeopardizes the future of our public schools.

What is most frustrating is that much of this reading failure could be prevented if schools just applied what is known about beginning reading instruction. While the field of reading seems mired in contentious debate—principally pitting phonics against whole language as the best instructional approach—a powerful and persuasive consensus has developed among educational, cognitive and medical researchers, as well as our best teachers, about the causes and cures of reading failure.

Ripe for Improvement

These ideas have been successfully implemented in thousands of classrooms in diverse settings with spectacular results. They draw from the whole language movement but also include organized skill development components such as phonemic awareness, phonics and decoding. As such, effective reading programs use elements from both traditions that have proven successful while discarding those that have proven ineffective.

Although this comprehensive approach is not driving reading instruction in most classrooms, teachers are hungry for information about specifics and willing to apply them in their classrooms and schools. Reading instruction is ripe for improvement because teachers daily face children who are not learning to read, and they realize a gap in instruction exists. In such situations, administrative leadership is crucial.

Before change can occur, administrators need a detailed knowledge of the reading process so they don't get taken in by specious advice.

Although for most children the reading battle is lost in kindergarten and 1st grade, the best place to begin the search for remedies is to observe students who have difficulty reading in upper grades. In the course of working with school districts nationwide to improve reading performance, I have asked more than 10,000 teachers to describe such students. They uniformly state (consistent with the research) that reading-deficient children in the upper primary grades exhibit:

- poor decoding skills (students struggle with too many individual words and don't know how to effectively tackle a new word);
- weak vocabulary;
- the inability to read strategically and actively;
- poor spelling;
- too few reading opportunities outside of school; and
- poor motivation, lack of confidence or avoidance behavior, all stemming from experiencing too much reading failure.

Rule of Thumb

Recent research has developed a powerful explanatory theory of why poor readers exhibit these behaviors. The theory is based on the two ways that proficient readers gain meaning from text: (1) from the *word*—the vocabulary concept underlying an individual word and (2) from the *passage*—from stringing those words together and thinking about their meaning.

This research shows that in proficient reading, word recognition is primarily an automatic, unconscious and rapid process. Conversely, passage understanding is primarily an active, engaged, thinking process of weaving individual words into a meaningful whole, thinking about what the author is saying and connecting it to other ideas.

If readers take too much time and mental effort decoding individual words, they can't attend to passage meaning. The rule of thumb is this: A student should recognize 18 or 19 out of 20 words automatically or reading comprehension suffers, a construct referred to as automaticity. Additionally, by sixth grade if students are reading below 100

to 120 words a minute, they probably cannot attend to meaning properly. The 1992 National Assessment of Educational Progress showed that more than 40 percent of American 4th-graders read too slowly to understand what they were reading.

A balanced reading program should include strategies to develop both automatic word recognition *and* passage comprehension. Many reading programs used in schools fall short of this balanced approach. They de-emphasize the word side and the tools by which students become automatic with a growing number of words and over-rely on the passage side. These inadequate programs are based on the theory that the arduous instructional task of developing word recognition skills for many children can be avoided or minimized because the passage can supply word meaning. Vast amounts of research and experience now dispute this view.

One strand of studies, focusing on computer eye research, has disposed of the claims that proficient readers skip a large number of words. Actually, studies suggest, they read virtually every word and see all the letters in each word. (Try skipping a *not* in expository text.)

Other studies show that using context can help decode words only about 10 to 25 percent of the time and this rate is too slow for fluency. It is the poorer readers who rely on context-based decoding strategies. Finally, studies have demonstrated that using indirect methods first (such as context) and waiting to directly instruct those who fail to intuit the alphabetic system significantly decreases the odds that those struggling students will learn to read properly.

In 1st grade, recognizing individual words contributes about 80 percent of meaning. (The words and concepts of the story are simple and if the words are recognized the meaning of the story is apparent.) In later grades, other factors increase in importance such as strategic reading ability or the ability to discuss

10 Components for a Comprehensive Reading Strategy

A strong consensus has developed on the program components necessary to reduce reading failure and improve reading performance among students. No single program will suffice, but literature on the best practices in reading instruction points to 10 major interventions, all of which must be effectively organized and integrated in an elementary reading program if that school is to reach the standard that 85 to 90 percent of students can read grade-appropriate material from the end of first grade on.

The absence or ineffectiveness of any one of these components will lower the number of students who can handle grade-appropriate materials. Thus it is the cumulative effect of these elements that produces high literacy rates in a school. Some of these strands are ongoing: some are appropriate for a particular time.

No. 1: A pre-K to fifth grade (or ending elementary grade level) oral language program in which children read to a little above their reading level and ideas are discussed.

No. 2: A kindergarten to fifth grade writing program stressing both narrative and expository writing, which uses accepted rubrics (telling a story, organizing a report, arguing a point, etc.) and

writing as a means of discussing important ideas.

Decoding Tools

No. 3: Teaching each child to phonologically decode. Equipping each student with this tool (preferably by mid-first grade) requires:

● A kindergarten skills development program of basic phonemic awareness (hearing and manipulating sounds in spoken words), upper and lower-case letter recognition and concepts in print, especially recognizing a word in print. A supplemental phonemic awareness program is needed for those children not making progress by mid-kindergarten.

● A late-kindergarten/first-grade strand of organized and systematic phonics to teach students how the alphabetic system works. This strand should include enough of the letter/sound correspondence system to allow students to become automatic with a sufficient number of words. This phonics strand should also allow students to develop some proficiency in word attack skills (sounding out, seeing common letter patterns, seeing parts of words and generating and selecting from legitimate alternative pronunciations) to start to read beginning materials independently in which only about one in 20 words needs

to be figured out. It also should use decodable text to practice and perfect the recognition of words based on the patterns being taught and the use of spelling and word-building activities.

Most children should be able to read and understand non-predictable beginning materials by mid-first grade—some will require more time, others will have mastered these skills to be reading (not pretend reading) by late kindergarten. Continued support of enhancing these skills during late first and second grade also should be provided.

No. 4: An ongoing diagnostic assessment and intervention component to know which children are progressing and which need more intensive instruction. (Students who have learned to decode will get 18, 19 or 20 words right on a mid-first grade standard decoding test of simple pseudo-words, while students who don't understand the alphabetic system will get none, one or two right.) A tutoring or intervention program can assist students in kindergarten, first and later grades who, after intensified assistance by the teacher, still are not making proper progress.

No. 5: An independent reading program that gets students to read simple trade books in first grade and approximately 25 to 35 narrative and informational books a what has been read, but recognizing individual words still remains crucial to reading for understanding.

Decoding Skills
Becoming automatic with a growing number of words depends on knowing how to use the alphabetic system to decode words. (Decoding is the ability to read through a word from left to right, generate the sounds that are connected to all the letters or letter patterns in that word and manipulate those sounds until they connect to a word in the student's speaking vocabulary). This finding is one of the most validated in reading research and equipping each child with the ability to decode simple words should be a major goal of kindergarten and early 1st-grade reading instruction.

First-grade decoding ability predicts 80 to 90 percent of reading comprehension in 2nd and 3rd grade and still accounts for nearly 40 percent of reading comprehension by 9th grade!

Why should the ability to sound out a pseudo-word like *mot* in mid-1st grade and *lote* or *blar* by late 1st be so predictive of later reading ability? (A pseudo-word assures that the child has not seen and memorized the word and so is a true test of decoding ability.) The reason has to do with storing words efficiently in memory for subsequent rapid retrieval.

Thoroughly decoding a word the first few times it is read forces a reader to connect information about the unique pattern of each of the letter/sound combinations to the meaning of the word. When a word is read, the letters of the word are stored in one part of the brain, the sounds in another and the meaning of the word in another so it is necessary to establish neural connections among these parts. Subsequent successful readings strengthen these mental connec-

tions and quicken the retrieval process until it occurs automatically. Additionally, early readers who want to read for meaning independently need a strategy for figuring out words that they have not yet seen in print.

Theories that questioned the importance of alphabetic decoding of individual words have not withstood scientific and empirical scrutiny. Furthermore, the children's inability to figure out the sounds of printed words is implicated in most cases of reading deficiency. Compared to full alphabetic screening of a word, no other method produces fast enough retrieval for the huge numbers of words in English—there are too many words to memorize without using the generative nature of the alphabetic system. Contextual cues are essential for increasing

year beginning in second grade. Fifth grade elementary students need to read over a million words of text outside school assignments (approximately 20 minutes a night, four nights a week) to learn enough vocabulary words to stay grade-appropriate readers.

Discussion Opportunities
No. 6: An advanced skill development support in syllabication, word roots, fluency, more complex letter sound correspondences and mechanics from second grade on.

No 7: A comprehension development program that includes (1) teaching strategic reading, especially for expository text (emphasized in third through fifth) and (2) discussion or book club groups.

No. 8: Vocabulary instruction in word webs, word choice and word histories.

No 9: A developmental (linguistically based) spelling program starting in late first or early second grade.

No. 10: Parents and community involvement that encourages reading to children, having children read to them and turning off the TV for a nightly reading period.

Diagnostics, Too
This comprehensive, strategic approach has several implications.

In early primary grades it is important that enough time for both skill and language-rich activities be allocated (at least

two to three hours a day, including reading in the subject matter areas in early primary). Schools must purchase a mix of good literature (both narrative and informational text), predictable text and decodable text and ensure that the support programs, such as Chapter 1 and tutoring, are integrated into teaching reading right from the start.

This strategy also requires a diagnostic

approach. Programs should allow for some skill grouping because such groups are essential for diagnostic teaching and children learn the alphabetic principle at different rates.

You need to know which children are making satisfactory progress and which are not and do something to correct the deficiencies quickly.

—*Bill Honig*

Dealing with Non-English-Speaking Learners

Some educators question whether young students who are learning to speak English also can be taught to read in English and can profit by phonemic awareness, phonics and decoding instruction in kindergarten and first grade.

The pedagogical argument against skills instruction is that these children are so overwhelmed by learning English that teaching them phonics will be confusing and interfere with their oral language learning. Consequently, many school programs for second-language learners are strong on oral language development but weak on reading skills.

A large body of evidence now refutes this hypothesis. The research shows that kindergarten and first grade children benefit tremendously by skills instruction. By neglecting these skills, many will not learn to read well and will be deprived of the very tool (fluent reading) that will enable them to build their English vocabulary.

Development Classes

In English language development classes or sheltered English classes, students can learn to decode in about the same time as English-speaking children (perhaps lagging a month or two) because even limited oral vocabularies are enough to teach the alphabetic principle.

As such, they are much like children who come from extremely low socio-economic conditions. Both groups have limited English oral vocabularies but are taught to read in first grade by teachers using the best practices described here.

One added component is necessary for these children: Teachers must ascertain if the child knows the meaning of the word being decoded since decoding and becoming automatic with that word requires connecting letters, sounds and the meaning of the word.

A recent series of studies (which can be obtained from Dale Willows, School of Education, Ontario Institute of Studies in Education, 252 Bloor Street West, Toronto, Ontario, Canada M5S 1V6) have shown that contrary to the prevailing dogma, second-language students who receive decoding early do just as well as English speakers who receive the same training in learning to read in English,

and they significantly outperform English speakers who do not receive such instruction. Second-language learners who do not receive skill instruction lag way behind the other three groups—another example of the harm that neglect or indirection does for our most vulnerable children.

Bilingual Programs

In Latin America, Spain and the most effective bilingual programs in the United States, beginning reading is now incorporating specific instruction in phonemic awareness, phonics and decoding since Spanish also is an alphabetic system. Spanish traditionally has been taught using syllables—*ma, me, mi, mo, mu, ba, be, bi*, etc. Since Spanish has only a limited number of syllables and they are short and regular, many students can learn to read by memorizing the syllables, reading and intuiting the alphabetic system.

However, even in Spanish many children are hampered by low levels of phonemic awareness and an incomplete understanding of how sound maps to print. They, too, will be helped by decoding instruction. A good bilingual program using these techniques should have almost all children actually reading simple materials and cracking the code by late kindergarten.

Many new bilingual materials contain these decoding strategies, while others have not budged from relying solely on the more traditional syllable-driven instructional strategy.

One weak part of bilingual programs is the absence of a transition strategy. Many programs move students into third and fourth grade just when English materials begin to contain large numbers of new words not in the student's speaking vocabulary and more complex linguistic patterns. Many English-speaking students who have not reached basic fluency by the end of third grade go into a fourth-grade slump because they flounder with too many basic words.

Similarly, many bilingual students who have not had a strong English-as-a-second-language component starting in the early grades and have not become automatic in print with a core group of English words have an extremely difficult year when they transition. These students are forced to do double duty be simultaneously trying to learn to read basic words while struggling with the huge number of new words appearing in text that are not in their speaking vocabulary. Reading scores of many students who read well in Spanish plummet during their transition years because of the lack of proper preparation to read in English.

—*Bill Honig*

vocabulary, resolving ambiguity in decoded words or confirming a decoded word ("Does it make sense or does it sound right?"). But context-driven decoding even if aided by partial alphabetic clues is too slow and unreliable to serve as a fluent decoding tool.

For example, a recent large-scale study in New Zealand found that 1st-graders who use sounding-out strategies for new words as opposed to context-based strategies (skipping the word, reading to the end of the sentence etc.) read significantly better in 2nd and 3rd grades than do poorer and second-language learners. These more vulnerable children tended to use the less-effective context-based method.

Extensive research and practical experience has demonstrated that learning to read does not come as naturally to most children as learning to speak does. It needs to be taught. As many as 50 percent of children will intuit the alphabetic system from the instructional strategies now in vogue—exposure to print and print activities and mini-lessons in the context of reading a story. However, many students need an organized program that teaches phonemic awareness, letter sound correspondences and decoding skills to learn to read. This need is especially true of the dyslexic, low socioeconomic and second-language children who fail under our present emphasis on indirect strategies.

Moreover, many 1st-grade students may seem to be progressing because they are memorizing words. Yet many remain unable to decode words and will subsequently suffer reading problems. Thus, every student needs to be evaluated to determine if he or she understands and can use the alphabetic system. Finally, almost all students' learning will be accelerated or consolidated by helping them understand the alphabetic system.

Decoding ability, vocabulary level and spelling are extremely highly correlated with reading comprehension. Pedagogically, they are connected. The best method for building vocabulary is to read extensively, and children cannot read extensively, especially when text becomes conceptually and structurally more difficult in 3rd and 4th grade, unless they have become automatic with a large number of words and proficient at decoding and learning new words. Similarly, learning spelling patterns helps accelerate decoding and developing automaticity with written words.

A vast amount of research also has shown that learning decoding and independent reading of simple non-predictive text in 1st grade is developmentally appropriate. (Approximately 95 percent of children are mature enough to learn basic phonemic awareness and letter recognition in kindergarten and phonics and decoding in 1st grade.) These studies also found that if students are not taught these skills early, most will never recover. Only one out of eight children reading below grade level by the end of 1st grade will ever read grade-appropriate materials, though expensive and well-designed intervention can beat these odds.

Decoding gives students a sense of success, confidence and independence in figuring out and remembering a new word. This independence leads to real, not pretend, reading: Students know they can look at a previously unread simple text and read it. Non-decoders seldom experience this success and continually experience frustration in attempting to read.

Researchers estimate that nearly half of special education students would not need that expensive program if they were vowels) and the patterns of words using these sounds. They also master a core of high-frequency words and phonograms, how to map sounds to letter/letter patterns in sequence in written words (blending or sounding out) and how to apply this knowledge in figuring out a word that has not been read before but is in the student's speaking vocabulary.

Many students figure out how to sound out or blend after a few attempts; many others find this skill difficult and need several months to master this skill. In late 1st and 2nd grades, students need to extend their letter-sound knowledge to the more complex patterns and learn to use larger orthographic patterns when they sound out a word.

Four major deficiencies in reading instruction prevent students from learning how to decode:
● Nearly 20 percent of our students do not develop threshold levels of phonemic awareness in kindergarten. (This means they can not distinguish the discrete sounds in words and manipulate and sequence them, which is necessary to connect sounds and letters in words.) And, these children were not diagnosed and given assistance.
● Students were not taught enough about the main letter/sound correspondences and thus did not learn the alphabetic system.
● About a third of our students have

" ... in proficient reading, word recognition is primarily an automatic, unconscious and rapid process."

taught initially to read properly. Unfortunately, few schools make the ability to decode a primary objective in 1st grade, check to see which children can do it and then help the ones who can't.

Instructional Implications
To acquire the ability to decode a simple word by mid-1st grade, students must have reached basic levels of phonemic awareness (the ability to hear and manipulate the sounds in spoken words), recognize letters and have acquired basic concepts in print, preferably by the end of kindergarten. Then, by mid-1st grade, they learn about half of the basic letter/sound correspondences (at least the consonants and short vowels and a smattering of blends, long vowels and more complex

difficulty in learning how to read through a word or how to sound it out and have not been taught how to do it.
● Students have not had the opportunity to practice reading a large number of words based on the beginning letter/sound patterns in text. As a result, they have not become automatic at recognizing those words.

Phonemic Awareness

One critical breakthrough in the reading field in the past decades is how important being able to hear and manipulate the discrete sound parts of words—phonemic awareness—is to learning to read. Most phonemic awareness is learned in the process of learning how print maps to sound in phonics instruction. However, threshold levels are necessary to learn phonics. If a child cannot tell what the last sound in *cat* is, that child is going to find it impossible to connect that sound with the written symbol *t* or to read through a word while keeping the letters and sounds in proper sequence.

Most children acquire basic phonemic awareness in kindergarten by such activities as rhyming and sound-word games. Unfortunately, about a sixth of our children have phonological wiring problems. Without assistance of about 12-14 hours (about 20 minutes a day) during the latter third of the kindergarten year, they will not acquire basic phonemic awareness. Many of these children end up in special education or Title I programs because they never were taught properly at the outset, and many others flounder with their reading problems remaining undetected. The implications are obvious—kindergarten programs must identify and assist those children who, without intervention, will have an extremely

difficult time learning to read.

One reason for the growth of the whole language movement was the reality that many children never seemed able to learn phonics and decoding. Educators naturally were inclined to find other ways for them to learn to read. As mentioned earlier, these other ways (predictions using context and first-letter cues) are too slow and inaccurate to replace phonological decoding, and teaching children to rely on them produced large numbers of poor readers. Now we know that one key reason why many of these students didn't learn to decode was that they could not hear and abstract the sounds. The obvious solution is to ensure that children are properly prepared to learn phonics and decoding.

Phonics Instruction

Most children need an organized program that directly teaches the basic consonant/vowel combinations and that follows principles of linguistic sequencing. Such a program introduces words based on short vowel patterns and simple consonants in early 1st grade and then follows with the more complicated vowel marker patterns (*e* controlled, *r* controlled and vowel combinations and consonant blends and digraphs, such as *ch*). Those basic high-frequency words that cannot be sounded out also need to be taught in some sequence.

The sound/symbol correspondences (and high-frequency words) must be practiced and reinforced extensively in connected or decodable text. These materials contain good stories but are designed to contain large numbers of words easy enough for children to read because they represent the patterns previously taught. For example, changing the gingerbread man with its difficult "g" sound to the pancake man, which reinforces short and long "a" sounds. The problem is this: Many materials in use for teaching reading in 1st grade are highly predictable in their vocabulary with too few decodable words. Thus, the materials are not effective for developing independent decoding skills. The opposite problem is no better; literature books that contain too many difficult words are too hard for many children beginning to read.

Finally, activities that allow students to spell and manipulate words by sorting, and changing them (change *sit* to *set* to *sat*) are an essential part of the curriculum for beginning readers. Just allowing students to play with the structure of words will help many students to understand the alphabetic principle.

Studies have shown that programs in-

corporating these elements (as well as reading to children, discussions and language-rich activities) are about twice as effective as the more indirect or unfocused methods now in wide use.

Massive Retraining

The other major reasons for the growth of whole language approaches that deemphasized decoding were the sterile, unproductive nature of much phonics instruction (worksheets and paucity of connected text), and the lack of motivational and authentic reading experiences accompanying skills instruction. The decoding instruction being advocated today is much more akin to a thinking phonics program that strives for understanding of the alphabetic principle and uses engaging activities to help students learn it.

Secondly, in the latest synthesis, decoding instruction is only part of a broader language arts curriculum that does stress reading to children, writing, shared reading activities and discussion of literature.

None of these ideas will be simple to implement. They call for the use of the right materials, restructuring of schools around these ideas and massive retraining of teachers. (A high percentage of those who have graduated from university teacher training programs in the past 10 years have minimal understanding of linguistics, spelling and teaching the alphabetic code.) Without aware and dedicated leadership, this problem will not be corrected. ∎

Bill Honig is author of *Teaching Our Children to Read: The Role of Skills in a Comprehensive Reading Program*, published by Corwin Press. He is visiting distinguished professor of education at San Francisco State University and president of the Consortium of Reading Excellence, 5500 Shellmound St., Suite 140, Emeryville, Calif. 94608. E-mail: Honig@sirius.com

From *The School Administrator,*
September 1997

Statement of Dr. G. Reid Lyon

April 28, 1998: Overview of Reading and Literacy Initiatives

Chief Child Development and Behavior Branch
National Institute of Child Health and Human Development
National Institutes of Health
9000 Rockville Pike, Bethesda, Maryland 20892
Committee on Labor and Human Resources
Room 428, Senate Dirksen Office Building, Washington, DC

am Dr. Reid Lyon, the Chief of the Child Development and Behavior Branch of the National Institute of Child Health and Human Development at the National Institutes of Health. I am pleased to have the opportunity to present to you information about the results of the extensive research that our Institute has supported on the process of learning to read in our nation's schools.

Chairman Jeffords and members of the committee, some children learn to read and write with ease. Even before they enter school, they have developed an understanding that the letters on a page can be sounded out to make words and some preschool children can even read words correctly that they have never seen before and comprehend what they have read. As Marilyn Adams has reported, before school, and without any great effort or pressure on the part of their parents, they pick up books, pencils, and paper, and they are on their way, almost as though by magic.

However, the magic of this effortless journey into the world of reading is available to only about 5% of our nation's children. It is suggested in the research literature that another 20% to 30% learn to read relatively easily once exposed to formal instruction, and it seems that youngsters in this group learn to read in any classroom, with any instructional emphasis.

Unfortunately, it appears that for about 60% of our nation's children, learning to read is a much more formidable challenge, and for at least 20% to 30% of these youngsters, reading is one of the most difficult tasks that they will have to master throughout their schooling. Why is this so unfortunate? Simply because if you do not learn to read and you live in America, you do not make it in life. Consider that reading skill serves as the major avenue to learning about other people, about history and social studies, the language arts, science, mathematics, and the other content subjects that must be mastered in school. When children do not learn to read, their general knowledge, their spelling and writing abilities, and their vocabulary development suffers in kind. Within this context, reading skill serves as the major foundational skill for all school-based learning, and without it, the chances for academic and occupational success are limited indeed. Because of its importance and visibility, particularly during the primary grades, difficulty learning to read squashes the excitement and love for learning that many youngsters enter school with. It is embarrassing and even devastating to read slowly and laboriously and to demonstrate this weakness in front of peers on a daily basis. It is clear from our NICHD-supported longitudinal studies that follow good and poor readers from kindergarten into young adulthood that our young poor readers are not used to such failure. By the end of the first grade, we begin to notice substantial decreases in the children's self-esteem, self-concept, and motivation to learn to read if they have not been able to master reading skills and keep up with their age-mates. As we follow the children through elementary and middle-school grades these problems compound, and in many cases very bright youngsters are unable to learn about the wonders of science, mathematics, literature, and the like because they can not read the grade-level textbooks. By high school, these children's potential for entering college has decreased to almost nil, with few choices available to them with respect to occupational and vocational opportunities. These individuals constantly tell us that they hate to read, primarily because it is such hard work, and their reading is so slow and laborious. As one adolescent in one of our longitudinal studies remarked recently, "I would rather have a root canal than read."

While failure to learn to read adequately is much more likely among poor children, among nonwhite children, and among nonnative speakers of English, recent data derived from the National Assessment of Educational Progress (1994) reveals an alarming trend. In the State of California, 59% of fourth grade children had little or no mastery of the knowledge and skills necessary to perform reading activities at the fourth grade level, compared to a national average of 44% below basic reading levels. Even more alarming is that this evidence of serious reading failure cuts across all ethnic and socioeconomic variables. While 71% of African-Americans, 81% of Hispanics, and 23% of Asians were reading below basic levels, 44% of white students in the fourth grade were also below the basic reading level necessary to use reading as a skill. Moreover, 49% of the fourth grade children in California who were reading below basic levels were from homes where the parents had graduated from college. In fact, the children of college-educated parents in California scored lowest with respect to their national cohort. These data underscore the fact that reading failure is a serious national problem and cannot simply be attributed to poverty, immigration, or the learning of English as a sec-

ond language. The psychological, social, and economic consequences of reading failure are legion.

It is for this reason that the National Institute of Child Health and Human Development (NICHD) within the National Institutes of Health (NIH) considers reading failure to reflect not only an educational problem, but a significant public health problem as well. Within this context, a large research network consisting of 41 research sites in North America, Europe, and Asia are working hard to identify (1) the critical environmental, experiential, cognitive, genetic, neurobiological, and instructional conditions that foster strong reading development; (2) the risk factors that predispose youngsters to reading failure; and (3) the instructional procedures that can be applied to ameliorate reading deficits at the earliest possible time. The NICHD has supported research to understand normal reading development and reading difficulties continuously since 1965. During the past 33 years, NICHD supported scientists have studied the reading development of 34,501 children and adults. Many studies have been devoted to understanding the normal reading process, and 21,860 good readers have participated in investigations, some for as long as 12 years. Significant effort has also been deployed to understand why many children do not learn to read. To address this critical question, 12,641 individuals with reading difficulties have been studied, many for as long as 12 years. In addition, since 1985, the NICHD has initiated studies designed to develop early identification methods that can pinpoint children during kindergarten and the first grade who are at-risk for reading failure. These studies have provided the foundation for several prevention and early intervention projects now underway at 11 sites in the U.S. and Canada. Since 1985, 7,669 children (including 1,423 good readers) have participated in these reading instruction studies, and 3,600 youngsters are currently enrolled in longitudinal early intervention studies in Texas, Washington, Georgia, Massachusetts, New York, Florida, Colorado, North Carolina, and Washington, D.C. These studies have involved the participation of 1,012 classroom teachers, working in 266 schools and 985 classrooms. (A summary of the NICHD Reading Research Program is included with this testimony.)

With this as background, my remaining testimony will focus on addressing several major questions that may be of interest to the Committee on Labor and Human Resources on the topic of Reading and Literacy Initiatives. These questions are:

1. How Do Children Learn to Read?

2. Why Do Some Children (and Adults) Have Difficulties Learning to Read?

3. For Which Children Are Which Teaching Approaches Most Beneficial at Which States of Reading Development?

How Do Children Learn to Read?
Understanding How Sounds Are Connected to Print

In general, learning to read the English language is not as easy as conventional wisdom would suggest. Every type of writing system, whether it be a syllabic system as used by the Japanese, a morphosyllabic system as used by the Chinese (where a written symbol represents a unit of meaning), or an alphabetic system that is used in English, Spanish, and Scandinavian languages (to name a few), present challenges to the beginning reader. For example, in an English alphabetic system, the individual letters on the page are abstract and meaningless, in and of themselves. They must eventually be linked to equally abstract sounds, called phonemes, blended together and pronounced as words, where meaning is finally realized. To learn to read English, the child must figure out the relationship between sounds and letters. Thus, the beginning reader must learn the

connections between the 40 or so sounds of spoken English (the phonemes) and the 26 letters of the alphabet. What our NICHD research has taught us is that in order for a beginning reader to learn how to connect or translate printed symbols (letters and letter patterns) into sound, the would-be reader must understand that our speech can be segmented or broken into small sounds (phoneme awareness) and that the segmented units of speech can be represented by printed forms (phonics). This understanding that written spellings systematically represent the phonemes of spoken words (termed the alphabetic principle) is absolutely necessary for the development of accurate and rapid word reading skills.

Why is phoneme awareness so critical for the beginning reader? Because if children cannot perceive the sounds in spoken words—for example, if they cannot "hear" the "at" sound in "fat" and "cat" and perceive that the difference lies in the first sound—they will have difficulty decoding or "sounding out" words in a rapid and accurate fashion. This awareness of the sound structure of our language seems so easy and commonplace that we take it for granted. But many children do not develop phoneme awareness, and for some interesting reasons that we are now beginning to understand. Unlike writing, the speech we use to communicate orally does not consist of separate sounds in words. For example, while a written word like "cat" has three letter-sound units, the ear hears only one sound, not three, when the word "cat" is spoken aloud. This merging and overlapping of sounds into a sound "bundle" makes oral communication much more efficient. Consider how long it would take to have a conversation if each of the words that we uttered were segmented or "chopped" into their sound structures. In essence we would be spelling aloud the words that we were speaking. From the NICHD studies that were initiated in 1965 to understand how the reading process develops, we now have strong evidence that it is not the ear that understands that a spoken word like "cat" is divided into three sounds and that these discrete sounds can be linked to the letters C-A-T, it is the brain that performs this function. In some youngsters, the brain seems to have an easy time processing this type of information. However, in many children, the skill is only learned with difficulty, and thus must be taught directly, explicitly, and by a well-trained and informed teacher. It has also become clear to us that the development of these critical early reading-related skills such as phoneme awareness and phonics are fostered when children are read to at home during the preschool years, when they learn their letter and number names, and when they are introduced at very early ages to concepts of print and literacy activities.

Does this mean that children who have a difficulty understanding that spoken words are composed of discrete individual sounds that can be linked to letters suffer from brain dysfunction or damage? Not at all. It simply means that the neural systems that perceive the phonemes in our language are less efficient than in other children. This difference in neural efficiency can also be hypothesized to underlie the individual differences that we see every day in learning any skill such as singing, playing an instrument, constructing a house, painting a portrait, and the like. In some cases, our NICHD studies have taught us that the phonological differences we see in good and poor readers have a genetic basis. In other children, the differences seem to be attributable to a lack of exposure to language patterns and literacy-based interactions and materials during the preschool years.

As pointed out, the development of phoneme awareness, the development of an understanding of the alphabetic principle, and the translation of these skills to the application of phonics in reading words are non-negotiable beginning reading skills that ALL children must master in order to understand what they read and to learn from their reading sessions. Printed letters and words are the basic data on which reading depends, and the emerging reader must be able to recognize accurately and quickly spelling patterns and their mappings to speech. To recapitulate, these skills are supported nicely when children receive an abundance of early literacy experiences in the home and in preschool. But the development of phoneme awareness and phonics, while necessary, are not sufficient for learning to read the English language so that meaning can be derived from print. In addition to learning how to "sound out" new and/or unfamiliar words, the beginning reader must eventually become proficient in reading, at a very fast pace, larger units of print such as syllable patterns, meaningful roots, suffixes, and whole words.

The Development of Reading Fluency

While the ability to read words accurately is a necessary skill in learning to read, the speed at which this is done becomes a critical factor in ensuring that children understand what they read. As one child recently remarked, "If you don't ride a bike fast enough, you fall off." Likewise, if the reader does not recognize words quickly enough, the meaning will be lost. Although the initial stages of reading for many students require the learning of phoneme awareness and phonics principles, substantial practice of those skills, and continual application of those skills in text, fluency and automaticity in decoding and word recognition must be acquired as well. Consider that a young reader (and even older readers for that matter) has only so much attentional capacity and cognitive energy to devote to a particular task. If the reading of the words on the page is slow and labored, readers simply cannot remember what they have read, much less relate the ideas they have read about to their own background knowledge. Children vary in the amount of practice that is required for fluency and automaticity in reading to occur. Some youngsters can read a word only once to recognize it again with greater speed; others need more than 20 or more exposures. The average child needs between four and 14 exposures to automatize the recognition of a new word. Therefore, in learning to read, it is vital that children read a large amount of text at their independent reading level (95% accuracy), and that the text format provide specific practice in the skills being learned.

Constructing Meaning from Print

The ultimate goal of reading instruction is to enable children to understand what they read. Again, the development of phoneme awareness, phonics skills, and the ability to read words fluently and automatically are necessary but not sufficient for the construction of meaning from text. The ability to understand what is read appears to be based on several factors. Children who comprehend well seem to be able to activate their relevant background knowledge when reading—that is, they can relate what is on the page to what they already know. Good comprehenders also have good vocabularies, since it is extremely difficult to understand something you cannot define. Good comprehenders also have a knack for summarizing, predicting, and clarifying what they have read, and frequently use questions to guide their understanding. Good comprehenders are also facile in employing the sentence structure within the text to enhance their comprehension.

In general, if children can read the words on a page accurately and fluently, they will be able to construct meaning at two levels. At the first level, literal understanding is achieved. However, constructing meaning requires far more than literal comprehension. Children must eventually guide themselves through text by asking questions like, "Why am I reading this and how does this information relate to my reasons for doing so?" "What is the author's point of view?" "Do I understand what the author is saying and why?" "Is the text internally consistent?" and so on. It is this second level of comprehension that leads readers to reflective, purposeful understanding.

The development of reading comprehension skills, like the development of phoneme awareness, phonics, and fluency, needs to be fostered by highly trained teachers. Recent research shows that the teacher must arrange for opportunities for students to discuss the highlights of what they have read and any difficulties they have had when reading. Because the grammatical structures of written text are more varied and complex than those of casual, oral language (speaking to one another), regular exploration and explicit instruction on formal syntax is warranted. Children's reflections on what they have read can also be directly fostered through instruction in comprehension strategies. These sorts of discussions and activities should be conducted throughout a range of literacy genres, both fiction and nonfiction, and should be a regular component of the language arts curriculum throughout the children's school years.

Other Factors That Influence Learning to Read

Our research continues to converge on the following findings. Good readers are phonemically aware and understand the alphabetic principle and can apply these skills to the development and application of phonics skills when reading words, and can accomplish these applications in a fluent and accurate manner. Given the ability to rapidly and automatically decode and recognize words, good readers bring strong vocabularies and good syntactic and grammatical skills to the reading comprehension process, and actively relate what is being read to their own background knowledge via a variety of strategies. But what factors can provide a firm foundation for these skills to develop?

It is clear from research on emerging literacy that learning to read is a relatively lengthy process that begins very early in development and clearly before children enter formal schooling. Children who receive stimulating literacy experiences from birth onward appear to have an edge when it comes to vocabulary development, an understanding of the goals of reading, and an awareness of print and literacy concepts. Children who are read to frequently at very young ages become exposed in interesting and exciting ways to the sounds of our language, to the concept of rhyming, and to other word and language play that serves to provide the foundation for the development of phoneme awareness. As children are exposed to literacy activities at young ages, they begin to recognize and discriminate letters. Without a doubt, children who have learned to recognize and print most letters as preschoolers will have less to learn upon school entry. The learning of letter names is also important because the names of many letters contain the sounds they most often represent, thus orienting youngsters early to the alphabetic principle, or how letters and sounds connect. Ultimately, children's ability to understand what they are reading is inextricably linked to their background knowledge. Very young children who are provided opportunities to learn, think, and talk about new areas of knowledge will gain much from the reading process. With understanding comes the clear desire to read more and to read frequently, ensuring that reading practice takes place.

Why Do Some Children (and Adults) Have Difficulties Learning to Read?

Difficulties learning to read result from a combination of factors. In general, children who are most at-risk for reading failure are those who enter school with limited exposure to language and who have little prior understanding of concepts related to phonemic sensitivity, letter knowledge, print awareness, the purposes of

reading, and general verbal skills, including vocabulary. Children raised in poverty, youngsters with limited proficiency in English, children with speech and hearing impairments, and children from homes where the parent's reading levels are low are relatively predisposed to reading failure. Likewise, youngsters with subaverage intellectual capabilities have difficulties learning to read, particularly in the reading comprehension domain. Given this general background, recent research has been able to identify and replicate findings which point to at least four factors that hinder reading development among children irrespective of their socioeconomic level and ethnicity. These four factors include deficits in phoneme awareness and the development of the alphabetic principle (and the accurate and fluent application of these skills to textual reading), deficits in acquiring reading comprehension strategies and applying them to the reading of text, the development and maintenance of motivation to learn to read, and the inadequate preparation of teachers.

Deficits in Phoneme Awareness and the Development of the Alphabetic Principle

In essence, children who have difficulties learning to read can be readily observed. The signs of such difficulty are a labored approach to decoding or "sounding" unknown or unfamiliar words and repeated misidentification of known words. Reading is hesitant and characterized by frequent starts and stops and multiple mispronunciations. If asked about the meaning of what has been read, the child frequently has little to say. Not because he or she is not smart enough—in fact, many youngsters who have difficulty learning to read are bright and motivated to learn to read, at least initially. Their poor comprehension occurs because they take far too long to read the words, leaving little energy for remembering and understanding what they have read.

Unfortunately, there is no way to bypass this decoding and word recognition stage of reading. A deficiency in these skills cannot be appreciably offset by using context to figure out the pronunciation of unknown words. In essence, while one learns to read for the fundamental purpose of deriving meaning from print, the key to comprehension starts with the immediate and accurate reading of words. In fact, difficulties in decoding and word recognition are at the core of most reading difficulties. To be sure, there are some children who can read words accurately and quickly yet do have difficulties comprehending, but they constitute a small portion of those with reading problems.

If the ability to gain meaning from print is dependent upon fast, accurate, and automatic decoding and word recognition, what factors hinder the acquisition of these basic reading skills? As mentioned above, young children who have a limited exposure to both oral language and print before they enter school are at-risk for reading failure. However, many children with robust oral language experience, average to above-intelligence, and frequent interactions with books since infancy show surprising difficulties learning to read. Why?

In contrast to good readers who understand that segmented units of speech can be linked to letters and letter patterns, poor readers have substantial difficulty developing this "alphabetic principle." The culprit appears to be a deficit in phoneme awareness—the understanding that words are made up of sound segments called phonemes. Difficulties in developing phoneme awareness can have genetic and neurobiological origins or can be attributable to a lack of exposure to language patterns and usage during the preschool years. The end result is the same, however. Children who lack phoneme awareness have difficulties linking speech sounds to letters—their decoding skills are labored and weak, resulting in extremely slow reading. This labored access to print renders comprehension impossible. Thus the purpose for reading is nullified because the children are too dysfluent to make sense out of what they read.

In studying approximately 34,501 children over the past 33 years, we have learned the following with respect to the role that phonemic awareness plays in the development of phonics skills and fluent and automatic word reading:

1. Phonemic awareness skills assessed in kindergarten and first grade serve as potent predictors of difficulties learning to read. We have learned how to measure phonemic awareness skills as early as the first semester in kindergarten with tasks that take only 15 minutes to administer—and over the past decade we have refined these tasks so that we can predict with approximately 80% to 90% accuracy who become good readers and who will have difficulties learning to read.

2. We have learned that the development of phonemic awareness is a necessary but not sufficient condition for learning to read. A child must integrate phonemic skills into the learning of phonics principles, must practice reading so that word recognition becomes rapid and accurate, and must learn how to actively use comprehension strategies to enhance meaning.

3. We have begun to understand how genetics are involved in learning to read, and this knowledge may ultimately contribute to our prevention efforts through the assessment of family reading histories.

4. We are entering very exciting frontiers in understanding how early brain development can provide a window on how reading develops. Likewise, we are conducting studies to help us understand how specific teaching methods change reading behavior and how the brain changes as reading develops.

5. We have learned that just as many girls as boys have difficulties learning to read. Until five years

ago, the conventional wisdom was that many more boys than girls had such difficulties. Now females should have equal access to screening and intervention programs.

6. We have learned that for 90% to 95% of poor readers, prevention and early intervention programs that combine instruction in phoneme awareness, phonics, fluency development, and reading comprehension strategies, provided by well-trained teachers, can increase reading skills to average reading levels. However, we have also learned that if we delay intervention until nine years of age (the time that most children with reading difficulties receive services), approximately 75% of the children will continue to have difficulties learning to read throughout high school. To be clear, while older children and adults can be taught to read, the time and expense of doing so is enormous.

Deficits in Acquiring Reading Comprehension Strategies

Some children encounter obstacles in learning to read because they do not derive meaning from the material that they read. In the later grades, higher-order comprehension skills become paramount for learning. Reading comprehension places significant demands on language comprehension and general verbal abilities. Constraints in these areas will typically limit comprehension. In a more specific vein, deficits in reading comprehension are related to: (1) inadequate understanding of the words used in the text; (2) inadequate background knowledge about the domains represented in the text; (3) a lack of familiarity with the semantic and syntactic structures that can help to predict the relationships between words; (4) a lack of knowledge about different writing conventions that are used to achieve different purposes via text (humor, explanation, dialogue, etc.); (5) verbal reasoning ability which enables

the reader to "read between the lines," and (6) the ability to remember verbal information.

If children are not provided early and consistent experiences that are explicitly designed to foster vocabulary development, background knowledge, the ability to detect and comprehend relationships among verbal concepts, and the ability to actively employ strategies to ensure understanding and retention of material, reading failure will occur no matter how robust word recognition skills are.

Our current understanding of how to develop many of these critical language and reasoning capabilities related to reading comprehension is not as well developed as the information related to phoneme awareness, phonics, and reading fluency. We have not yet obtained clear answers with respect to why some children have a difficult time learning vocabulary and how to improve vocabulary skills. Our knowledge about the causes and consequences of deficits in syntactical development is sparse. A good deal of excellent research has been conducted on the application of reading comprehension strategies, but our knowledge of how to teach children to apply these strategies in an independent manner and across contexts is just emerging.

The Development and Maintenance of Motivation to Learn to Read

A major factor that aids or limits the amount of improvement that a child may make in reading is highly related to their motivation to persist in learning to read despite difficulties. Very little is known with respect to the exact timing and course of motivational problems in reading development, but it is clear that reading failure has a devastating effect on children. In the primary grades, reading activities constitute the major portion of academic activities undertaken in classrooms, and children who struggle with reading are quickly noticed by peers and teachers.

Although most children enter formal schooling with positive attitudes and expectations for success, those who encounter difficulties learning to read clearly attempt to avoid engaging in reading behavior as early as the middle of the first grade year. It is known that successful reading development is predicated on practice in reading, and obviously the less a child practices, the less developed the various reading skills will become.

To counter these highly predictable declines in the motivation to learn to read, prevention and early intervention programs are critical.

Inadequate Preparation of Teachers

As evidence mounts that reading difficulties originate in large part from difficulties in developing phoneme awareness, phonics, reading fluency, and reading comprehension strategies, the need for informed instruction for the millions of children with insufficient reading skills is an increasingly urgent problem. Unfortunately, several recent studies and surveys of teacher knowledge about reading development and difficulties indicate that many teachers are underprepared to teach reading. Most teachers receive little formal instruction in reading development and disorders during either undergraduate and/or graduate studies, with the average teacher completing only two reading courses. Surveys of teachers taking these courses indicate: (1) teachers rarely have the opportunity to observe professors demonstrate instructional reading methods with children; (2) coursework is superficial and typically unrelated to teaching practice; and (3) the supervision of student teaching and practicum experiences is fragmentary and inconsistent. At present, motivated teachers are often left to obtain specific skills in teaching phonemic awareness, phonics, reading fluency, and comprehension on their own by seeking out workshops or specialized instructional manuals.

Teachers who instruct youngsters who display reading difficulties must be well versed in understanding the conditions that have to be present for children to develop robust reading skills. They also must be thoroughly trained to assess and identify children at-risk for reading failure at early ages. Unfortunately, many teachers and administrators have been caught between conflicting schools of thought about how to teach reading and how to help students who are not progressing easily. In reading education, teachers are frequently presented with a "one size fits all" philosophy that emphasizes either a "whole language" or "phonics" orientation to instruction. No doubt, this parochial type of preparation places many children at continued risk for reading failure, since it is well established that no reading program should be without all the major components of reading instruction (phoneme awareness, phonics, fluency, reading comprehension) and the real question is which children need what, how, for how long, with what type of teacher, and in what type of setting.

It is hard to find disagreement in the educational community that the direction and fabric of teacher education programs in language arts and reading must change. However, bringing about such change will be difficult. In addition, if teacher preparation in the area of language and reading is expected to become more thoughtful and systematic, changes in how teaching competencies and certification requirements are developed and implemented is a must. Currently, in many states, the certification offices within state departments of education do not maintain formal and collaborative relationships with academic departments within colleges of education. Thus, the requirements that a student may be expected to satisfy for a college degree may bear little relationship to the requirements for a teaching certificate. More alarming is the fact that both university and state department of education requirements for the teaching of reading may not reflect, in any way, the type and depth of knowledge that teachers must have to ensure literacy for all.

For Which Children Are Which Teaching Approaches Most Beneficial at Which Stages of Reading Development?

1. Learning to read is a lengthy and difficult process for many children, and success in learning to read is based in large part on developing language and literacy-related skills very early in life. A massive effort needs to be undertaken to inform parents and the educational and medical communities of the need to involve children in reading from the first days of life—to engage children in playing with language through nursery rhymes, storybooks, and writing activities; to bring to children as early as possible experiences that help them understand the purposes of reading, and the wonder and joy that can be derived from reading. Parents must become intimately aware of the importance of vocabulary development and the use of verbal interactions with their youngsters to enhance grammar, syntax, and verbal reasoning.

2. Young preschool children should be encouraged to learn the letters of the alphabet, to discriminate letters from one another, to print letters, and to attempt to spell words that they hear. By introducing young children to print, their exposure to the purposes of reading and writing will increase and their knowledge of the conventions of print and their awareness of print concepts will increase.

3. Reading out loud to children is a proven activity for developing vocabulary growth and language expansion, and plays a causal role in developing both receptive and expressive language capabilities. Reading out loud can also be used to enhance children's background knowledge of new concepts that may appear in both oral and written language.

4. Our NICHD prevention and early intervention studies in Houston, Tallahassee, Albany, Syracuse, Atlanta, Boston, Seattle, and Washington, D.C., all speak to the importance of early identification and intervention with children at-risk for reading failure. Procedures now exist to identify such children with good accuracy. This information needs to be widely disseminated to schools, teachers, and parents.

5. Kindergarten programs should be designed so that all children will develop the prerequisite phonological, vocabulary, and early reading skills necessary for success in the first grade. All children should acquire the ability to recognize and print both upper- and lowercase letters with reasonable ease and accuracy, develop familiarity with the basic purposes and mechanisms of reading and writing, and develop age-appropriate language comprehension skills.

6. Beginning reading programs should be constructed to ensure that adequate instructional time is allotted to the teaching of phonemic awareness skills, phonics skills, the development of reading fluency and automaticity, and the development of reading comprehension strategies. All of these components of reading are necessary but not sufficient in and of themselves. For children demonstrating difficulty in learning to read, it is imperative that each of these components be taught within an integrated context and that ample practice in reading familiar material be afforded. For some children, our research demonstrates that explicit, systematic instruction is crucial in helping them to understand and apply critical phonemic, phonics, fluency, and reading comprehension skills. Even for children who seem to grasp reading concepts easily, learning to read is not a natural process—reading instruction must be thoughtful, planned, and must incorporate the teaching of all the critical reading skills.

7. A major impediment to serving the needs of children demonstrating difficulties learning to

read is current teacher preparation practices. Many teachers lack basic knowledge about the structure of the English language, reading development, and the nature of reading difficulties. Major efforts should be undertaken to ensure that colleges of education possess the expertise and commitment to foster expertise in teachers at both preservice and inservice levels.

8. The preparation of teachers and the teaching of reading in our nation's classrooms must be based upon research evidence of the highest caliber and relevance. Research that is used to guide policy and instructional practice should be characterized by methodological rigor and the convergence of studies demonstrated to be representative, reliable, valid, and described with sufficient clarity and specificity to permit independent replication. Moreover, we must realize that no one study should be used to guide practice. To reiterate a significant point, the research knowledge that is employed to guide policy and practice must inform us how different components of reading behavior are best developed by various approaches to reading instruction for children of differing backgrounds, learning characteristics, and literacy experiences.

Keith E. Stanovich

Romance and reality

Stanovich reviews significant findings from his research and speculates on differential responses to his work. He argues that we must let scientific evidence answer questions about the reading process.

When, in preparation for this essay, I began thinking about the various components of my research program over the past 20 years, I realized that they could be divided into two categories: Research I have done that almost everyone likes and research I have done that not everybody likes. I thought that this distinction might be worth exploring in this essay because it may well say more about the current state of the field of reading than it does about my research itself.

Research I have done that almost everyone likes

In this category would go some of my research that has demonstrated that certain ways of classifying children having reading difficulties may be untenable. For example, one idea that has a long history in the learning disabilities field is that less-skilled readers who display a discrepancy with a measure of "aptitude" (typically defined as performance on an intelligence test) are different from poor readers who do not display such a discrepancy. It was thought that the reading-related cognitive characteristics of these groups were different and that they needed different types of treatment. Nevertheless, recent research and theory has brought these assumptions into question (Siegel, 1989; Stanovich, 1988, 1991).

It appears that children having difficulties in reading who have aptitude/achievement discrepancies have cognitive profiles that are surprisingly similar to children who do not. Also, to a large extent, these groups respond similarly to various educational interventions. Although some in the learning disabilities community have not found this research to be palatable, IRA audiences and the vast majority of teachers have not only felt very comfortable with these research conclusions, but also vindicated by them.

Even more popular has been my work on Matthew effects in reading development (Stanovich, 1986). The term Matthew effects derives from the Gospel according to Matthew: "For unto every one that hath shall be given, and he shall have abundance; but from him that hath not shall be taken away even that which he hath" (XXV:29). It is used to describe rich-get-richer and poor-get-poorer effects that are embedded in the educational process. Herb Walberg (Walberg & Tsai, 1983) had focused attention on the process by which early educational achievement spawns faster rates of subsequent achievement, and in a 1986 paper I specifically explored the idea of Matthew effects in the domain of reading achievement. I outlined a model of how individual differences in early reading acquisition were magnified by the differential cognitive, motivational, and educational experiences of children who vary in early reading development.

In that particular paper, I detailed several developmental mechanisms that are of continuing theoretical and empirical interest. Put simply, the story went something like this: Children who begin school with little phonological awareness have trouble acquiring alphabetic coding skill and thus have difficulty recognizing words. Reading for meaning is greatly hindered when children are having too much trouble with word recognition. When word recognition processes demand too much cognitive capacity, fewer cognitive resources are left to allocate to higher-level processes of text integration and comprehension. Trying to read without the cognitive resources to allocate to understanding the meaning of the text is not a rewarding experience. Such unrewarding early reading experiences lead to less involvement in reading-related activities. Lack of exposure and practice on the part of the less-skilled reader further delays the development of automaticity and speed at the word recognition level. Thus, reading for meaning is hindered, unrewarding reading experiences multiply, practice is avoided or merely tolerated without real cognitive involvement, and the negative spiral of cumulative disadvantage continues. Troublesome

emotional side effects begin to be associated with school experiences, and these become a further hindrance to school achievement.

Conversely, children who quickly develop efficient decoding processes find reading enjoyable because they can concentrate on the meaning of the text. They read more in school and, of equal importance, reading becomes a self-chosen activity for them. The additional exposure and practice that they get further develops their reading abilities. I speculated that reading develops syntactic knowledge, facilitates vocabulary growth, and broadens the general knowledge base. This facilitates the reading of more difficult and interesting texts. Thus, the increased reading experiences of these children have important positive feedback effects that are denied the slowly progressing reader.

My description of the different developmental trajectories due to differences in the ease of early reading acquisition struck a responsive chord of recognition with many practitioners who thought that the theoretical description captured some things that they had observed. Critiques by researchers were also largely supportive. Subsequent work in which I have tried to generate empirical sup-

Certain ways of classifying children having reading difficulties may be untenable.

port for the role of print exposure in cognitive development has been equally well received. My research group has tried to develop alternative methods of assessing differences in amount of print exposure in children and adults (Allen, Cipielewski, & Stanovich, 1992; Cunningham & Stanovich, 1991; Stanovich & West, 1989). Using some new methods, as well as some instruments designed by other investigators, we have documented an important role for print exposure in cognitive development (Stanovich, 1993; Stanovich & Cunningham, 1992, in press). Amount of print exposure is a potent predictor of vocabulary growth, knowledge acquisition, and a host of other verbal skills. Exposure to print does seem to be implicated in some educational Matthew effects.

More optimistically, however, we have found that exposure to print seems to be efficacious regardless of the level of the child's cognitive and reading abilities. Using some fairly sophisticated statistical analyses, we found that print exposure was a significant predictor of verbal growth even after the children had been equated on their general cognitive abilities. Print exposure was a strong predictor of cognitive growth in even the least advantaged children in our research samples. Thus, the child with limited reading skills and low general ability will build vocabulary and cognitive structures through immersion in literacy activities just as his or her high-achieving counterpart does. An encouraging message for teachers of low-achieving children is implicit here, and this research program of mine has been almost universally well received. Not so, however, with some other research that I have done.

Research I have done that not everyone likes

One of the first research problems in reading that I investigated was the role of context in word recognition. At the time I began these investigations with my colleague Richard West (in the early 1970s), several popular theories posited that the ability to use contextual information to predict upcoming words was an important factor in explaining individual differences in reading ability. Fluent readers were said to have attained their skill because of a heavy reliance on context in identifying words. Reading difficulties were thought to arise because some readers could not, or would not, use context to predict upcoming words.

To our surprise at the time (West and I had started these investigations thinking that the context view was correct), our initial investigations of this problem revealed just the opposite: It was the less-skilled readers who were more dependent upon context for word recognition (Stanovich, West, &

Feeman, 1981; West & Stanovich, 1978). The reason for this finding eventually became apparent: The word recognition processes of the skilled reader were so rapid and automatic that they did not need to rely on contextual information.

Over 10 years later, this finding is one of the most consistent and well replicated in all of reading research. It has been found with all types of readers, in all types of texts, and in a variety of different paradigms (e.g., Bruck, 1988; Leu, DeGroff, & Simons, 1986; Nicholson, 1991; Nicholson, Lillas, & Rzoska, 1988). Reviews of the dozens of different studies that converge on this conclusion are contained in Perfetti (1985), Rayner and Pollatsek (1989), and Stanovich (1980, 1984, 1986, 1991).

Perhaps understandably, at the time our initial findings were published they were not warmly received by researchers invested in the context-use theory that the results falsified. Today, however, the implications of these results have been incorporated into all major scientific models of the reading process (e.g., Just & Carpenter, 1987; Rayner & Pollatsek, 1989). Scientifically, the results are now uncontroversial. However, they are still not welcomed by some reading educators who would perpetuate the mistaken view that an emphasis on contextual prediction is the way to good reading.

It should be noted here that the findings I have referred to concern the use of context as an aid to word recognition rather than as a mechanism in the comprehension process. Although good readers employ contextual information more fluently in the comprehension process, they are not more reliant on contextual information for word recognition. A tendency to conflate these two levels of processing in discussions of context effects has caused enormous confusion among both researchers and practitioners.

Additional confusion has been caused by the use of imprecise labels such as "word calling." Despite the frequency with which this term occurs in reading publications, it is rare to find authors who spell out exactly what they mean by the term "word caller." However, the implicit assumptions behind its use appear to be as follows: (a) Word calling occurs when the words in the text are efficiently decoded into their spoken forms without comprehension of the passage taking place. (b) This is a bad thing, because (c) it means that the child does not understand the true purpose of reading, which is extracting meaning from the text. (d) Children engaging in word calling do so because they have learned inappropriate reading strategies. (e) The strategic difficulty is one of overreliance on phonemic strategies.

The idea of a word-caller embodying the assumptions outlined above has gained popularity despite the lack of evidence that it applies to an appreciable number of poor readers. There is no research evidence indicating that decoding a known word into a phonological form often takes place without meaning extraction. To the contrary, a substantial body of evidence indicates that even for young children, word recognition automatically leads to meaning activation (Ehri, 1977; Stanovich, 1986) *when the meaning of the word is adequately established in memory.* The latter requirement is crucial. Reports of word calling rarely indicate whether the words that are called are even in the child's listening vocabulary. If the child would not understand the meaning of the word or passage when spoken, then overuse of decoding strategies can hardly be blamed if the child does not understand the written words. In short, a minimal requirement for establishing word calling is the demonstration that the written material being pronounced is within the listening comprehension abilities of the child.

Secondly, it is necessary to show that the word calling is not a simple consequence of poor decoding. Although reasonably efficient decoding would appear to be an integral part of any meaningful definition of word calling, decoding skills are rarely assessed carefully before a child is labeled a word caller. It is quite possible for accurate decoding to be so slow and capacity-demanding that it strains available cognitive resources and causes comprehension breakdowns. Such accurate but capacity-demanding decoding with little comprehension should not be considered word calling as defined above. To the contrary, it is a qualitatively different type of phenomenon. Comprehension fails not because of overreliance on decoding, but because decoding skill is not developed enough.

Examples of phonological awareness tasks

Phoneme deletion: What word would be left if the /k/ sound were taken away from *cat*?

Word to word matching: Do *pen* and *pipe* begin with the same sound?

Blending: What word would we have if you put these sounds together: /s/, /a/, /t/?

Sound isolation: What is the first sound in *rose*?

Phoneme segmentation: What sounds do you hear in the word *hot*?

Phoneme counting: How many sounds do you hear in the work *cake*?

Deleted phoneme: What sound do you hear in *meat* that is missing in *eat*?

Odd word out: What word starts with a different sound: *bag, nine, beach, bike*?

Sound to word matching: Is there a /k/ in *bike*?

Another line of my research that has not been universally applauded concerns the role of phonological skills in early reading acquisition. Early insights from the work of Chall, Roswell, and Blumenthal (1963), Bruce (1964), and Liberman, Shankweiler, Fischer, and Carter (1974) came to fruition in the early 1980s when numerous investigators began to document the importance of phonological awareness skills in early reading acquisition. Our own work (e.g., Stanovich, Cunningham, & Cramer, 1984; Stanovich, Cunningham, & Feeman, 1984) was part of the "second generation" of research on these processes.

Reading researchers have for years sought the cognitive predictors of individual differences in early reading acquisition. The list of candidate processes and behaviors is long (short-term memory, intelligence, processes of contextual prediction, etc.). In the last 10 years, researchers have come to a strong consensus about the cognitive processes that best predict reading progress in the earliest stages. These cognitive processes have been called phonological awareness and they are measured by some of the tasks briefly summarized in the Table.

The term phonological awareness refers to the ability to deal explicitly and segmentally with sound units smaller than the syllable. Researchers argue intensely about the meaning of the term and about the nature of the tasks used to measure it. However, in the present context, it is critical to establish only that phonological awareness is indicated by performance on the generic type of tasks that we see in this Table. These tasks vary in difficulty. Some can be successfully completed before others. But all are highly correlated with each other. Most importantly, they are the best predictors of the ease of early reading acquisition—better than anything else that we know of, including IQ.

The latter is a somewhat startling finding if you think about it. Consider that I can spend an hour and a half giving a child any of a number of individually administered intelligence tests; then I can take about 7 minutes and administer 15 items of the type illustrated in the Table. And, when I am done, the 7-minute phonological awareness test will predict ease of initial reading acquisition better than the 2-hour intelligence test! This is why both researchers and practitioners have been greatly interested in research on phonological awareness.

Additionally, research has shown that phonological awareness appears to play a causal role in reading acquisition—that it is a good predictor not just because it is an incidental correlate of something else, but because phonological awareness is a foundational ability underlying the learning of spelling-sound correspondences. Numerous training studies have demonstrated that preschool and kindergarten children exposed to programs designed to facilitate phonological awareness become better readers (Ball & Blachman, 1991; Bradley & Bryant, 1985; Cunningham, 1990; Lie, 1991; Lundberg, Frost, & Peterson, 1988). Programs incorporating aspects of phonological awareness have recently been described in the pages of *The Reading Teacher* (e.g., Griffith & Olson, 1992; Yopp, 1992).

Like my findings on context use in reading—but unlike my research on Matthew effects and print exposure—my research on phonological awareness was less than welcome in some quarters of the reading education community. What accounts for these differential responses to research emanating from the same investigator? It is certainly possible that when I did the work on print exposure I had a "good day" and that when I did the work on phonological awareness and

context effects I was having a "bad day." However, those who have followed the dreadful "reading wars" in North American education will be aware that there is a more parsimonious explanation: Research topics that I investigated that were closer to the heart of the Great Debate over reading education were more controversial.

The Great Debate—again

Simply put, the work on phonological awareness and context effects contradicted the philosophical tenets of the more "hard line" whole language advocates. Although almost all teachers recognize from their own experience that encouraging "contextual guessing" in those children experiencing early reading difficulty does not help, heavy reliance on context to facilitate word recognition is still emphasized by some whole language proponents. Similarly, phonological awareness training violates a fundamental tenet because it isolates components of the reading process.

What really is the heart of this controversy? I hesitate here, because so much contention and vitriol has surrounded the "phonics vs. whole language" debate that I almost balk at the thought of contributing to it further. Nevertheless, ever the optimist, in what follows I offer a five-step strategy for attenuating the dispute. My strategy has the following logic:

1. First look for points of agreement between opposing positions.

2. When doing so, invoke a "spirit of charity" whereby all sides are encouraged to stretch their principles to the maximum to accommodate components of the other position.

3. Step back and take a look at what might be a larger degree of agreement than anyone supposed.

4. Next, isolate the crucial differences. Try to make these few in number but clearly defined so that they are amenable to scientific test.

5. However, before arguing about the outcomes of the tests, both sides should take a look at the set of defining differences and ask themselves whether they are worth the cost of war.

It is really not difficult to demonstrate

that there is more agreement among reading educators than is sometimes apparent to those obsessively focused on the so-called reading wars. For example, Chall (1989) has repeatedly pointed out that many of the recommendations and practices that are commonly associated with whole language have appeared repeatedly in her writings. She reminds us that "Teaching only phonics—and in isolation—was not a recommendation of the Great Debate in 1967 or 1983" (p. 525). Chall is at pains to remind her readers that, in common with many whole language advocates, she "also recommended that library books, rather than workbooks, be used by children not working with the teacher and that writing be incorporated into the teaching of reading" (p. 525). Chall (1989) has no compunctions about admitting that "Some teachers may inadvertently overdo the teaching of phonics, leaving little time for the reading of stories and other connected texts," but she notes that "The history of reading instruction teaches us that literature, writing, and thinking are not exclusive properties of any one approach to beginning reading" (p. 531).

Clearly there is plenty of scope for the "principle of charity" to operate here. Corresponding to Chall's statement that "some teachers may inadvertently overdo the teaching of phonics" we simply need the companion admission that some children in whole language classrooms do not pick up the alphabetic principle through simple immersion in print and writing activities, and such children need explicit instruction in alphabetic coding—a concession having the considerable advantage of being consistent with voluminous research evidence (Adams, 1990; Vellutino, 1991). It seems inconceivable that we will continue wasting energy on the reading wars simply because we cannot get both sides to say, simultaneously, "some teachers overdo phonics" and "some children need explicit instruction in alphabetic coding."

Adams (1991) is likewise boggled at what, seemingly, is the cause of all our strife. She points to the defining features of the whole language philosophy that Bergeron (1990) gleaned from an extensive review of the literature:

> Construction of meaning, wherein an emphasis is placed on comprehending what is read; functional

language, or language that has purpose and relevance to the learner; the use of literature in a variety of forms; the writing process, through which learners write, revise, and edit written works; cooperative student work; and an emphasis on affective aspects of the students' learning experience, such as motivation, enthusiasm, and interest. (p. 319)

Adams (1991) asks rhetorically "Is this what the field has been feuding about?" (p. 41). Probably not. Instead, she argues that:

> the whole language movement carries or is carried by certain other issues that do merit serious concern....these issues are: (1) teacher empowerment, (2) child-centered instruction, (3) integration of reading and writing, (4) a disavowal of the value of teaching or learning phonics, and (5) subscription to the view that children are naturally predisposed toward written language acquisition. (p. 41)

Educators working from a variety of different perspectives might well endorse points #1 to #3. Clearly the key points of difference are issues #4 and #5. However, Adams (1991) makes the seemingly startling—but actually very wise—suggestion that the:

> positions of the whole language movement on teaching and learning about spellings and sounds are historical artifacts. Although they are central to its rhetoric and focal to its detractors, they may well be peripheral to the social and pedagogical concerns that drive the movement....Yet their continuing centrality to the rhetoric of the movement may be owed no less to their historical precedence than to the fact that...they were tightly connected to the other issues of teacher empowerment, child-centered education, and the reading-writing connection. I believe, moreover, that it is these latter issues that inspire the deepest commitment and passion of the movement....To treat it today as an issue of phonics versus no phonics is not only to misrepresent it, but to place all of its valuable components at genuine risk. (pp. 42, 51)

Adams is pointing toward some dangers that lie in wait for whole language advocates but also toward a possible rapprochement within the reading education community. The danger is this. In holding to an irrationally extreme view on the role of phonics in reading education—for failing to acknowledge that some children do not discover the alphabetic principle on their own and need systematic direct instruction in the alphabet principle, phonological analysis, and alphabetic coding—whole language proponents threaten all of their legitimate accomplishments. Eventually—perhaps not for a great while, but eventually—the weight of empirical evidence will fall on their heads. That direct instruction in alphabetic coding facilitates early reading acquisition is one of the most well established conclusions in all of behavioral science (Adams, 1990; Anderson, Hiebert, Scott, & Wilkinson, 1985; Chall, 1983, 1989; Perfetti, 1985; Stanovich, 1986). Conversely, the idea that learning to read is just like learning to speak is accepted by no responsible linguist, psychologist, or cognitive scientist in the research community (see Liberman & Liberman, 1990). To stand, Canute-like, against this evidence is to put at risk all of the many hard-won victories of the whole language movement:

> The whole language movement should be a movement that is a core component of a long overdue and highly constructive educational revolution. It should be about restoring the confidence and authority of teachers. It should be an affirmation that education can only be as effective as it is sensitive to the strengths, interests, and needs of its students....It should be about displaying such outmoded instructional regimens with highly integrated, meaningful, thoughtful, and self-engendering engagement with information and ideas. If, in fact, these are goals that drive the whole language movement then they must be supported wholeheartedly by all concerned. These goals are of paramount importance to our nation's educational health and progress. At the same time, however, they are strictly independent from issues of the nature of the knowledge and processes involved in reading and learning to read. Only by disentangling these two sets of issues, can we give either the attention and commitment that it so urgently deserves. (Adams, 1991, p. 52)

Future historians will find it difficult to explain how the political goal of restructuring educational resources got tied up with the issue of whether teachers should say, "S makes the /s/ sound."

"Only by disentangling these issues" is the key phrase here. The whole language movement is currently burdened with, shall we say, entangling alliances—in particular, an alliance with an extreme view on the role of direct instruction of decoding skills that is seriously out of step with current evidence. I would give essentially the same medical advice that Adams is pointing to: Only amputation will save the patient. And, make no

mistake, we do risk losing the patient. Several months ago, in the same Distinguished Educator Series in which the current essay appears, Goodman (1992) excoriated the Bush administration for its hostility to universal public education and pointed to a

> group of individuals who want to limit education to a small elite group of technicians needed to run our industry....The Bush initiative would further the development of a two-tiered work force by limiting educational expense for those not needed as technicians. (p. 198)

I share all of Goodman's concerns, and I am in sympathy with his indictment of the Bush administration and the many special interest groups with a vested interest in privatized education (The Edison Project of the Whittle Corporation comes to mind). The "savage inequalities" (Kozol, 1991) in American education are indeed a national disgrace and deserve a revolutionary political response. But future historians will find it difficult to explain how the political goal of restructuring educational resources got tied up with the issue of whether teachers should say "*s* makes the /s/ sound."

But, paradoxically, the latter point does relate—in an unexpected way—to some broader political issues such as the integrity of the public education system. Parents with children who have trouble in early reading acquisition and who have not been given instruction in alphabetic coding will add fuel to the movement toward privatized education in North America. "Parents Question Results of State-Run School System" (Enchin, 1992) is an increasingly frequent newspaper headline in Canadian provinces (e.g., Ontario) where phonics instruction is neglected or deemphasized. The January 11, 1993, cover of *Maclean's,* Canada's weekly newsmagazine, was titled "What's Wrong at School?" and featured numerous reports of parents seeking private education for children struggling in reading due to a lack of emphasis on alphabetic coding in school curricula. Featured stories in the magazine had titles such as "Angry Parents Press for Change," and photographs were highlighted with labels such as "Accusing the Schools of Taking Part in a Costly, Failed Experiment." It is reported that Canada's private school enrollment jumped 15% in the single year of 1992. In short, parents who notice that their second and third graders cannot decode simple words will become the unwitting pawns of the corporate advocates of privatized education whose motives Goodman rightly questions.

I have faith, though, that in the end, teachers will save us from some of the more nefarious goals of the Bush administration (now thankfully gone) and its like-minded allies. Teachers, like scientists, are committed pragmatists. They single-mindedly pursue "what works"—ignoring philosophical strictures along the way. The scientists of 50-60 years ago ignored positivist restrictions on the extent of their theorizing. A population now enjoying the fruits of fiber-optic technology is glad they did. Currently, those of us who hope for medical cures for our health problems will be reassured to know that biochemists in their laboratories are blissfully unaware of constructivist arguments against the idea that one criterion of a good theory is that it should correspond to physical reality.

Teachers are similarly pragmatic, and I am confident that they will find a middle way between the rhetorical blasts and political posturings of our field. Increasingly we are seeing examples of practitioners and teacher-educators finding the middle way—some in the pages of this very journal (Spiegel, 1992; Stahl, 1992; Trachtenberg, 1990).

Mosenthal (1989) has characterized whole language as a "romantic" approach to literacy, and its affinities with Rousseauan ideas are commented upon by both advocates and detractors. But we are all aware that a shockingly high number of romantically inspired marriages end in divorce. Often, a little reality testing in the early stages of a romance can prevent a doomed marriage. Better yet, some early reality testing and adjustment can sometimes prolong a romance. Appropriately chosen direct instruction in the spelling-sound code is the reality that will enable our romance with whole language to be a long-lasting one.

The connecting thread: Science

Although I have dichotomized my research projects in this essay, I really do not think of them this way. The projects, to me, are all similar in a mundane way: They are interesting problems about the reading process that were amenable to scientific test.

And the latter point is really the common thread. I believe in letting scientific evidence answer questions about the nature of the reading process. Nothing has retarded the cumulative growth of knowledge in the psychology of reading more than the failure to deal with problems in a scientific manner.

Education has suffered because its dominant model for adjudicating disputes is political (with corresponding factions and interest groups) rather than scientific. Education's well-known susceptibility to the "authority syndrome" stems from its tacit endorsement of a personalistic view of knowledge acquisition: the belief that knowledge resides within particular individuals who then dispense it to others. Knowledge in science is publicly verifiable (see Stanovich, 1992) and thus depersonalized in the sense that it is not the unique possession of particular individuals or groups (Popper, 1972).

An adherence to a subjective, personalized view of knowledge is what continually leads to educational fads that could easily be avoided by grounding teachers and other practitioners in the importance of scientific thinking for solving educational problems. This training should include an explicit discussion of some of the common misconceptions that people hold about science, for example, that the idea of objective, depersonalized knowledge in the social sciences dehumanizes people. Such facile slogans compromise both research and practice in many educational domains.

What science actually accomplishes with its conception of publicly verifiable knowledge is the democratization of knowledge, an outcome that frees practitioners and researchers from slavish dependence on authority; and it is subjective, personalized views of knowledge that degrade the human intellect by creating conditions in which it is inevitably subjugated to an elite whose "personal" knowledge is not accessible to all (Bronowski, 1956, 1977; Medawar, 1982, 1984, 1990; Popper, 1971).

The scientific criteria for evaluating knowledge claims are not complicated and could easily be included in teacher-training programs, but they usually are not (thus a major opportunity to free teachers from reliance on authority is lost right at the beginning). These criteria include the publication of findings in refereed journals (scientific publications that employ a process of peer review), the duplication of the results by other investigators, and a consensus within a particular research community on whether or not there is a critical mass of studies that point toward a particular conclusion. These mechanisms are some of the best consumer protections that we can give teachers.

Teachers should also be introduced to the values of science. Although the technological products of science are value free in that they can be used for good or ill, it is not true that the process of science is value free (Bronowski, 1956, 1977). For example, objectivity is a value that is fundamental to science and simply means that we let nature speak for itself without imposing our wishes on it. The fact that this goal is unattainable for any single human being should not dissuade us from holding objectivity as a value (this would be confusing what is the case with what ought to be). The sorry state of fields that have abandoned objectivity is perhaps the strongest argument for holding to it as a value. To use a convenient and well-known example, the inability of parapsychologists to screen out subjective wishes and desires from their observations has filled their field with charlatans and scandal, made progress impossible, and alienated a scientific world that was once quite supportive of the field (Alcock, 1990; Hines, 1988).

My view on these matters is considered old fashioned in many educational circles. There is much loose talk in education now about paradigms, incommensurability, frameworks, and such. The whole melange is sometimes termed constructivism and it is commonly employed to support various relativistic doctrines such as the view that there is no objective truth, that all investigators construct their evidence from what they already know is true, that we all live in different realities, that correspondence to reality is not a valid scientific criterion, etc.—or, more technically, that "equally rational, competent, and informed observers are, in some sense, free (of external realist and internal innate constraints) to constitute for themselves different realities" (Shweder, 1991, p. 156).

These ideas have unfortunately come into education half baked and twice distorted. Legitimate philosophy of science was picked up and reworked by scholars in a variety of humanities disciplines who were not philosophers by training and who used the work for their own—often political—agendas. Educational theorists have taken these worked-over ideas and recooked them once again so that they are now almost unrecognizable from the original. For example, constructivist theorists in education cite Thomas Kuhn constantly. They are greatly enamored with Kuhn's (1970) incommensurability thesis in philosophy of science: the idea that competing frameworks "cannot be compared and evaluated on rational grounds" (Bechtel, 1988, p. 55). These theorists seem unaware of the facts that Kuhn's concept of incommensurability has been seriously disputed by numerous historians and philosophers of science (Gutting, 1980; Lakatos & Musgrave, 1970; Laudan, 1990; Leplin, 1984; Siegel, 1980; Suppe, 1984) and that Kuhn has largely abandoned the idea (see the 1970 Postscript to *The Structure of Scientific Revolutions* and the commentary on the Postscript by Musgrave, 1980; see also Siegel, 1980).

Numerous philosophers of science—the very scholars who did the original work that the educational theorists are parodying—have objected to the distortion of their work by social scientists and educators. For example, Ian Hacking (1983), a leading contributor to these debates in philosophy of science, has written of how

> slightly off-key inferences were drawn from work of the first rank...Kuhn was taken aback by the way in which his work (and that of others) produced a crisis of rationality. He subsequently wrote that he never intended to deny the customary virtues of scientific theories. Theories should be accurate, that is, by and large fit existing experimental data. They should be both internally consistent and consistent with other accepted theories. They should be broad in scope and rich in consequences. They should be simple in structure, organizing facts in an intelligible way. (pp. 2, 13)

Larry Laudan, another key figure in the debate within philosophy of science, echoes Hacking's comments that:

> Many who are not philosophers of science (from cultural philosophers like Rorty and Winch to sociologists like Barnes and Collins) appear to believe that contemporary philosophy of science provides potent arguments on behalf of a radical relativism

about knowledge in general and scientific knowledge in particular....My belief, by contrast, is that strong forms of epistemic relativism derive scant support from a clearheaded understanding of the contemporary state of the art in philosophy of science. I am not alone in that conviction; most of my fellow philosophers of science would doubtless wholeheartedly concur. But that consensus within the discipline apparently cuts little ice with those outside it....Many scientists (especially social scientists), literati, and philosophers outside of philosophy of science proper have come to believe that the epistemic analysis of science since the 1960s provides potent ammunition for a general assault on the idea that science represents a reliable or superior form of knowing....My larger target is those contemporaries who—in repeated acts of wish fulfillment—have appropriated conclusions from the philosophy of science and put them to work in aid of a variety of social cum political causes for which those conclusions are ill adapted. (1990, pp. viii-ix)

The worst example of this distortion is how the concept of incommensurability has been used. The dehumanizing implications of this concept seem not to have entirely escaped educational theorists in the literacy area. The seeming delight in the view that we are all "locked into our paradigms" is puzzling. The very thing that incommensurability seeks to deny—the cumulative nature of human knowledge—provides the key rationale that commands a member of the intellectual community to show respect for the ideas of others. Although the social and moral motivation for attempting to view the world from inside another person's framework is to gain a more humanized understanding of another individual, the intellectual motivation must be that by doing so I may gain a better (i.e., more accurate) view of the world.

If we, as educators, deny the last possibility, we will undercut the motivation to shift frameworks for even the first—the humanistic—purpose. It is one thing to deny the possibility of attaining certain knowledge. Most scientists admit this impossibility. It is another thing entirely to argue that we lose nothing by giving up even the attempt at attaining objective knowledge. Such a stratagem undermines the rationale for the scientific quest for knowledge and in this quest lies the only hope of escaping our continuing dilemma.

Stanovich is a professor at the Ontario Institute for Studies in Education, 252 Bloor Street West, Toronto, Ontario, Canada M5S 1V6. He has twice received from IRA the Albert J. Harris Award for outstanding contributions to the diagnosis or remediation of reading or learning disabilities.

References

Adams, M.J. (1990). *Beginning to read: Thinking and learning about print*. Cambridge, MA: MIT Press.

Adams, M.J. (1991). Why not phonics and whole language? In W. Ellis (Ed.), *All language and the creation of literacy* (pp. 40-52). Baltimore: Orton Dyslexia Society.

Alcock, J.E. (1990). *Science and supernature: An appraisal of parapsychology*. Buffalo, NY: Prometheus Books.

Allen, L., Cipielewski, J., & Stanovich, K.E. (1992). Multiple indicators of children's reading habits and attitudes: Construct validity and cognitive correlates. *Journal of Educational Psychology, 84*, 489-503.

Anderson, R.C., Hiebert, E.H., Scott, J., & Wilkinson, I. (1985). *Becoming a nation of readers*. Washington, DC: National Institute of Education.

Ball, E.W., & Blachman, B.A. (1991). Does phoneme segmentation training in kindergarten make a difference in early work recognition and developmental spelling? *Reading Research Quarterly, 26*, 49-66.

Bechtel, W. (1988). *Philosophy of science*. Hillsdale, NJ: Erlbaum.

Bergeron, B. (1990). What does the term whole language mean? Constructing a definition from the literature. *Journal of Reading Behavior, 22*, 301-329.

Bradley, L., & Bryant, P.E. (1985). *Rhyme and reason in reading and spelling*. Ann Arbor: University of Michigan Press.

Bronowski, J. (1956). *Science and human values*. New York: Harper & Row.

Bronowski, J. (1977). *A sense of the future*. Cambridge, MA: MIT Press.

Bruce, D. (1964). The analysis of word sounds by young children. *British Journal of Educational Psychology, 34*, 158-170.

Bruck, M. (1988). The word-recognition and spelling of dyslexic children. *Reading Research Quarterly, 23*, 51-69.

Chall, J.S. (1983). *Stages of reading development*. New York: McGraw-Hill.

Chall, J.S. (1989). Learning to read: The great debate 20 years later. *Phi Delta Kappan, 70*, 521-538.

Chall, J.S., Roswell, F., & Blumenthal, S. (1963). Auditory blending ability: A factor in success in beginning reading. *The Reading Teacher, 17*, 113-118.

Cunningham, A.E. (1990). Explicit versus implicit instruction in phonemic awareness. *Journal of Experimental Child Psychology, 50*, 429-444.

Cunningham, A.E., & Stanovich, K.E. (1991). Tracking the unique effects of print exposure in children: Associations with vocabulary, general knowledge, and spelling. *Journal of Educational Psychology, 83*, 264-274.

Ehri, L.C. (1977). Do adjectives and functors interfere as much as nouns in naming pictures? *Child Development, 48*, 697-701.

Enchin, H. (1992, December 29). Parents question results of state-run school system. *Toronto Globe and Mail*, p. 1.

Goodman, K.S. (1992). I didn't found whole language. *The Reading Teacher, 46*, 188-199.

Griffith, P.L., & Olson, M.W. (1992). Phonemic awareness helps beginning readers break the code. *The Reading Teacher, 45*, 516-523.

Gutting, G. (1980). *Paradigms and revolutions*. Notre Dame, IN: University of Notre Dame Press.

Hacking, I. (1983). *Representing and intervening*. Cambridge: Cambridge University Press.

Hines, T. (1988). *Pseudoscience and the paranormal*. Buffalo, NY: Prometheus Books.

Just, M., & Carpenter, P.A. (1987). *The psychology of reading and language comprehension*. Boston: Allyn and Bacon.

Kozol, J. (1991). *Savage inequalities*. New York: Crown.

Kuhn, T.S. (1970). *The structure of scientific revolutions* (2nd ed.). Chicago: University of Chicago Press.

Lakatos, I., & Musgrave, A. (1970). *Criticism and the growth of knowledge*. Cambridge: Cambridge University Press.

Laudan, L. (1990). *Science and relativism*. Chicago: University of Chicago Press.

Leplin, J. (1984). *Scientific realism*. Berkeley, CA: University of California Press.

Leu, D.J., DeGroff, L., & Simons, H.D. (1986). Predictable texts and interactive-compensatory hypotheses: Evaluating individual differences in reading ability, context use, and comprehension. *Journal of Educational Psychology, 78*, 347-352.

Liberman, I.Y., & Liberman, A.M. (1990). Whole language vs. code emphasis: Underlying assumptions and their implications for reading instruction. *Annals of Dyslexia, 40*, 51-77.

Liberman, I.Y., Shankweiler, D., Fischer, F.W., & Carter, B. (1974). Explicit syllable and phoneme segmentation in the young child. *Journal of Experimental Child Psychology, 18*, 201-212.

Lie, A. (1991). Effects of a training program for stimulating skills in word analysis in first-grade children. *Reading Research Quarterly, 26*, 234-250.

Lundberg, I., Frost, J., & Peterson, O. (1988). Effects of an extensive program for stimulating phonological awareness in preschool children. *Reading Research Quarterly, 23*, 263-284.

Medawar, P.B. (1982). *Pluto's republic*. Oxford: Oxford University Press.

Medawar, P.B. (1984). *The limits of science*. New York: Harper & Row.

Medawar, P.B. (1990). *The threat and the glory*. New York: HarperCollins.

Mosenthal, P.B. (1989). The whole language approach: Teachers between a rock and a hard place. *The Reading Teacher, 42*, 628-629.

Musgrave, A. (1980). Kuhn's second thoughts. In G. Gutting (Ed.), *Paradigms and revolutions* (pp. 39-53). Notre Dame, IN: University of Notre Dame Press.

Nicholson, T. (1991). Do children read words better in context or in lists? A classic study revisited. *Journal of Educational Psychology, 83*, 444-450.

Nicholson, T., Lillas, C., & Rzoska, M. (1988). Have we been misled by miscues? *The Reading Teacher, 42*, 6-10.

Perfetti, C.A. (1985). *Reading ability*. New York: Oxford University Press.

Popper, K.R. (1971). *The open society and its enemies* (Vols. 1 & 2). Princeton, NJ: Princeton University Press.

Popper, K.R. (1972). *Objective knowledge*. Oxford: Oxford University Press.

Rayner, K., & Pollatsek, A. (1989). *The psychology of reading*. Englewood Cliffs, NJ: Prentice Hall.

Shweder, R.A. (1991). *Thinking through cultures*. Cambridge, MA: Harvard University Press.

Siegel, H. (1980). Objectivity, rationality, incommensurability and more. *British Journal for the Philosophy of Science, 31*, 359-384.

Siegel, L.S. (1989). IQ is irrelevant to the definition of learning disabilities. *Journal of Learning Disabilities, 22*, 469-479.

Spiegel, D.L. (1992). Blending whole language and systematic direct instruction. *The Reading Teacher, 46*, 38-44.

Stahl, S. (1992). Saying the "p" word. *The Reading Teacher, 45*, 618-625.

Stanovich, K.E. (1980). Toward an interactive-compensatory model of individual differences in the development of reading fluency. *Reading Research Quarterly, 16*, 32-71.

Stanovich, K.E. (1984). The interactive-compensatory model of reading: A confluence of developmental, experimental, and educational psychology. *Remedial and Special Education, 5*, 11-19.

Stanovich, K.E. (1986). Matthew effects in reading: Some consequences of individual differences in the acquisition of literacy. *Reading Research Quarterly, 21*, 360-407.

Stanovich, K.E. (1988). Explaining the differences between the dyslexic and the garden-variety poor reader: The phonological-core variable-difference model. *Journal of Learning Disabilities, 21*, 590-612.

Stanovich, K.E. (1991). Word recognition: Changing perspectives. In R. Barr, M.L. Kamil, P. Mosenthal, & P.D. Pearson (Eds.), *Handbook of reading research* (Vol. 2, pp. 418-452). New York: Longman.

Stanovich, K.E. (1992). *How to think straight about psychology* (3rd ed.). New York: HarperCollins.

Stanovich, K.E. (1993). Does reading make you smarter? Literacy and the development of verbal intelligence. In H. Reese (Ed.), *Advances in child development and behavior* (Vol. 24, pp. 133-180). San Diego: Academic Press.

Stanovich, K.E., & Cunningham, A.E. (1992). Studying the consequences of literacy within a literate society: The cognitive correlates of print exposure. *Memory & Cognition, 20*, 51-68.

Stanovich, K.E., & Cunningham, A.E. (in press). Where does knowledge come from? Specific associations between print exposure and information acquisition. *Journal of Educational Psychology*.

Stanovich, K.E., Cunningham, A.E., & Cramer, B. (1984). Assessing phonological awareness in kindergarten children: Issues of task comparability. *Journal of Experimental Child Psychology, 38*, 175-190.

Stanovich, K.E., Cunningham, A.E., & Feeman, D.J. (1984). Intelligence, cognitive skills, and early reading progress. *Reading Research Quarterly, 19*, 278-303.

Stanovich, K.E., & West, R.F. (1989). Exposure to print and orthographic processing. *Reading Research Quarterly, 24*, 402-433.

Stanovich, K.E., West, R.F., & Feeman, D.J. (1981). A longitudinal study of sentence context effects in second-grade children: Tests of an interactive-compensatory model. *Journal of Experimental Child Psychology, 32*, 185-199.

Suppe, F. (1984). Beyond Skinner and Kuhn. *New Ideas in Psychology, 2*, 89-104.

Trachtenburg, P. (1990). Using children's literature to enhance phonics instruction. *The Reading Teacher,*

43, 648-654.

Vellutino, F.R. (1991). Introduction to three studies on reading acquisition: Convergent findings on theoretical foundations of code-oriented versus whole-language approaches to reading instruction. *Journal of Educational Psychology, 83*, 437-443.

Walberg, H.J., & Tsai, S. (1983). Matthew effects in edu-cation. *American Educational Research Journal, 20*, 359-373.

West, R.F., & Stanovich, K.E. (1978). Automatic contex-tual facilitation in readers of three ages. *Child Development, 49*, 717-727.

Yopp, H.K. (1992). Developing phonemic awareness in young children. *The Reading Teacher, 45*, 696-703.

From *The Reading Teacher, Vol. 47, No. 4, December 1993/January 1994*

The brain reads sound by sound

Research: Scientists can now watch what goes on in children's brains as they read. When the lights go on, it confirms an old theory: We learn to read by linking letters with sounds.

By KATHY LALLY AND DEBBIE M. PRICE : SUN STAFF

EW HAVEN, Conn. — A gigantic white magnet fills the room and a small blond boy lies very still inside it. A great ping-ping-ing noise, like the sonar echo of a submarine, begins as the magnet goes to work, taking pictures of the boy's brain.

Words flash on a screen before the child. He is asked to decide whether the words rhyme and push a button. Computers whir madly, processing the brain pictures and the boy's responses.

Together, the magnet, the computers and a team of scientists and doctors are working to solve one of the great mysteries of humankind.

They are watching the brain read.

With the cutting-edge technology of the magnetic resonance imaging (MRI) device — commonly called "the magnet" — scientists at Yale University's Center for Learning and Attention have found a window on the brain. Through this high-tech porthole, they can see what their predecessors had deduced by studying children in classrooms: The brain reads by breaking words into sounds.

The scientists, led by Yale physicians Sally and Bennett Shaywitz, have identified the parts of the brain used in reading. By observing the flow of oxygen-rich blood to working brain cells, they have found that people who know how to sound out words can rapidly process what they see.

These readers, asked to imagine "cat" without the "kah" sound, readily summon "at." And the MRI photographs show their brains lighting up like pinball machines.

When the brain gets it, the light bulbs really do go on.

Conversely, the brains of people who can't sound out words often look different on MRI pictures. There is less blood flow to the language centers of the brain and, in some cases, not much activity evident at all. Scientists are not sure why this is or what it means.

But simply put, without the ability to sound out words, the brain is stumped.

The Yale research offers more high-powered ammunition for the argument that beginning readers should be taught to discern the individual sounds within words.

It builds upon millions of dollars of research, conducted over the past 20 years under the aegis of the National Institutes of Health in Bethesda, that has documented similar conclusions: Children need to understand the sounds of the English language and sound-letter relationships — known as "phonics" — before they can learn to read. For some, this comes naturally; others must be taught.

What's more, NIH-sponsored studies are finding that at least 95 percent of even the poorest readers can learn to read at grade level if they are given early and proper instruction in sound-letter relationships.

By contrast, as many as 40 percent of school-age children remain poor readers, with half of them having serious trouble. In Maryland, two-thirds of the third-graders aren't meeting the state's standard in reading.

A key reason for this huge gap is that for years scientific research has been ignored by educators.

"The gap that exists between the level of knowledge and what we have implemented of that knowledge all across the board ... is absolutely awful and sad," says Sally Shaywitz, a pediatrician-scientist involved in reading research for almost two decades. "It would be a tremendous tragedy if, knowing what we know about how children learn, [that knowledge] were not put to work."

But in the academic arena, science has been no match for fad and fashion, infused with politics and religion. Since the 1970s, school districts across the country have abandoned phonics for enticing "whole-language" programs that promise to teach children to read by immersing them in literature.

The battles over the two reading methods have been ugly, and the casualties have been children.

Millions of children today read poorly or not at all because, as mounting scientific and academic evidence proves, they could have been taught better. While the pendulum is swinging back toward more phonics in many school districts, a generation has been damaged.

"When children don't learn to read, there's not much accountability," says G. Reid Lyon, a neuropsychologist in charge of the NIH's reading research. "People blame the kids, the teachers, the parents, the socioeconomic background, all kinds of things except the instructional procedures being used."

Two methods

Phonics or whole language? The methods derive from educational philosophies that are as different as night and day.

Pure phonics instruction is meticulous and begins with baby steps. Children are first taught the 44 basic sounds in the English language and how those sounds are formed by combinations of the 26 letters of the alphabet. Then they learn how to sound out or decode the words. Sentences, stories and books come linked to these particular skills.

At City Springs Elementary in Baltimore, which has adopted a rigorous phonics-based reading program, first-graders progressed in the first month of class from a review of sounds they learned in kindergarten to simple stories that employ limited sets of sounds, such as one titled "Lots of Pots."

In one City Springs class, first-graders were recently asked to circle the words on a work sheet that matched pictures. Most of the children were confused by a drawing of a jar with grapes on the label. Told that the picture was of "jam" — for many little children it's all jelly — several children were able to sound out the word quickly and select "jam" from look-alikes "gem" and "jab."

Their experience illustrates, phonics advocates say, that once children learn the rules, they can figure out words they've never seen. Meaning comes in time.

By contrast, whole language approaches reading instruction from the opposite direction. It holds that children learn to read by reading. Once exposed to literature and taught to love language, children will become readers.

Whole-language classrooms use books filled with broad vocabularies and more complex stories than the simple texts given to beginning phonics readers. When children come across unfamiliar words — rather than being encouraged to sound them out — they are often told to guess or look at an accompanying picture for clues.

In a first-grade classroom at Centennial Lane Elementary School in Ellicott City, for example, students recently were reading "The Best Dressed Bear" — a 3-foot-tall book on display in front of the room.

Before opening the cover, teacher Christina Haris asks students to predict what will happen based on the title of the book. Some suggest the bear will be going to a wedding. Others suggest the bear will enter a contest.

As Haris and the students read aloud together, she asks the students what strategy they're using to figure out words they don't know.

"The pictures," comes the reply.

"That's right. You're using the picture," Haris says. "The pictures tell the whole story themselves."

Reading research

About half of all children will eventually learn to read at their grade level, whether they're taught to sound out unfamiliar words or to look at pictures.

But for almost as many children — those who do not seem to have a natural ability to sort out the sounds within words — learning to read can be excruciating. The most severely challenged are often labeled dyslexic because, despite their often high intelligence, they have great difficulty deciphering the words on a page.

"You can have an IQ of 145, be a great reasoner and still be a poor reader," says NIH neuropsychologist Lyon. "Some of these bright kids can't get through a story, but if you take the book away and read them the story, they'll talk about it all day long."

Over the past 15 years, Lyon and his NIH colleagues have observed more than 10,000 children and have published more than 26 books and 2,000 articles in their quest to discover why some children read with ease and others do not.

They have launched clinical trials involving almost 5,900 children in 10 cities to determine which methods work best for teaching children with reading problems.

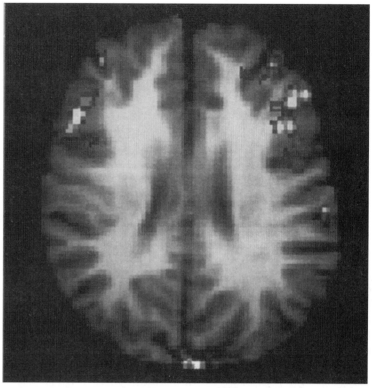

B.A. SHAYWITZ, ET AL., 1995, NMR/YALE MEDICAL SCHOOL

Brain at work: *An MRI image of a normal adult brain shows the highlighted language centers.*

They've learned to predict, even with kindergartners, which children will later have troubles based on their early inability to hear and repeat subtle sounds, identify letters and write their names.

And they have studied the ways that children learn, using pure phonics, pure whole-language programs and combinations of both.

Their conclusion: Children learn to read best if they're first given "phoneme-awareness" training in the sounds of the English language and then taught the letter-sound relationships of traditional phonics. All along, teachers should also expose children to literature by reading to them and giving them interesting books to read as in the whole-language method.

"To read the English language, there is no way to get around the fact that you have to decode it," Lyon says. "The key is the right mix and that you start early."

Once children have learned the code, Lyon says, they need to develop speed and accuracy so that they can comprehend what they are reading.

Particularly encouraging are classroom studies involving 3,000 children in Houston, Tallahassee, Fla., and Albany, N.Y., which have shown that all but the most severely disabled can learn to read at grade level. All but 5 percent of the poorest readers — regardless of income and race — can achieve average test scores after a year of intensive teaching 30 to 45 minutes a day in kindergarten and first grade.

For many children, even the first step is very difficult: hearing the distinct sounds within language.

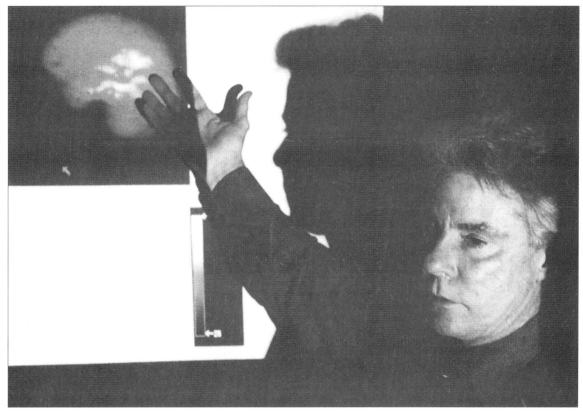

KIM HAIRSTON : SUN STAFF

Blood flow: *G. Reid Lyon of the National Institutes of Health uses an MRI image to show that blood flow is often more diffuse to a particular portion of the brains of problem readers. "To read the English language," he says, "there is no way to get around the fact that you have to decode it."*

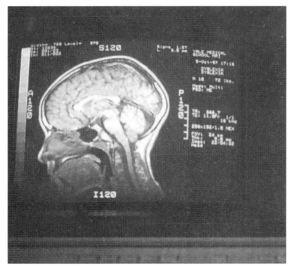

RICHARD MEI : SPECIAL TO THE SUN

Brain mapping: *A computer image of the brain. Using MRI technology, scientists have mapped the parts of the brain used to read.*

Lyon plays a videotape of young children in a classroom in Boston. Their teacher tells them to think of a zoo animal that rhymes with "miger."

"Giraffe!" a little girl says.

"That child," Lyon says, "is going to have trouble learning to read."

The child has difficulty comprehending the sounds of language. And scientists increasingly believe it is the brain's inability to process what it hears — not what it sees — that causes dyslexia.

Because dyslexics frequently confuse "b" and "d," they originally were thought to have vision problems. Scientists now believe that dyslexics confuse the two letters because they sound alike.

Dyslexia has been the focus of the MRI studies at Yale and four other sites. The Shaywitzes, co-directors of the Yale Center for Learning and Attention, wanted to see what was — or wasn't — happening within the brains of dyslexic children.

A functional MRI machine, a type that requires no injection of dye and is safe and painless, takes thousands of pictures of the brain, at rest and as it processes information. When brain cells go to work, oxygen-rich blood rushes to fuel their activity, much as gasoline fills the engine of a running car. Because this oxygenated blood has different magnetic properties, MRIs can discern it.

The MRI pictures are then color-coded by a computer. In the Yale study, for example, resting brain cells are blue. Blood rushing glucose and oxygen to brain cells at work is yellow and red.

The brains of people who have difficulty reading show a more diffuse blood flow, Lyon says.

By asking people to perform different tasks — identify single letters, pick out rhyming words or signal whether two words belong to the same category — researchers have been able to pinpoint the discrete sections of the brain used in reading.

One part of the brain, the extrastriate cortex, identifies letters. Another part, the inferior frontal gyrus, identifies the sounds associated with those letters. And a third section, the superior temporal gyrus, reaches for meaning.

Yale researchers see this difference explicitly when they show research subjects made-up words, such as "joat" and "mote," and ask them to signal whether they rhyme. To do so, they have to be able to sound out the words.

People who can't sound out words appear to have lighter blood flow to the language regions of their brains, Lyon says.

"We apparently don't get as much flow and volume in those regions of the brain" in dyslexics, Lyon says. "But it's very important to point out we don't know exactly why. All we know is there are brain differences in people who do not read well if they're dyslexic."

In February 1995, the Shaywitzes announced a major finding. They had identified and mapped the sections of the brain that process language. In so doing, they had discovered that men generally use only half of their brains for these tasks while women use both lobes.

As headlines around the globe trumpeted the "Battle of the Brains," the importance of the Shaywitzes' discovery about the brain's language processing was all but obscured by the popular appeal of the gender differences.

Much quieter but perhaps more significant has been their research into the ways that the brains of dyslexics differ from those of normal readers. The Shaywitzes are also beginning a trial with Syracuse University researchers to determine whether intensive training can improve the way dyslexics process information.

The Shaywitzes are reluctant to discuss unpublished findings, and they caution that it is still far too early to draw conclusions. But they say they hope one day to be able to demonstrate physical differences in the brain of a dyslexic.

"One reason we are so excited is that we do think we will be able to produce concrete evidence of this person's disability," says Sally Shaywitz. "It would be like an X-ray of a person's broken arm, something you could actually see. Reading disabilities for so long have been a hidden disability."

Jack Pikulski, a University of Delaware reading professor and president of the International Reading Association based in Newark, Del. — an organization that has promoted the whole-language approach — says the NIH research offers valuable insights. But he cautions against drawing conclusions from it about the general population and reading.

"Be careful. ... They concentrated on the 20 to 25 percent having difficulty," Pikulski says of the studies. "We shouldn't generalize about what is happening with the broader population."

Pikulski says he is working to bring balance to the reading debate. Whole-language proponents, he says, have been misled by their success with children for whom reading comes easily, incorrectly deducing that learning to read is as natural as learning to speak.

On the other hand, he also fears that the NIH research with children having serious reading problems will lead to intensive phoneme training and phonics in-

Four steps to reading

Research shows that people learning to read must first understand the sounds that make up words. Then they must link these sounds to letters, vocabulary and meaning. Studies suggest that problem readers have trouble sounding out words and are often blocked at that point.

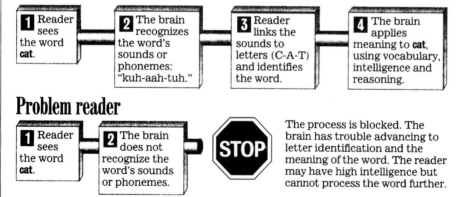
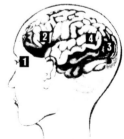

SOURCES: Scientific American, November 1996; Collins Medical Dictionary

EMILY HOLMES : SUN STAFF

struction for children who don't need it. "We have to be careful," Pikulski says, "that we don't say that everybody needs 20 minutes of phoneme-awareness training."

But Lyon disputes that the NIH studies' conclusions are restricted to poor readers: "Normal readers require phoneme awareness and phonics and whole language just as lousy readers do. ... We're finding that normal readers benefit as well."

Reading war

What leaves the scientific laboratory as a scholarly debate becomes a bare-knuckles brawl on the schoolyard.

"Brain dead!" Siegfried Engelmann of Oregon, creator of the phonics-based Direct Instruction program, calls proponents of whole language.

"This magic show that suggested that kids would learn to read if you immersed them in language!" he explodes. "I mean that is total, unmitigated b—s—."

In turn, Kenneth Goodman, author of "What's Whole About Whole Language," labels phonics a "flat-earth view of the world."

"To be opposed to phonics," says Goodman, who introduced whole language to U.S. schools, "is to be a kind of an anti-Christ. Phonics is surrounded by evangelical fervor."

Caught between the religious right and the humanist left, phonics has been sprinkled with holy water and splattered with mud — to the horror of scientists.

Liberal educators and humanists have been turned off by the perception that where there is phonics, Bible-reading in the classroom cannot be far behind. As de-

Phonics

Phonics — which stresses teaching children the sounds of words — dates to the 1700s. Since then, it has been eclipsed from time to time by the whole-language approach.

1700s – mid-1800s: Children are taught to read through memorization of the alphabet. Primary text: the Bible.

1783: Noah Webster publishes "The American Spelling Book," used for almost 100 years.

Mid-1800s – early 1900s: McGuffey Readers prevail. Very phonics oriented.

1910 – 1920: Ginn and Co.'s Beacon Readers, an "efficient and intelligent sequence of systemic phonics."

1955: "Why Johnny Can't Read," by Rudolf Flesch, attacks look-say instruction, urges a return to phonics. "We've thrown 3,500 years of civilization out the window," he writes.

1967: Jeanne S. Chall's "Learning to Read: The Great Debate," endorses direct instruction in phonics.

1981: Twenty-six years after "Why Johnny Can't Read," Rudolf Flesch publishes "Why Johnny Still Can't Read."

1984: The federal Commission on Reading issues "Becoming a Nation of Readers." "The issue is no longer, as it was several decades ago, whether children should be taught phonics," the commission said.

1995: California's "ABC" laws require instructional materials to include "systematic, explicit phonics, spelling and basic computational skills." North Carolina and Ohio follow suit.

1995 – 1997: "Word Identification" programs in most Maryland school systems include phonics.

Whole language

Whole-language — which stresses teaching children the meaning of words — dates to the mid-1800s.

Mid-1800s: Inspired by Jeffersonian democratic ideals, some educators say reading instruction should be "meaning based." Phonics comes under attack.

1930s: Look-say or whole word (not whole language) emerges, exemplified by Dick and Jane readers. Instruction emphasizes reading comprehension.

1940s – 1960s: Dick and Jane readers eventually grab 80 percent of the textbook market, helping teach 85 million children to read. "Copycat" readers appear, most with big, bold pictures and brother-sister teams — Alice and Jerry, Ned and Nancy, Susan and Tom, Bruce and Barbara, Janet and Mark.

1960s: Dick and Jane begin to fade but "look-say" readers dominate into the 1970s.

Late 1970s: Whole language emerges with intellectual roots in New Zealand, Europe and North America. Phonics de-emphasized. Greater emphasis placed on the meaning of text.

1982: "The Read-Aloud Handbook," by Jim Trelease, is published. This best seller places great emphasis on real literature.

1987: All California schools convert to whole language.

scribed by its foes, phonics is taught by modern-day Cotton Mathers who would drill little minds into submission.

Meanwhile, phonics proponents cast whole language as an illogical, scattershot approach that would be laughable if its consequences were not so tragic.

"In hindsight, whole language seems just bizarre," says Alice R. Furry, an administrator with the Sacramento County Office of Education, who helped change the California school system's curriculum from exclusively whole language to one that includes phonics. "The fact that we've taken this long to realize phonics is essential reading instruction is scandalous."

No one, phonics advocates note, would expect a beginning piano student to be able to play Chopin's "Minute Waltz" after simply listening to the composer's music. Scales, arpeggios and years of practice come first.

Yet, as Barbara Ruggles, a Chicago teacher and member of the American Federation of Teachers, testified last summer before Congress, that is essentially what advocates of whole language expect children to do: "If we are not teaching letter-sound relationships, blending, sounding out words _ then we are not giving our children the start they need to become fluent, independent readers," she said.

But even those who support phonics emphasize that not everything labeled phonics works. Children may turn away from reading if all they receive is drill. "If phonics had solved all the problems of the '70s," says Robert E. Slavin, a leading educational researcher at the Johns Hopkins University, "whole language wouldn't have dominated."

The moderates in the debate — and they risk being trampled by both sides — argue that the best reading instruction comes from a careful pairing of phonics and literature.

"Everyone wants to focus on the reading wars — whole language vs. phonics," Lyon says. "But there is no debate. At a certain stage of reading, phonics is necessary. Then children need literature to read. Why we polarize it is a mystery to me."

Little new

For all the dirt kicked up in the reading war, there is little new about phonics. American schools have taught children to read by sounding out words, off and on, for more than a century.

Studies compiled over the past 80 years have supported phonics as the best introduction to reading. Even the contentious 1984 Commission on Reading, formed by the equally divided National Academy of Education, came down on the side of phonics.

"Thus the issue is no longer, as it was several decades ago, whether children should be taught phonics," the commission wrote, but "how it should be done."

Even so, phonics instruction has been supplanted by one method after another, from the Dick-and-Jane "look-say" approach of the 1930s to the 1970s to the whole-language movement of the 1980s and '90s.

In his 1955 best seller, "Why Johnny Can't Read," Rudolf Flesch attacked American schools for abandoning phonics. Twenty-six years later, Flesch fired a second volley with "Why Johnny Still Can't Read."

While Flesch was hostile to educators — and lost some credibility — Jeanne S. Chall, professor emeritus at the Harvard Graduate School of Education and one of the nation's most respected reading experts, was measured and thorough.

Her 1967 book, "Learning to Read: The Great Debate," examined educational research going back to the beginning of the century and found that children who have difficulty learning to read have trouble making letter-sound connections. She endorsed systematic phonics.

"If you stress meaning at the beginning, you get just the opposite," Chall says. "If you stress reading words at the beginning, they get the meaning later."

Now, having spent her career trying to impose fact over fancy, Chall is writing a book on why the education world disregards research. "You have an accumulation of evidence and research," she says. "Then someone gets an idea. All of the research is ignored."

Recently, Lyon wrote to tell her that she ought to be pleased that NIH research argues for the pro-phonics findings she published 30 years ago.

"I'm not sure I feel so good about it," Chall says. "It's very unfortunate all this was known and ignored."

Sun staff writers Marego Athans, Mike Bowler and Howard Libit and research librarian Andrea Wilson contributed to this article.

From *Reading by 9, Part Two, The Baltimore Sun,*
November 3, 1997

SECTION II

Word Structure

 The History of the English Language

The History of the English Language

by Stephen Krensky

Language is something that most of us take for granted. Words seem to appear automatically in our heads; sentences pop out at our request. We hardly think about how and why we choose them. We read and write, speak and listen, as though we have done it always. This is not true, of course. We are not born with a language at the tip of our tongues, nor do we put on a language like a new winter coat. Learning a language is more like gathering leaves in October. We rake them up, either deliberately or at random, watching the pile grow larger as the leaves fall in ever increasing numbers.

Whether we remember it or not, there was a time for each of us before the leaves began to fall. A newborn baby does not speak a language; he simply gurgles. Gurgling is a sound he makes without thinking about it. But babies are smart. Soon they're imitating their parents, their brothers and sisters, and anybody else they meet. One thing all these people do is talk. They do not talk the same way everywhere, though. Different words are used in different places. In the United States a baby is a *baby,* but in France he is an *enfant* and in Germany a *Säugling.* A baby will naturally learn the language he hears. If it is French, he will come to speak French. If it is German, he will come to speak German. And if it is English, he will some day speak that.

The idea of language itself is a complicated one. When a baby cries for the first time, he is only reacting to discomfort. Babies cry when they're hungry or thirsty, frightened or hurt. Sometimes they cry because they're in a bad mood. Babies cry a lot. But when a baby realizes—as all babies do—that crying will bring help, he cries with a purpose. Crying has become an expression of his unhappiness. The deliberate use of this expression marks the beginning of the baby's language.

The notion of representing ideas with symbols can be traced back through recorded history, and undoubtedly it existed before the advent of writing. The existence of words, either written or spoken, is not as old as some other forms of language. Sign language, for example, probably preceded it. Even today we know the difference between an angry face and a smiling one without the need for words. And we still wave at people to greet them or to get their attention.

Sign language, though, is hampered by its need to be seen. A sign for help cannot be noticed at a distance, and it is useless at night. A cry for help would be heard in both instances. The development of speech might have followed when one particular cry for help was used by a group of people living together. At the same time, someone may have started mimicking the hiss of a snake or the crackle of burning wood. Before long a hiss might mean *snake,* and a crackling noise might stand for *fire.* And the creation of a few words would soon lead to others. We cannot prove that speech began in this fashion, but it's entirely possible.

Speech alone, though, is difficult to examine and even harder to preserve. Written languages do not have these drawbacks. These advantages undoubtedly led to their development, beginning with picture writing. The idea behind it was simple: a picture of an object identified that object. Rather than write *cow* to mean the four-legged animal that gives us milk, people drew a picture of a cow. We still draw pictures, though most of us don't think of them in terms of language. But the famous old saying "One picture is worth a thousand words" shows that words and pictures have been related for a long time. And if one picture could identify one object, a series of pictures could tell a story—the tale of a successful hunt or of building a home. A lengthy story, however, would take many pictures, an awkward practice. And some things are more complicated to draw than a cow. How would anybody draw a picture of right and wrong? Or how would we draw pictures to explain the history of the English language?

What was needed were written symbols to represent the sounds in spoken words. An alphabet is a collection of written symbols, each of which represents a different sound. When individual letters are grouped together, they form a word. A word can represent anything. *Love, hate, funny, sad, dog, run,* and *yellow* are all words, but they have different meanings. These words are formed with the Roman alphabet, which was passed along by the Romans during their European conquests. The Romans had not invented it, though. They had adapted it, as they adapted so many ideas, from the Greeks. The Greeks, however, had not invented it, either. Their alphabet had come from the Phoenicians and the Hebrews, who lived in the Middle East. The word *alphabet* itself comes from the first two letters of the Greek alphabet: *alpha* and *beta.* These names echo those of the first two letters of the Hebrew alphabet: *'aleph* and *bēth.*

The borrowing and adapting that have led to the modern Roman alphabet are similar to the evolution that has marked the English language as a whole. Neither has stood alone in its development. English is related to other languages, just as we are related to other people. We share

features and habits of our parents and grandparents, our brothers and sisters, and even our cousins. Our inheritance may be the shape of a nose, the color of our eyes, or a particular sense of humor. For English the features and habits show up in its vocabulary, pronunciation, and sentence structure.

The influences that contributed to English are not without some confusing legacies. Words that sound alike, such as *waste* and *waist,* are not spelled alike; nor do they mean the same thing. And what about separate words with identical spellings but different meanings? We take a *bow* by bending at the waist, but a *bow* is also the front of a ship. Then, too, we shoot a *bow* and arrow. It's enough to make anybody dizzy. But beneath the confusion is a rich and varied pattern, the work of many tribes and nations over thousands of years. Yet English was hardly constructed with careful planning, as the Romans built their roads or the Egyptians raised their pyramids. It was not created by any one people, but created by many. Most of all, it was a by-product of invasion and conquest.

The common ancestor of English and many other languages is the Indo-European language. It was spoken in east-central Europe over five thousand years ago. Other languages were spoken then in other places, but they had no influence on the birth of English. Although the Indo-European language was not written down, we know which modern languages stem from it because they share certain similarities. One clue is in the vocabulary. Words like *father* and *winter,* for example, are similar even in languages that exist thousands of miles apart. So, while Persian and French, or English and Sanskrit, look and sound very different from one another, they are not as different as they seem.

The differences between them arose when the speakers of Indo-European broke up into smaller groups that migrated through Europe and Asia. The Indo-European people ended up spread out over two continents, and any language stretched that far was bound to snap into separate parts.

Some of the migrating people settled in and around what is now Germany. Their language, Germanic, divided into three main sections: East Germanic, North Germanic, and West Germanic. It is from West Germanic that English—as well as Dutch, Flemish, and Frisian—came.

Fifteen hundred years ago three tribes speaking a form of West Germanic lived among the lowlanders on the North Sea coast. Their languages were closely related, and the three tribes—known as the Angles, the Saxons, and the Jutes—understood one another. At about that time most of Europe was overrun by German tribes—Ostrogoths, Vandals, and Visigoths among them. It was continental Europe that attracted their attention, though, leaving Britain (as England was then known) to be invaded by the Angles, the Saxons, and the Jutes.

The natives of Britain were the Celts. They had been conquered over four hundred years earlier by the Romans, who had left some time before. The Celts were not at all united, apparently satisfied to fight among themselves. This proved their undoing. By the year 600 the Germanic invaders had driven the Celts into Wales, taken them into captivity, or killed them. And while the Romans had looked on Britain as merely an outpost, the Angles, the Saxons, and the Jutes had come to stay. In fact the Angles, being the biggest and most widely settled of the three tribes, eventually gave their name to the land, people, and language of their new home. *Engle* they were soon called, and *Engla land* their country. In time the name would shorten to *England*.

The Germanic invasion overlapped the Christian conversion of Britain. By 700 most of the Anglo-Saxons, as we call the descendants of the three tribes, had been adopted into the Roman Catholic Church.

The first manuscripts written in English appeared during this period. The Germanic invaders had originally brought their own alphabet with them, but English clerics, newly converted to Christianity, chose instead to record English speech with Latin, or Roman, letters. The next two centuries witnessed the development of Old English. (Old English is the name we give to the first phase of the English language.) It had four major dialects. Northumbrian and Mercian were spoken by the Angles, Kentish by the Jutes, and West Saxon by the Saxons. The most famous example of Old English literature, *Beowulf,* comes from Northumbrian. It is a long poem that tells of the Viking warrior-king Beowulf, who kills the monster, Grendel, and Grendel's mother, with a magic sword. He later sets out to defeat a ravaging dragon, and though he is successful, the victory costs him his life.

Many of the objects and ideas described in Old English in *Beowulf* and other works have remained with us. These words concern such integral parts of daily life that they have proven impossible to dislodge. *Day, night, father, mother, work, love, hate,* and *summer* would not be exactly recognizable in their Old English forms, but the similarities are clear. Old English parents were a *faeder* and a *mōdor.* The *grund* Beowulf walked on is the *ground* we walk on now. The seemingly mysterious *weorc,* which looks like something magical, is only the *work* we all know far too well. Not every word has changed, though. *Winter,* for example, is the same cold and snowy season today that it was a thousand years ago.

Beginning in about the eighth century the Vikings began to trouble the Anglo-Saxons. They were great explorers, the Vikings. Five hundred years before Columbus bumped into North America while searching for India, the Vikings had come and gone. But clearly not all Vikings enjoyed long sea voyages, and England was conveniently nearby.

The Viking attacks united the Anglo-Saxons

against their common enemy. Their combined strength was greatest under Alfred the Great (849-899), who succeeded to the West Saxon throne in 871. He defeated the northern invaders regularly until they were discouraged enough to give Anglo-Saxons some years of peace. Once he secured his domain, Alfred turned his attention to scholarship. The story is told that when he was a young boy, his mother promised a book of Anglo-Saxon poems to the first of her children who learned to read. Though Alfred had several older brothers, he won the book. His early affection for learning stayed with him his whole life. Because of Alfred and his successors the bulk of Old English writings are known to us in West Saxon. And Alfred was not satisfied with recording only English works. He began a translation of important Latin manuscripts (into what was then called *Englisc*), promoted an enlightened code of laws, and commanded all young freemen who had the means to learn to read. As a result England had a written standard of language and a richness of expression long before other European countries.

While King Alfred had confined the Vikings to one part of England during his reign, after his death they finally defeated the Anglo-Saxons. The fate of the conquered people, however, was not the one the Celts had suffered. There were bonds between the Vikings and the Anglo-Saxons that had not existed between the Anglo-Saxons and the Celts. The Viking language was also Germanic in origin, and their heritage had things in common with Anglo-Saxon customs. Also, the cultural and physical similarities made it easier for both the peoples and their languages to mingle. The legacy of this mingling is evident in the English vocabulary. The Vikings' other contributions reflect in sound and meaning their harsh life and cold homeland. *Rotten* eggs would only smell bad, monsters wouldn't be *ugly*, and we would not *gasp* or *gape* in surprise had not the Vikings come to England.

While some Vikings were invading England others were invading the rest of Europe. One such group secured for themselves the northwest part of France. Northmen they were called, having come from the north, but Normans they became. The Normans quickly took on French customs and attitudes, but they were not content for long with their French holdings. They invaded England under William the Conqueror in 1066, an invasion that was more than simply another Viking attack. The Normans were not interested in mingling with the Anglo-Saxons; they wished to rule them. After their victory at the Battle of Hastings the Normans soon achieved this aim. They replaced most of the English nobles with their own leaders and took control of the Church. Norman French became the language of everything important—literature, commerce, law, and religion. Latin remained the language of learning, but only because the Normans studied with it as well.

The barriers that had risen around Old English were as strong as the walls of any castle. No one in authority either spoke it or wrote it, no one was recording it, and anyone who cared about its past assuredly did so in secret. The peasants alone spoke English freely, which divided them even further from the Norman lords. While Robin Hood and his merry men, for example, spoke an Old English dialect when planning an ambush, the Sheriff of Nottingham was plotting against them in Norman French. But a language needs more than merry men to preserve it. Despite the wagging peasant tongues, had these barriers remained around English for five hundred years, it might have disappeared altogether.

That English survived was through some lucky circumstances. First, in 1204 the French captured the Norman holdings in France. This left the Normans to look on England not as a colonial possession but as their home. The situation worsened when some newly arrived French nobles tried to change the language of the English court from Norman French to Parisian French, the language of Paris. It didn't matter that the Normans had done the same thing to the Anglo-Saxons two hundred years earlier. They were certainly not going to tolerate any notions of French superiority. In protest, many of them turned to the unpretentious language of their subjects.

The Black Death also did its part. This plague swept through England killing thousands and thousands of people. Its worst effects were felt in the cities, where the Normans were concentrated. Once the plague passed, Anglo-Saxons began filling some professional posts because there were no longer enough Normans to fill the posts alone. Consequently English resurfaced above the lower classes. Meanwhile the ongoing Hundred Years' War (1337-1453) widened the breach between England and France, severing the political ties that remained.

The language that rose in the wake of the French retreat was not the Old English of King Alfred, however. There is a well-known parlor game that illustrates what had happened. In a roomful of people—perhaps twenty or more—one person thinks of a message and whispers it to whoever is next to him, who in turn passes it down the line. The first person writes down the message he whispered, and the last person speaks aloud the message he received. The two messages rarely match. In passing from person to person words have been added or dropped, heard wrong, or said badly. So, too, the English language had drifted. Three centuries of passing it down the line had wrought certain changes. Sentences were simpler and sentence construction more flexible. Complicated word endings had been nibbled at by repeated mumbling, and both long and short words had been disguised by changing pronunciation.

Middle English (the name we give to the second phase of the English language) was the language that emerged. The strong influence of Norman French was its most apparent feature.

Not surprisingly, this influence was strongest in areas of Norman concern and weakest in areas they ignored. For example, tending livestock was a chore mostly left to the Anglo-Saxon peasants. And so *cows* and *sheep* retained their native English names. The Normans, though, did take a great interest in their meals. *Beef* and *mutton* were Norman French words that Middle English adopted, as were the ways of preparing them— *roast, boil, stew,* and *fry.* A peasant might *eat* his meal in a *house,* but a Norman could *dine* in a *palace.* And after the meal, while the Anglo-Saxon was busy trying to keep *warm,* a Norman spent his time *painting, dancing,* and writing *poetry.*

As Middle English absorbed these words further events ensured its stature. In 1349 English was reinstated in the schools, and in 1362 it became the language of the courts. New literary works also supported the language's claim to respectability. Foremost among the writers of the time was Geoffrey Chaucer. Although he knew several languages, he chose to write in English. His most famous book, *The Canterbury Tales,* particularly captured the full flavor of Middle English while revealing it as a language of transition.

In Chaucer's writings and in other places Middle English words were not spelled uniformly. The development of printing, though, helped to end the resulting confusion. William Caxton printed the first book in English in 1475, beginning a tradition that greatly enlarged the permanent record of the language. Hand-written manuscripts, though beautiful, took a long time to complete. As a result their numbers were relatively few, and they were unavailable to the general population. Only the rich or scholarly had the means to afford them, and so these manuscripts basically reflected only their interests and their speech patterns. Printing made the written page accessible to many more people— people who enriched the language with new words and experiences. The printers' influence extended even to spelling, which achieved some printed uniformity that spread when other people began following their example.

This widening of background prepared the way for the beginning of Modern English (the name we give to our current speech). One major difference between Middle and Modern English is in how words are pronounced. In 1400 the final *e* in such words as *space* was pronounced. It sounded like the *e* in *father*. By 1600 the final *e* was silent. Similarly, the *ed* in words like *looked* and *cooked* was pronounced. *Lookedd* and *cookedd*, Chaucer would have said. Now, of course, we say *lookt* and *cookt*. A more sweeping change was the Great Vowel Shift, which is our name for what happened to the pronunciation of *a, e, i, o,* and *u.* For example, Chaucer said *about* like we say *aboot.* The shift finally stopped in the seventeenth century, and the basic sound of English hasn't altered much since. An enormous growth in vocabulary has also marked Modern English. In the eighth century English clerics seeking converts to Christianity used native words instead of Latin whenever possible. By doing so they hoped to make the conversion seem more familiar. Fourteenth- and fifteenth-century scholars, however, were trying to make their writings seem impressive, not familiar. Latin was still impressive, even if an increasing number of things were being written in English. It was not unusual to add a Latin or Latin-based word to an English text in the hope of improving its appearance. Whether or not any improvement took place, English gained a lot of words in the process. Before long people were adding Greek words to the language as well. At times the additions weren't necessary. Today a sad person can receive both *sympathy* and *compassion* from a considerate friend. He won't feel any better knowing that the first comes from the Greek and the second from Latin, but he probably won't feel any worse, either.

One thing that did not affect Modern English was another conquest. The defeat of the Spanish Armada in 1588 ended the last threat to English sovereignty that might have decidedly changed the language. And while England was establishing itself politically its literature was delivering the final blow to anybody who thought English inferior to other languages. The works of Sidney, Spenser, Jonson, Milton, and, most of all, Shakespeare displayed a solid literary foundation that the English people could point to with pride. In the late 1600's English even began competing with Latin as the language of scholarship. Sir Isaac Newton wrote about the laws of motion and gravity in his *Principia Mathematica,* a Latin work. Seventeen years later his study of light, *Optiks,* was published In English.

The stability that English had reached by the eighteenth century was unmatched in its earlier history. Some people were so pleased with it that they proposed freezing the language in place. They feared that importing more foreign words would corrupt the perfect state English had achieved. But how many foreign words are really too many? And how does one freeze a language? Their idea melted away in the realization that it was impossible to carry out.

It was true, though, that English had reached a juncture where rules setting forth its grammar and usage would prove useful. Looming large was the need for precise word definitions. An early English dictionary by Robert Cawdrey had appeared in 1604. It briefly defined about twenty-five hundred words, hardly enough for most purposes. Several other dictionaries were published in the next hundred and fifty years, with varying success, but none equaled the dictionary of Samuel Johnson, published in 1755. Dr. Johnson had spent eight years completing it. The dictionary contained forty thousand precise definitions, studded with a hundred and sixteen thousand quotations from literature to help illustrate meanings. It was a unique achievement. Mirroring the thoughts of his peers, Dr. Johnson had at first set out to secure the language permanently. By the time he had finished, he knew that language could not be caged, however noble the intent of the warden.

The establishment of dictionaries and other linguistic tools helped mold the general shape of the English language. In the last few hundred years most of the changes English has undergone have resulted from its geographic expansion. The isolation that fractured the ancient Indo-European language could not do the same thing to English. Such isolation no longer exists; the advances in transportation and communication have seen to that. Nonetheless some adjustments were inevitable.

American English is a notable example. Over two hundred million people speak it, far more than all the other English-speaking peoples put together. Their diverse cultural and ethnic backgrounds have decidedly influenced our language. The native Americans were the first to have an impact. They had names for things they made, like *moccasins* and *tomahawks,* and for animals unknown in Europe, like *moose, raccoons,* and *skunks.* The colonists had enough to do without thinking up new names, so they borrowed the existing ones. Later developments—after the American Revolution, when British influence had lessened—led to differences in spelling and vocabulary. We write *center* when the British write *centre;* we also write *color* for *colour, connection* for *connexion,* and *traveler* for *traveller.* The pattern of *-er* for *-re, -or* for *-our,* and one *l* for two is repeated in many words. The wrinkles in vocabulary are more complicated. While Americans find their way through the dark with a *flashlight,* the British use an electric *torch.* British babies ride around in *prams,* not *baby carriages,* and British *constables* keep law and order across the ocean from American *policemen.* These and other differences, however, affect the flavor more than the body of the language. Even a thick accent cannot prevent an Englishman from understanding his American counterpart.

The British Empire, of course, was not confined to North America, and English has grown in response to its far-flung contacts. From Arabic have come such words as *syrup* and *magazine;* the Chinese gave us *tea;* the native Australians threw us a *boomerang;* while from the West Indies hail the unlikely pair of *hurricane* and *barbecue.* Of all the world's languages only English remains important in so many countries. It is the predominant language of Canada, Australia, and New Zealand, as well as a major force in India, Pakistan, South Africa, and other former British territories.

Today the ages of conquest and exploration are over, but English continues to expand. Its growth is not the wild and unpredictable one of medieval times, yet it retains some surprises. New words have been formed with practical inventiveness. *Greenhouse* and *blackboard* were made by joining together existing words. *Laser* comes from another source; it is the sum of the first initials of *L*ight *A*mplification by *S*timulated *E*mission of *R*adiation. We can easily see why it was shortened. Other words, especially in the sciences, have been named for people. We *pasteurize* milk because Louis Pasteur invented the process. And the *watt,* a unit of electrical power, is named after James Watt, who invented the steam engine. Meanwhile words like *television* are created when the things they represent enter our experience.

English is now a language of over five hundred thousand words. In keeping with its history, about a third of these come from Old English and the Viking language, and two-thirds from the more recent French and Latin. We're not sure, in fact, whether some words came to English directly from Latin or passed through French along the way. The problem is like receiving a gift through the mail and deciding after it's been unwrapped whether it came first class or special delivery. But whatever their origin, English words currently make up the vast majority of the world's books and newspapers. Only Chinese is spoken by more people. Its influence, though, is essentially confined to mainland China.

We can never be certain about a language's future. Old English disappeared in England after the Norman invasion, but a cousin of it lives on in Modern Icelandic. Middle English gave way under the pressure of a growing vocabulary and changes in pronunciation, yet certain Scottish dialects retain much in common with it. About Modern English we can at least say that it will probably not undergo any radical transformations. Still, new words will be coined and old ones dusted off to be used again so long as people continue to write and speak. Definitions will shift, shrink, and expand depending on generations of interpretation. Following the course of the English language is like following a path through uncharted territory. It is easy to get lost along the way. A dictionary can't show us where the path ends, but like a good compass, it will always help us to keep our bearings.

Sound/Print Connection

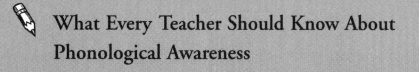

What Every Teacher Should Know About Phonological Awareness

by Joseph K. Torgesen and Patricia Mathes

Phonological awareness is rapidly becoming one of the most important educational "buzzwords" of this decade. Teachers are talking about it, parents are trying to understand it, and publishers of early reading materials are trying to include it. Yet, it is a concept that is easily misunderstood. Some confuse it with "phonics," and others consider it to be a part of general print awareness, and it is neither of these things. We must also be careful about how we teach it to children; unless we thoroughly understand the concept and its role in reading development, we may easily teach it in ways that produce no real benefit. This short essay is an attempt to share what is currently known about the nature of phonological awareness, why it is important in reading growth, why children differ from one another in their ability to acquire it, and how we may most effectively incorporate it into reading instruction. Although we currently know a great deal about this concept, there is still much that is not known, so we shall try to point out some of the questions along the way.

What is phonological awareness?

In order to understand the concept of phonological awareness, we must first know what a phoneme is. A phoneme is the smallest unit of sound in our language that makes a difference to its meaning. For example, the word *cat* has three phonemes, /k/-/a/-/t/. By changing the first phoneme, we can produce the word *bat*. Changing the second phoneme creates the word *cot*, and we can obtain the word *cab* by altering the final phoneme. Words in English (in fact, in all languages) are composed of strings of phonemes. This is fortunate, because it allows us to create all the words we will ever need by using various combinations of just 44 different speech sounds!

Speech scientists have discovered that the human brain is specifically adapted for processing many different kinds of linguistic information, and one part of our biological endowment allows us to process the complex phonological information in speech without actually being aware of the individual phonemes themselves. This is one of the human abilities that makes acquiring speech a natural process, so that almost everyone in the world learns to speak a language with very little direct instruction. As we will explain more fully later, learning to read requires that children become consciously aware of phonemes as individual segments in words. In fact, phonological awareness is most commonly defined as one's sensitivity to, or explicit awareness of, the phonological structure of words in one's language. In less formal language, it involves the ability to notice, think about, or manipulate the individual sounds in words.

One of the early signs of emerging sensitivity to the phonological structure of words is ability to play rhyming games and activities. In order to tell whether two words rhyme, the child must attend to the sounds in words rather than their meaning. In addition, the child must focus attention on only one *part* of a word rather than the way it sounds as a whole. As children grow in awareness of the phonemes in words, they become able to judge whether words have the same first or last sounds, and with further development, they become able to actually pronounce the first, last, or middle sounds in words. At its highest levels of development, awareness of individual phonemes in words is shown by the ability to separately pronounce the sounds in even multi-syllable words, or to tell exactly how two words like *task* and *tacks* are different (the order of the last two phonemes is reversed).

Acquiring phonological awareness actually involves learning two kinds of things about language. First, it involves learning that words can be divided into segments of sound smaller than a syllable. Second, it involves learning about individual phonemes themselves. As children acquire more and more conscious knowledge of the distinctive features of phonemes (how they sound when they occur in words, or how they feel when they are pronounced), they become more adept at noticing their identity and order when they occur in words. For example, while children in the first semester of first grade might be able to notice the first or last sound of a word like *man,* by the end of first grade, most children can easily, and relatively automatically, notice all the sounds in a more complex word like *clap*. At both beginning and more advanced levels, phonological awareness strongly supports learning about the ways that the words in our language are represented in print.

Why is phonological awareness important in learning to read?

When children learn to read, they must acquire two different kinds of skills. They must learn how to identify printed words, and they must learn how to comprehend written material. Their major challenge when they first enter school is to learn to accurately identify printed words, and

this brings them face to face with the alphabetic principle. English is an alphabetic language, meaning that words are represented in print roughly at the level of phonemes. For example, the word *cat* has three phonemes, and three letters are used to represent them; the word *which* has three phonemes, but five letters are used to represent them.

In our language, the alphabetic principle presents two important learning challenges to children. First, individual phonemes are not readily apparent as individual segments in normal speech. When we say the word *dog,* for example, the phonemes overlap with one another (they are coarticulated), so that we hear a single burst of sound rather than three individual segments. Coarticulating the phonemes in words (i.e., starting to pronounce the second phoneme (/r/) in the word *frost* while we are still saying the first phoneme (/f/) makes speech fluent, but it also makes it hard for many children to become aware of phonemes as individual segments of sound within words.

The second challenge presented by the alphabetic principle in our language is that there is not always a regular one-to-one correspondence between letters and phonemes. For example, some phonemes are represented by more than one letter (i.e., ch, sh, wh, ai, oi). In addition, sometimes the phoneme represented by a letter changes, depending on other letters in the word (*not* vs. *note, fit* vs. *fight, not* vs. *notion*), or pronunciation of parts of some words may not follow any regular letter-phoneme correspondence patterns, such as in *yacht* or *choir.* Variations in the way that phonemes are represented by letters present problems for some children in learning *phonics* skills in reading, while the coarticulation of phonemes in spoken language makes acquisition of *phonological awareness* a challenge for many children.

If understanding and utilizing the alphabetic principle in reading words presents such learning challenges for children, the obvious question, and one that has been repeatedly asked over the last century, is whether it is really necessary for children to understand the principle and master its use in order to become good readers. On the basis of research on reading, reading development, and reading instruction conducted over the past twenty years, we now know that the answer to this question is very strongly in the affirmative (Beck & Juel, 1995). Children who quickly come to understand the relationships between letters and phonemes, and who learn to utilize this information as an aid to identifying words in print, almost invariably become better readers than children who have difficulty acquiring these skills (Share & Stanovich, 1995).

There are at least three ways that phonological awareness is important in learning beginning word reading skills. These are:

1. *It helps children understand the alphabetic principle.* Without at least a beginning level of phonological awareness, children have no way of understanding how the words from their oral language are represented in print. Unless they understand that words have sound segments at the level of the phoneme, they cannot take advantage of an alphabetic script (Liberman, Shankweiler & Liberman, 1989). They will also not be able to understand the rationale for learning individual letter sounds, and the common request to "sound out" words in beginning reading will not make sense to them.

2. *It helps children notice the regular ways that letters represent sounds in words.* If children can notice all four phonemes in the word *flat,* it helps them to see the way the letters correspond to the sounds. This ability to notice the match between the letters and sounds in words has two potential benefits to children learning to read. First, it reinforces knowledge of individual letter-sound correspondences, and second, it helps in forming mental representations of words so

they can be accurately recognized when they are encountered in print again. Research has shown that the associations children form between the letters and sounds in words creates the kind of "sight word" representations that are the basis of fluent reading (Ehri, 1997).

3. *It makes it possible to generate possibilities for words in context that are only partially "sounded out."* For example, consider a first grade child who encounters a sentence such as "John's father put his bicycle in the car," and cannot recognize the fifth word. A relatively early level of phonological awareness supports the ability to search one's mental dictionary for words that begin with similar sounds. Thus, if the child knows the sound represented by the letter *b,* he/she can mentally search for words that begin with that sound and fit the context. As children acquire more knowledge of "phonics" and can "sound out" more letters in words, their search for words with similar phonemes in them can proceed much more accurately.

As should be clear from this analysis, phonemic awareness has its primary impact on reading growth through its effect on children's ability to phonetically decode words in text. Although phonetic decoding skills should never be considered the end goal of reading instruction (phonetic decoding is too slow and effortful to support fluent reading and good comprehension), research now shows that, for most children, these skills are a critical step along the way toward effective reading skills.

To illustrate concretely the impact that deficient phonological awareness can have on the growth of reading skills, Figure 1 (see following page) presents information on the growth of word reading ability in a group of children who began first grade with relatively low levels of phonological awareness (Torgesen, Wagner & Rashotte, 1994). At the beginning of first grade, these children's performance on measures of phonological awareness was in the bottom 20% of a large group of children who all had estimated general verbal ability in the normal range. The numbers at the right of the graphs represent average grade level score at the end of fifth grade of children above and below the 20th percentile. From the top panel, we can see that children with weak phonological awareness ended up about two grade levels below their peers in sight word reading ability, and the bottom panel shows that their phonetic reading skills were more than three grade levels below their peers. On a measure of reading comprehension, the children with weak phonological awareness obtained a grade score of 3.9, which was three years behind the score of 6.9 obtained by their peers.

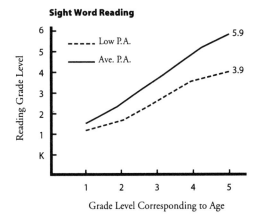

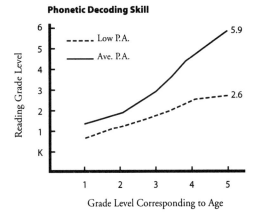

FIG. I: *Growth of sight word and phonetic decoding skill in children who begin first grade below the 20th percentile in phonological awareness*

Before we leave this section, it is important to remind ourselves that phonological awareness is not the only knowledge or skill required to learn to read. Longitudinal research has shown that phonological awareness is *necessary*, but not *sufficient* for becoming a good reader. Other phonological abilities may also affect children's ability to acquire phonetic decoding ability and sight word fluency, and a good vocabulary, general knowledge about the world, good thinking skills, and an interest in reading are clearly important in the development of reading comprehension.

What is the normal developmental course for phonological awareness?

Although reliable information about normal growth rates in phonological awareness is one of the questions remaining for further research, it is possible to outline some broad benchmarks of development for the early school years. There is even less information available for the preschool years, although a few studies have demonstrated beginning levels of phonological awareness in children as young as two-and-a-half to three years of age.

It is important to recognize that when we speak of phonological awareness in children as young as three years old, we are speaking of a very different level of this ability than is shown by most first grade children. The tasks used to assess phonological awareness in young children differ in at least two important ways from those used with older children. First, many of these tasks assess sensitivity to syllables and rhyme, which are more global aspects of the phonological structure of words than phonemes. These measures assess general *phonological sensitivity* rather than *phonemic awareness*. Second, some tasks, such as those that involve judging whether words have similar beginning sounds, require a less fully explicit knowledge of phonemes than tasks that ask children to pronounce or manipulate individual phonemes in words. Tasks that assess a more general level of phonological sensitivity (such as awareness of syllables or sensitivity to rhyme) are not as predictive of reading growth as measures that specifically assess awareness or sensitivity to phonemes in words.

Normally developing children enter kindergarten prepared to easily learn to play rhyming games and activities, and most of them can divide simple words into syllables by mid-year (thus showing good general *phonological* awareness). By the end of kindergarten, a child who is developing normally in phonological awareness should be able to judge rhyming words and generate new words that rhyme with a given word. They should also be able to respond to measures of *phonemic* awareness that require them to compare words on the basis of their first sounds. Most children can also pronounce the first phoneme of simple words when asked a question like, "What is the first sound in the word *man*?"

By midway in the first semester of first grade, children who are developing normally in phonological awareness can reliably blend phonemes together to produce two-phoneme words such as *on, in, at,* or *bee.* Children at this stage of development can also say what word is left if a given sound is dropped from the beginning or end of a three-phoneme word (i.e., say *man* without saying the /m/ sound).

With the beginning of reading instruction, most children's ability to perform on measures of phonemic awareness increases rapidly. By the end of first grade, average children who have received at least a moderate degree of instruction in "phonics" can pronounce all the sounds in a three-phoneme word such as *dog, hat,* or *fan.* Their phoneme-blending skills are also much better by this time, and, without too much trouble, they can blend words containing three and four phonemes. From this point, further development in phonemic awareness occurs primarily in the form of increasing accuracy and fluency in the skills acquired during first grade.

What causes differences among children in phonological awareness?

When children enter school, there is substantial variability in their level of phonological awareness, and their response to instruction in kindergarten produces an even larger range of individual differences by the end of the school year. The factors that cause individual differences among children in phonological awareness when they enter school are genetic endowment and preschool linguistic experience.

Research conducted over the last 20 years has shown that children vary significantly "in the phonological component of their natural capacity for language" (Liberman, Shankweiler & Liberman, 1989). This phonological ability, or talent, is a trait that is strongly heritable. In other words, children can vary in their talent for processing the phonological features of language in the same way that they vary among one another in musical ability, height, or hair color. In fact, large-scale studies involving identical twins have shown that about half of all the variation in linguistically related phonological skills is inherited (Olsen, Forsberg & Wise, 1994).

Talent in the area of phonological processing can vary quite independently from other areas of intellectual ability, although many studies show that it is at least moderately correlated with general learning ability. It is clearly possible, for example, to be average or above average in general intelligence while being severely deficient in the ability to acquire phonological awareness. Sometimes a lack of talent for processing the phonological features of language produces noticeable effects on language and speech development prior to school entry, but frequently it does not. In other words, it is possible to have a genetically transmitted weakness in the area of phonological processing that does not affect speech, but does affect early reading development. The reason for this is that reading requires children to become consciously aware of the phonemic segments in words while speech does not. With this said, it is nevertheless true that subtle speech difficulties are a common correlate of early problems in acquiring phonetically based reading skills (Catts, 1993).

The child's preschool linguistic environment can also exert a strong influence on sensitivity to the phonological structure of words at the time of school entry. Early experience with nursery rhymes, for example, can help children begin to notice and think about the phonological structure of words. Several research studies have shown that children who know more about nursery rhymes at age three are those that tend to be more highly developed in general phonological awareness at age four, and in phonemic awareness at age six (Bryant, MacLean, Bradley & Crossland, 1990). There is also consistent evidence that children from different socioeconomic backgrounds enter school with significantly different levels of sensitivity to the phonological structure of words. Some very recent work has begun to verify that children who come from backgrounds in which they have been more frequently exposed to letters and their names and to various kinds of reading activities show more advanced phonological awareness upon school entry than those with less experience in these areas.

After children enter school, the growth of their phonological awareness depends not only on what they are taught, but on their response to that instruction. Reading programs that contain explicit instruction in "phonics" produce more rapid growth in phonological awareness than approaches that do not provide direct instruction in this area. In addition, children who respond well to early reading instruction grow much more rapidly in phonological awareness than those who experience difficulties learning early

reading skills. In this sense, phonological awareness is both a *cause* and a *consequence* of differences among children in the rate at which they learn to read. Those who begin reading instruction with sufficiently developed phonological awareness understand the instruction better, master the alphabetic principle faster, and learn to read quite easily. In contrast, those who enter first grade with weak phonological awareness do not respond well to early reading instruction and thus do not have the learning experiences or acquire the reading knowledge and skill that stimulates further growth and refinement of phonological awareness.

Can direct instruction in phonological awareness help children learn to read more easily?

There have now been many research studies showing that it is possible to stimulate growth in phonological awareness by direct training. Even when the phonological awareness training contains only oral language activities (does not include letters or instruction in letter-sound correspondences), it can have a positive effect on general growth of early reading skills (Lundberg, Frost & Peterson, 1988). However, we also know that the effectiveness of oral language training in phonological awareness is significantly improved if, at some point in the training, children are helped to apply their newly acquired phonological awareness directly to reading and spelling tasks (Bradley & Bryant, 1985). While most instructional programs in phonemic awareness begin with oral language activities, most also conclude by leading children to apply their newly acquired ability to think about the phonemic segments in words to reading and spelling activities. *This is a very important point.* Training in phonological awareness should never be considered an isolated instructional end in itself. It will be most useful as part of the reading curriculum if it is blended seamlessly with instruction and experiences using letter-sound correspondences to read and spell words.

We also know from recent research that training programs in this area must go beyond beginning levels of phonological awareness to activities that draw attention to the phonemes in words. Thus, programs that only teach rhyme or syllable awareness will not be as effective as those that require children to become aware of individual phonemes in words.

Unfortunately, it is in the area of instruction in phonological awareness that many of our most important unanswered questions still lie (Blachman, 1997). This, of course, does not mean that we should delay implementing what we know, but rather that we should be open to refinements in our knowledge in this area as research progresses. For example, we do not yet have specific information, beyond the simple distinction already made, about how much phonological awareness is optimal for beginning reading instruction. We might say, "the more the merrier," but if we concentrate too much time in developing more phonological awareness than is needed before we begin actual instruction in reading, this may be a waste of valuable instructional time. Further, it is not yet clear what the optimal combination of training tasks might be. We know that training using oral language activities can stimulate the growth of phonological awareness, but it is also clear that direct instruction in "phonics" and spelling can also produce development in this area.

Another important question is whether training in phonological awareness prior to the beginning of reading instruction can actually prevent serious reading disabilities. We know that classroom-level training or small group training in phonological awareness consistently produces improvements in reading growth for groups of children. However, in all studies conducted thus far, there has always been a large range of individual differences in response to the instruction, with the most phonologically impaired children showing the least growth in response to training.

It is very likely that classroom-level instruction in phonological awareness will not be sufficient to prevent reading disabilities in children who have serious deficiencies in phonological talent. These children will require more intensive, detailed, and explicit instruction in order to achieve the levels of phonemic awareness required to support good reading growth. Although we do not know precisely what such instruction might eventually look like, one program that has been used successfully to stimulate phonological awareness in severely impaired children and adults actually helps them to discover the mouth movements or articulatory gestures that are associated with each phoneme (Lindamood & Lindamood, 1984). One of the goals of this method of instruction is to provide a way for individuals to "feel" the sounds in words as well as hear them.

On the basis of very substantial and consistent research findings, it is clear at this point that instruction to enhance phonological awareness should be part of reading instruction for every child. This instruction will accelerate the reading growth of all children, and it appears to be vital in order for at least 20% of children to acquire useful reading skills. However, it is also clear that this instruction is only one small part of an effective overall reading curriculum. Good training in phonological awareness should be combined with systematic, direct, and explicit instruction in "phonics" as well as rich experiences with language and literature to make a strong early reading curriculum. This "balanced" reading curriculum should also include early and consistent experiences with writing, both as a means to help children learn more about the alphabetic principle and to enhance their awareness of reading and writing as meaningful activities. Of course, all this instruction should be provided within a supportive, rewarding context that provides instructional adjustments for children depending upon the different ways they respond to the basic reading curriculum.

References and Further Reading

Beck, I.L., & Juel, C. (1995). The role of decoding in learning to read. *American Educator, 19,* 8-42.

Blachman, B.A. (1997). Early intervention and phonological awareness: A cautionary tale. In B. Blackman (Ed.). *Foundations of Reading Acquisition and Dyslexia: Implications for Early Intervention.* Mahwah, NJ: Lawrence Erlbaum Associates.

Bradley, L., & Bryant, P. (1985). *Rhyme and Reason in Reading and Spelling.* Ann Arbor: University of Michigan Press.

Bryant, P., MacLean, M., Bradley, L., & Crossland, J. (1990). Rhyme and alliteration, phoneme detection and learning to read. *Developmental Psychology, 26,* 429-438.

Catts, H.W. (1993). The relationship between speech-language impairments and reading disabilities. *Journal of Speech and Hearing Research, 36,* 948-958.

Ehri, L.C. (1997). Grapheme-phoneme knowledge is essential for learning to read words in English. In J. Metsala & L. Ehri (Eds.). *Word recognition in beginning reading.* Hillsdale, NJ: Erlbaum.

Liberman, I.Y., Shankweiler, D., & Liberman, A.M. (1989). The alphabetic principle and learning to read. In Shankweiler, D. & Liberman, I.Y. (Eds.). *Phonology and reading disability: Solving the reading puzzle* (pp. 1-33). Ann Arbor, MI: University of Michigan Press.

Lindamood, C.H., & Lindamood, P.C. (1984). *Auditory Discrimination in Depth.* Blacklick, Ohio: SRA.

Lundberg, I., Frost, J., & Peterson, O. (1988). Effects of an extensive program for stimulating phonological awareness in pre-school children. *Reading Research Quarterly, 23,* 263-284.

Olsen, R., Forsberg, H., & Wise, B. (1994). Genes, environment, and the development of orthographic skills. In V.W. Beringer (Ed.). *The varieties of orthographic knowledge I: Theoretical and developmental issues* (pp. 27-71).

Share, D.L., & Stanovich, K.E. (1995). Cognitive processes in early reading development: A model of acquisition and individual differences. *Issues in Education: Contributions from Educational Psychology, 1,* 1-57.

Torgesen, J.K., Wagner, R.K., & Rashotte, C.A. (1994). Longitudinal studies of phonological processing and reading. *Journal of Learning Disabilities, 27,* 276-286.

Francine R. Johnston

The reader, the text, and the task: Learning words in first grade

How do predictable texts fit with children's early reading experiences? In this article, Johnston explores three important factors in facilitating young children's word learning: the reader, the text, and the task.

I began teaching first grade when basal reading programs were standard in most classrooms. I was bothered by the fact that my students had to learn a great many sounds and sight words before they read anything, but I didn't know an alternative. I was introduced to predictable texts and the shared book approach (Holdaway, 1979) in a university reading course in 1986. That fall I taught all my children to read *The Cat on the Mat* by Brian Wildsmith (1982) on the first day of school. Of course the children could not actually read it in a conventional sense. They had quickly memorized it and with the help of pictures could recite it accurately, but they were, I felt sure, on their way to becoming engaged and confident readers.

It was not until I worked with an older child that my faith in predictable text began to falter. Eliza was a third grader reading at a beginning level, but she was bright and had good language skills. After we read a predictable book together she reread it easily, but I could see she was paying only superficial attention to the print on the page even when I asked her to slow down and point to the words.

One more event had an important influence on my thinking about predictable text. Pat Crook, my professor of children's literature, told me about her grandson, Kenny. His kindergarten class had been reading *Brown Bear, Brown Bear, What Do You See?* (Martin, 1967), and he recited the entire text to her over the phone. Pat's response was, "Kenny, you are learning to read." But Kenny replied, "I don't have to read it; I already know it." Despite his love for and mastery of the language in this predictable book, Kenny knew reading involved something more than memorization. He was right, of course. In order to read we must be able to identify the words on the page, and to read well we must be able to identify those words effortlessly and accurately.

While contextual cuing strategies (Clay, 1985) have captured the attention of the reading community, a large and stable sight vocabulary continues to be the hallmark of a successful reader. Good evidence exists that only beginning and struggling readers rely upon context to identify words (Biemiller, 1970; Nicholson, 1991; Stanovich, 1994). Extensive and automatic word knowledge frees fluent readers to focus on the meaning of what they read rather than figuring out or guessing at unfamiliar words (Perfetti, 1985).

I grappled with the question of how to facilitate word learning as a classroom teacher and now as I instruct future teachers. From the reading and research I have done, as well as from my experiences working with students in the early stages of reading, I have identified three critical factors: the reader, the text, and the task.

The reader

The young reader brings varying amounts of word knowledge and print skills to the task of recognizing and learning words. This developmental continuum has been well researched by Ehri (1994, 1995) and Juel (1991). Children with little or no alphabet knowledge and weak phonological awareness have been described as "pre-alphabetic" readers by Ehri or "visual cue" readers by Juel. These emergent readers rely upon nonphonetic graphic cues as a guide to word recognition. They might recognize the name of their favorite fast food restaurant on a cup emblazoned with a familiar print style or logo but would not be able to recognize that word somewhere else.

Beginners who have some understanding of letter-sound relationships and a concept of word are described by Ehri as "partial alphabetic" readers. These beginning readers might confuse *lion* and *leopard* in a story about big cats found at the zoo because they often use only initial letters as a cue for word recognition. As children's knowledge of letters and sounds grows to include more consonants and vowels, they are known as "full alphabetic" readers by Ehri or "decoders" by Juel. These more advanced beginners might confuse words like *boot* and *boat* or *past* and *paste* if seen in isolation.

With experience students acquire knowledge of vowel spelling patterns (such as *ai* and *ay* for the long sound of *a*) and orthographic chunks (such as *-ing* and *-tion*) and are able to make sense of and remember a large number of words. These students have reached an "automatic" stage as described by Juel or a "consolidated alphabetic" phase as described by Ehri, where there is little evidence of conscious word analysis. They have a large sight vocabulary that can be accessed immediately and accurately without reference to contextual cues. It is only occasionally that they confront unknown words that require decoding strategies.

We know that children do not learn large numbers of words by sight in the sense that they simply memorize the graphic form in a holistic way as an unanalyzed series of letters (Venezky & Massaro, 1979). Instead, children construct a complex system of storing and retrieving words, which grows ever more sophisticated, accurate, and automatic as they see the same words over and over in various contexts and as their word knowledge grows (Ehri, 1992, 1994). While only a partial representation of a word may be stored initially, repeated encounters and advancing word knowledge help to "fill in" the letter-sound details.

The first and most important information we need to know is where beginning readers are on the developmental continuum in order to plan instruction that will enhance word learning. Teachers can get a good sense of this development by noting reading errors, children's invented spellings, and word identification ability in isolation. For example, a child who reads *favorite* as *flavor* in the sentence "Chocolate is my favorite," spells it as FAVRT, and names it as *fort* when she sees it in isolation is clearly using consonant and vowel knowledge to make logical sense of the word. These partially correct efforts offer us valuable insights into her word knowledge.

The text

A substantial body of recent research supports the developmental nature of word learning, but there is little research on how the nature of the reading material influences word learning. The work that has been done suggests that this is an important issue. Juel and Roper/Schneider (1985) found that the type of text used by first graders played an important role in their word identification strategies. Children who used a decodable basal developed a phonological strategy based on letter-sound correspondences, and those using a high-frequency basal adopted a primarily visual strategy for word identification. The decodable basal group could read significantly more of the core words from the high-frequency basal series than vice versa.

Traditional basal text was designed to facilitate word learning by using words that were high in utility or frequency, repeated in a cumulative fashion, and easily decodable. Controlled vocabulary led to rather contrived text, and the basal program became lockstep, when ease of reading depended upon the cumulative mastery of words at earlier levels.

The nature of text considered appropriate and easy for beginning readers has undergone dramatic change as reflected in the recent first-grade materials created by basal publishers (Hoffman et al., 1994). Anthologies of predictable literature have replaced preprimers, and the vocabulary control of the past is hardly evident. Word recognition is supported by the illustrations, by patterned repetitive language, by rhythm and rhyme, and by the child's ability to anticipate and quickly memorize the language. Word learning is assumed to happen as children read and reread the text (Bridge, Winograd, & Haley, 1983), but evidence for this is limited.

The nature of text considered appropriate and easy for beginning readers has undergone dramatic change.

Bridge et al. (1983) found that first graders reading in predictable materials learned significantly more target words than children reading basal text; however, another study of kindergarten children (Bridge & Burton, 1982) found no significant difference. My experience with Eliza led me to wonder if word learning was negatively affected when reading became more a matter of memorization than attention to print. Although predictable text facilitates the beginner's efforts to identify words, it may not optimize word learning.

Despite my growing concern with predictable text I still felt that it offered needed support for beginning readers. Perhaps word learning in predictable text could be enhanced by the manner in which these materials were used and the follow-up activities employed. The instructional methods or tasks constitute the third critical factor.

The tasks

Beginners may zip through predictable books with joyous familiarity (Martin &

Brogan, 1971) without paying much attention to the print. Attention is important if they are to learn the words. A number of studies offer evidence that children learn words faster and more completely when those words are studied in isolation (Ehri & Roberts, 1979; Ehri & Wilce, 1980; Nemko, 1984). Ehri and Roberts (1979) attributed this learning to the notion of processing depth. Retention is a function of the depth to which a stimulus has been processed (Craik & Lockhart, 1972). Adams (1990) has warned that, "Where context is strong enough to allow quick and confident identification of the unfamiliar word, there is little incentive to pore over its spelling. And without studying the word's spelling, there is no opportunity for increasing its visual familiarity" (p. 217).

Activities such as flashcard drill, worksheets, writing words in sentences, decoding exercises, and most recently "word walls" (Cunningham, 1995) help focus children's attention on the printed form of words in isolation. However, Holdaway's shared book approach (1979) offers a whole-to-part model aligned with current literature-based practices. Children begin with the full support of the text, but they also work with sentences, words, letters, and sounds in a way that demands close attention to print. I wondered if this model might be used to compensate for any disadvantages associated with predictable text.

A study of word learning in predictable text

I developed a study to compare three word learning tasks using predictable text (Johnston, 1995). Each task represented a different point on the whole-to-part continuum and required a different degree of attention to print: (a) repeated readings (RR) of familiar text in which students had the full support of context, (b) working with sentence strips (SC) in which students had some support from the context, and (c) a modified word bank approach (WB) in which students worked with words in isolation. I selected these tasks because they seemed to be congruent with current practices. Repeated readings (Chomsky, 1976; Samuels, 1979) have been well researched with older readers and are frequently used by teachers. Word banks are a long-standing tradition associated with the Language Experience Approach developed by Stauffer (1970). Whole-to-part activities have been described by a number of practitioners in addition to Holdaway (e.g., Heald-Taylor, 1987; McCracken & McCracken, 1979, 1986; Rhodes, 1981) but have not been tested experimentally.

In addition to tasks, I wanted to examine the nature of the text by analyzing the kinds of words that occurred and which words were learned most readily. Words were rated according to four features: repetition, general word frequency, decodability, and concreteness. Concreteness was added because meaningful words such as *cakes* or *alligator* may be more memorable than abstract words like *you* or *some* (Ashton-Warner, 1963).

I also collected information about each student's reading ability in an individually administered assessment prior to the implementation of the study. The *Early Reading Screening Instrument* (ERSI) developed by Morris (1992) tests beginners' print-related word knowledge in terms of alphabet, concept of word, phonemic awareness, and word recognition.

Subject and materials. Participants included 51 children in three first-grade classrooms at a U.S. public school serving primarily low- and middle-income families. For 3 weeks the regular classroom teachers used my plans and materials, substituting for the variety of books, chart stories, and poetry they had been using in the first 2 months of school. Each week the students read three predictable books from the Story Box collection (1990), a widely used set of predictable books equivalent to preprimer text. The three books for each week were similar in terms of difficulty and vocabulary load but did not have more than a few words in common.

Procedures. All three books were introduced to the students in a similar fashion on the first day each week using the shared book approach. The teachers discussed the title and cover with the students, read the book aloud, and invited the children to react to and discuss it. The children then read along with the teacher in their own copies of the book two times before attempting an independent reading.

After the first day, each book was used for a different task for the rest of the week. This meant that the teachers used all three books and all three tasks during the 30 minutes allotted to reading instruction, each book and task getting 10 minutes. They repeated the same lesson with three small groups, making some minor adjustments for differing degrees of literacy skills.

The books used in the repeated readings task (RR) were read 10 times over a 4-day period, always in the original context. In addition, the students participated in some simple dramatic interpretations. These typically involved acting the story out with stick puppets and story boards as one or more children read the story aloud.

The books used in the sentence context (SC) treatment were reread in context each day, but in addition the students read the text on a chart without the support of pictures. They also worked to rebuild the story using both large sentence strips that were put in a pocket chart and small individual sets of sentence strips.

The books used in the word bank task (WB) were also reread each day, but each child received a text-only copy of the story to read and selected known words by underlining them. The teacher then held up a small slip of paper or card with one of the selected words written on it. If the child could name the word it went into his or her word bank. On the third day students read through their words, using the book to look up any they did not know. They also had a chance to acquire additional words. On the fourth day students reviewed their words again and did a brief word study activity in which the teacher asked them to find words with a particular feature. For example, the teacher might say; "If you have a word that starts with *f* hold it up" or "Hold up a word that rhymes with *not*."

The students were pretested and posttested each week to determine the number of new words acquired in each task. They read from a list of all the words contained in the set of three books.

Findings. I will report the findings in terms of the three factors that appear to be critical aspects of beginning readers' ability to learn words.

• *The task.* Students learned significantly more words when they used sentence strips and word banks than when they simply read and reread the story, and they learned the most words using word banks (see Figure 1). These findings support the idea that word learning can be enhanced by planning whole-to-part tasks that increase the reader's need to attend

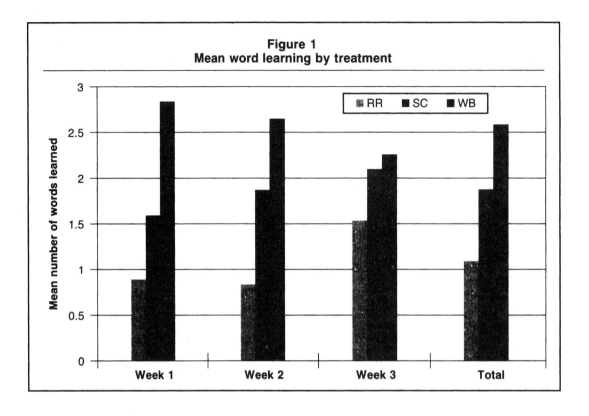

**Figure 1
Mean word learning by treatment**

to and process the print. My hypothesis had been confirmed, but I was disappointed to find that, despite reading the books 10 times over 4 days, students did not, on the average, seem to learn a great many words in any treatment. The average number of words learned in the word bank treatment each week was only 2.6. This was better than the average in the reread treatment, which was 1.0, and the sentence strip treatment, which was 1.8, but was still low enough to raise questions about the predictable text itself.

• *The text.* I examined the nature of the words used in the predictable texts. The difference between traditional basal materials and predictable text is very evident in terms of word repetition. Over half of the words in these predictable books (52%) appeared only one time, and the average number of repetitions was only 3.3. In the 1985 study of basal preprimers reported by Juel and Roper/ Schneider, the core vocabulary words repeated an average of 15 times in one series and an average of 26 times in another.

Two hundred words account for 50% of the words in reading materials (Carroll,

Davies, & Richmond, 1971). These high-frequency words accounted for slightly less than the 50% of the words in the predictable books chosen for the study, but this difference was small. About a third of the words were single syllable and phonetically regular (e.g., *box, bite, sleep, that*). Concrete nouns (e.g., *possum* or *chairs*) with clear referents accounted for about 40% of the words.

I explored the relationship between features of words and students' word learning through intercorrelations and a multiple regression analysis (see Table). It is not surprising that general word frequency and repetitions were correlated, because high-frequency words repeat a lot in text. But concreteness was negatively correlated with all the other factors, especially with frequency. A large variety of concrete words occurred in these texts, and many occurred only once. Only three of the factors were positively and significantly correlated with word learning: general word frequency, repetitions, and decodability. I concluded that while beginners are more likely to learn words that repeat and are easily decodable, these words were not the

Intercorrelations between features of words and posttest word recall					
	Posttest word identifications	Repititions	General word Frequency	Concreteness	Decodability
Posttest word identification	1.00	.45	.50	−.33	.30
Repetitions		1.00	.42	−.37	.05
General word Frequency			1.00	−.65	.07
Concreteness				1.00	−.09
Decodability					1.00

most common words in the predictable books I used. This may partially account for why word learning overall was low.

• *The reader.* I explored the "reader" factor by looking at how children with varying degrees of print skill differed in terms of word learning. The initial assessment scores revealed a range of ability, but no children were beyond the beginning reader stage. The children with the lowest scores were still unable to identify all their letters and had only rudimentary phonetic awareness as shown in their ability to represent a few initial consonant sounds in an invented spelling task. These children would be considered "pre-alphabetic" or at best "partial alphabetic" readers. Children with the highest scores knew all the letters and could represent initial, final, and some medial sounds in their invented spelling. They would be considered "partial" to "full alphabetic" readers. Not surprising, the better children did on the ERSI, the more words they learned (see Figure 2). Children with knowledge about letters and how letters map to sounds were in the best position to acquire and retain words.

The word bank did give the students in each achievement level a slight edge over the students in the next higher level who simply read and reread the text. The least able readers learned an average of 3.6 words using word banks, while the middle achievers learned 2.8 by simply reading and rereading. The middle achievers learned an average of 6.1 words us-ing word banks, while the best readers averaged only 5.6 reading and rereading.

Implications for teaching

I found three critical factors for word learning: the reader, the text, and the task. Teachers need to know their students' ability to process print, they need to select books that support students' word recognition but at the same time enhance their word learning, and they need to structure learning tasks that further facilitate word learning by drawing attention to the printed form of words. Many ways to do this are possible both in the context of reading and in whole-to-part follow-up activities.

The reader and the tasks. Prealphabetic and partial alphabetic readers have a limited store of sight words and will need considerable support from predictable text and shared reading. In the shared book approach the teacher typically reads the entire text several times; prealphabetic readers need this memory support. Partial alphabetic readers need only a little support from shared reading, and students in the full alphabetic phase don't need shared reading at all because they have a core of sight words and should be able to read some predictable books independently.

All beginning readers will benefit from whole-to-part tasks that increase their attention to print. Teachers should see that every child is engaged in such activities. Even in small groups, turn taking means that most of the group is sitting unengaged while another child

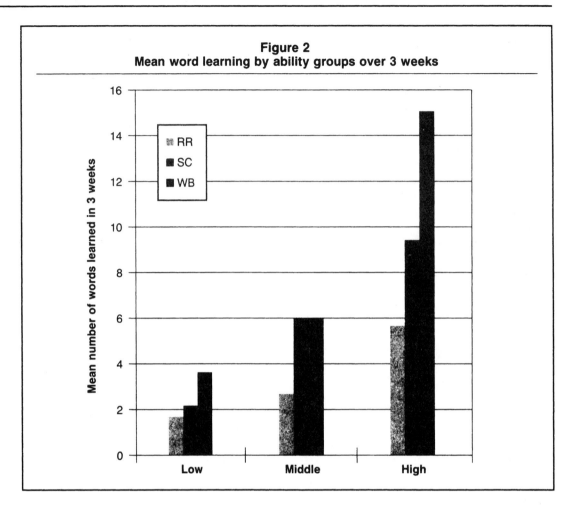

Figure 2
Mean word learning by ability groups over 3 weeks

reads aloud, finds a word on a chart, or puts a sentence strip in a pocket chart. When children have their own copies of the text, of sentence strips, and of word cards, it is more likely they will be examining the print carefully for themselves. Here are some specific suggestions for enhancing word learning:

1. Introduce new words in context. Predictable reading materials provide a rich and meaningful context that supports beginning readers' efforts, no matter their level of word knowledge. The entire class can enjoy and take part in shared reading with predictable books even when ability is diverse.

2. Take away the pictures. After several readings of a predictable text, remove the support of the illustrations by covering the pictures or by working with a large chart containing the text. Better still, give the students text-only copies. They can follow the words with their own fingers as they read or

listen to others read, which increases the visual familiarity of the print. Many publishers will grant permission for teachers to make these copies for use in classrooms. Students can accumulate a collection of these stories to illustrate and bind into their own books.

3. Examine words in context. When children hunt for known words to underline, as in the word bank approach used in this study, they must attend carefully to the print. Students might be asked to touch words the teacher calls out, or the children might take turns naming words for their classmates to find. For example, the teacher may ask each child to point to and name their favorite word, a word that begins with a particular letter, or a word that rhymes with a given word. The masking technique described by Holdaway (1979) is another way of isolating words in context for careful examination.

4. Work with sentence strips. Ask the students to read the sentence strips and to rebuild the text in sequence. Students may need to refer back to the chart or book in order to do this. Although large sentence strips can be used with the whole group, children also need their own sets of sentences so that everyone can be involved in the task at the same time. Individual sets can be made from text-only copy in which each sentence is on a different line. Run a different color of crayon or marker down each paper before cutting it into strips, and then students can easily identify which sentence strips are theirs when they work side by side.

5. Examine words in isolation. A word bank approach accomplishes this nicely as children write words on cards or slips of paper for their own personal collections. Word bank activities encourage students to focus upon words in context with the goal of finding words they know. Remember, too, children may use only partial cues to identify a word initially, but repeated encounters facilitate a more complete representation of a word in their memories.

6. Review words over time. When word bank words are kept from week to week, the students can review known words over a long period of time. In the absence of cumulative word review in the reading material itself, this might be an especially important advantage of word banks. Words are stored in an envelope or bag and reviewed two or three times a week. Unknown words may be identified by returning to the book in which they occurred. Children can review them on their own, with a buddy, or with an assistant or volunteer helper by going through and sorting the words into those known and unknown.

Words that the child repeatedly fails to name should be taken out of the word bank so that reviewing the words remains a rewarding task. An alternative to simply discarding those words is to lay a collection of them face up and name a word for the student to find. This activity is a good way to review unknown words because it allows the student to use partial phonetic cues to find the words.

7. Sort words into categories. Words can be examined for common features such as words that begin with particular sounds; words that rhyme; or words that share semantic similarities such as animal words, color words, or

Figure 3
A reproducible wordsheet for stories beginners will read

Mom	me	him
said	looked	is
for	here	under
clock	in	the
not	toy	rug
box	he	chimney
she	teapot	no
David		

action words. Word sorting activities (Bear, Invernizzi, Templeton, & Johnston, 1995) reinforce the recognition of familiar words and offer students the opportunity to make generalizations about graphophonic and orthographic characteristics of words. In the absence of phonetically controlled text, these word study activities are very important.

8. Create word sheets for favorite books (see Figure 3). Students can cut these up and select the words they know. These words can then be quickly checked by the teacher or an assistant so that only known words go into the word bank. Every new word needn't go into the word bank and be kept forever. In this study good results were found in the use of word banks even though the number of words children could acquire was limited and the words were kept for only 1 week.

9. Use word banks only with children who need them the most. Word banks can be discontinued when children have between 150 and 250 words, because students with over 200 words in a word bank probably have internalized their own efficient system for storing and retrieving words mentally. They will still benefit from the study of words (e.g., Bear et al., 1995) but do not need word banks.

10. Words can be examined in many other ways in isolation. Cut sentence strips apart into words and ask children to rebuild the sentence.

Glue library pockets into the back of books to hold word cards from the text, and students can go through these words on their own as part of independent reading. Hold up word cards for students to name, but do this only with the original context available for reference so that the prealphabetic or partial alphabetic reader can employ context cues as a way of figuring out unknown words. This is in contrast to the traditional flashcard drill, which is often more of a testing situation than a learning situation.

The text. Predictable text may be problematic in terms of word learning. It offers considerable support from context, making it easy to read, but it may not encourage careful processing of the print. In addition, the words used to write predictable text may not be the words children find easiest to learn. Traditional basal text was designed to facilitate word learning, but it often lacked appeal. I believe it is possible to use texts that combine the best of both kinds of materials or to use different kinds of materials for different purposes.

Many publishers of beginning reading materials, including basal publishers, are creating little books that combine predictable elements with phonetically regular words (e.g., Ready Readers by Modern Curriculum Press). These decodable readers can be used to match instruction in phonics with experiences in text as suggested by Juel and Roper/Schneider (1985). Rigby has a new line of little books called the PM Collection that features cumulative exposure to high-frequency words in a series that becomes less and less predictable.

One characteristic of traditional basal instruction was that children read very little other than their preprimers or primers. Now we can offer children a variety of reading experiences; the use of controlled-language texts seems well advised, especially for children who find learning to read difficult. Here are a few specific recommendations:

1. Limit the use of the shared reading model. When the reading material itself offers lots of support, students can work their way through the text independently and in the process attend carefully to the words. There is no reason to read everything in advance, even to prealphabetic readers, when the text itself is highly patterned and predictable. Often a well-planned book introduction (Clay, 1992) may suffice, or the teacher may read aloud only the first few pages to establish the pattern.

2. Move toward the use of less predictable text. As soon as students acquire a sizeable sight vocabulary and show evidence that they can read some material independently, move them into less predictable text. The majority of reading material is not especially predictable, and young readers must learn to rely less on context to be successful readers.

3. Use controlled-language texts. Although predictable text, especially top-quality literature, may form the core of the reading program in kindergarten and early first grade, students should also read texts that introduce and repeat high-frequency words in a cumulative fashion or include lots of phonetically regular words. I would not use such text exclusively, unless it is also good literature, but when students are studying a particular phonetic feature, such as short vowels, they benefit from lots of opportunities to read words with short vowels in the context of meaningful stories.

Conclusions

Teachers should reflect carefully on the reader, the text, and the tasks as they plan instruction to enhance word learning. New programs and books are flooding the market, but there is little research about how these texts interact with word learning or other reading tasks. This is an area ripe for further exploration.

Word study can be meaningful and rewarding. One of the teachers in my study reported that "the kids really seemed to love the word bank." The others agreed and expressed their belief that the children enjoyed the sense of accomplishment that came from getting tangible evidence of their learning. The focus of any reading program should be upon finding meaning in delightful stories, but children will not be able to enjoy reading and construct meaning unless they are able to read the words effortlessly.

Author notes

I would like to thank the first-grade teachers at George Rodgers Clark Elementary School in Charlottesville, Virginia, USA, who assisted me with this study: Donna Stokes, Becky Silvers, and Stephenie Mullaney Lee. I'd also like to thank Herbert Richards who helped me with the data analysis.

A first-grade teacher for 12 years, Johnston now teaches courses in reading and language arts at the University of North Carolina at Greensboro (School of Education, PO Box 26171, Greensboro, NC 27402, USA).

References

Adams, M.J. (1990). *Beginning to read: Thinking and learning about print.* Cambridge, MA: MIT Press.

Ashton-Warner, S. (1963). *Teacher.* New York: Simon & Schuster.

Bear, D., Invernizzi, M., Templeton, S., & Johnston, F.R. (1995). *Words their way: Word study for phonics, spelling and vocabulary growth.* New York: Merrill.

Biemiller, A. (1970). The development of the use of graphic and contextual information as children learn to read. *Reading Research Quarterly, 6*, 75 – 96.

Bridge, C.A., & Burton, B. (1982). Teaching sight vocabulary through patterned language materials. In J.A. Niles & L.A. Harris (Eds.), *New inquiries in reading research and instruction* (pp. 119 – 123). Washington, DC: *National Reading Conference.*

Bridge, C.A., Winograd, P.N., & Haley, D. (1983). Using predictable materials vs. preprimers to teach beginning sight words. *The Reading Teacher, 36*, 84 – 91.

Carroll, J.B., Davies, P., & Richmond, B. (1971). *The American heritage word frequency book.* New York: Houghton Mifflin.

Chomsky, C. (1976). After decoding, what? *Language Arts, 53*, 288 – 296.

Clay, M.M. (1985). *The early detection of reading difficulties* (3rd ed.). Portsmouth, NH: Heinemann.

Clay, M.M. (1992). Introducing a new storybook to young readers. *The Reading Teacher, 45*, 264 – 273.

Craik, F.I.M., & Lockhart, R.S. (1972). Levels of processing: A framework for memory research. *Journal of Verbal Learning and Verbal Behavior, 11*, 671 – 684.

Cunningham, P.M. (1995). *Phonics they use: Words for reading and writing.* New York: HarperCollins.

Ehri, L.C. (1992). Reconceptualizing the development of sight word reading and its relationship to recoding. In P. Gough, L. Ehri, & R. Treiman (Eds.), *Reading acquisition* (pp. 383 – 417). Hillsdale, NJ: Erlbaum.

Ehri, L.C. (1994). Development of the ability to read words: Update. In R. Ruddell, M. Ruddell, & H. Singer (Eds.), *Theoretical models and processes of reading* (4th ed.) (pp. 323 – 358). Newark, DE: International Reading Association.

Ehri, L.C. (1995). Phases of development in reading words. *Journal of Research in Reading, 18*, 116 – 125.

Ehri, L.C., & Roberts, K.T. (1979). Do beginners learn printed words better in context or in isolation? *Child Development, 50*, 675 – 685.

Ehri, L.C., & Wilce, L.S. (1980). Do beginners learn to read function words better in sentences or in lists? *Reading Research Quarterly, 15*, 675 – 685.

Heald-Taylor, G. (1987). Predictable literature selections and activities for language arts instruction. *The Reading Teacher, 41*, 6 – 12.

Hoffman, J.V., McCarthey, S.J., Abbott, J., Christian, C., Corman, L., Curry, C., Dressman, M., Elliott, B., Matherne, D., & Stahle, D. (1994). So what's new in the new basals? A focus on first grade. *Journal of Reading Behavior, 26*, 47 – 73.

Holdaway, D. (1979). *The foundations of literacy.* New York: Ashton Scholastic.

Johnston, F.R. (1995). *Enhancing beginners' word acquisition in predictable reading materials.* Unpublished doctoral dissertation, University of Virginia, Charlottesville, VA.

Juel, C. (1991). Beginning reading. In P.D. Pearson, R. Barr, M.L. Kamil, & P. Mosenthal (Eds.), *Handbook of reading research* (vol. 2). New York: Longman.

Juel, C., & Roper/Schneider, D. (1985). The influence of basal readers on first grade reading. *Reading Research Quarterly, 20*, 134 – 152.

Martin, B. (1967). *Brown bear, brown bear, what do you see?* New York: Holt.

Martin, B., & Brogan, P. (1971). *Teacher's guide to instant readers.* New York: Holt.

McCracken, M.J., & McCracken, R.A. (1979). *Reading, writing, and language: A practical guide for primary teachers.* Winnipeg, MB: Peguis.

McCracken, R.A., & McCracken, M.J. (1986). *Stories, songs and poetry to teach reading and writing.* Winnipeg, MB: Peguis.

Morris, D. (1992). What constitutes at-risk: Screening children for first grade reading intervention. *Best Practices in School Speech-Language Pathology, 2*, 43 – 51.

Nemko, B. (1984). Context versus isolation: Another look at beginning readers. *Reading Research Quarterly, 19*, 461 – 467.

Nicholson, T. (1991). Do children read words better in context or in lists? A classic study revisited. *Journal of Educational Psychology, 83*, 444 – 450.

Perfetti, C.A. (1985). *Reading ability.* New York: Oxford University Press.

Rhodes, L.K. (1981). I can read! Predictable books as resources for reading and writing instruction. *The Reading Teacher, 35*, 511 – 518.

Samuels, S.J. (1979). The method of repeated readings. *The Reading Teacher, 32*, 403 – 408.

Stanovich, K.E. (1994). Romance and reality. *The Reading Teacher, 47*, 280 – 291.

Stauffer, R.G. (1970). *The language-experience approach to the teaching of reading.* New York: Harper & Row.

Story box in the classroom: Stage I. (1990). San Diego, CA: The Wright Group.

Venezkey, R.L., & Massaro, D.W. (1979). The role of orthographic regularity in word recognition. In L. Resnick & P. Weaver (Eds.), *Theory and practice of early reading* (pp. 85 – 107). Hillsdale, NJ: Erlbaum.

Wildsmith, B. (1982). *The cat on the mat.* New York: Oxford University of Press.

Publishers mentioned

Rigby, PO Box 797, Crystal Lake, IL 60039, USA. Telephone 1-800-822-8661.

Modern Curriculum Press, 4350 Equity Drive, PO Box 2649, Columbus, OH 43216, USA. Telephone 1-800-321-3106.

From *The Reading Teacher, Vol. 51, No. 8, May 1998*

Cross-Language Transfer of Phonological Awareness

Aydin Y. Durgunoğlu, William E. Nagy, and Barbara J. Hancin-Bhatt

The number of students from linguistically diverse backgrounds who are enrolled in U.S. schools is increasing rapidly (Hakuta & García, 1989). For these students, learning to read in English is one of the crucial components of academic success. Hence, how these students' first-language knowledge may affect their reading in a second language is of great pedagogical importance. In addition, the effects of first language on second-language reading (i.e., cross-language transfer) is also of theoretical interest, as evidenced by the increase in research devoted to this issue in the last few years. After two decades of little attention to cross-linguistic transfer, researchers in the area of second-language acquisition have returned to studying acquisition and production of second-language structures as a function of the characteristics of the first language (for reviews, see Gass & Selinker, 1983; Kellerman & Sharwood Smith, 1986; Odlin, 1989). However, despite a resurgence of interest in the effects of cross-language transfer on second-language reading, there has been very little systematic research on the role of first-language cognitive strategies and knowledge on beginning reading in a second language (for exceptions, see Faltis, 1986; Kendall, Lajeunesse, Chmilar, Shapson, & Shapson, 1987).

Cross-Language Transfer

Research with monolingual beginning readers has convincingly demonstrated the relationship between phonological awareness and reading acquisition. In this study, we have replicated this finding with Spanish-speaking children and have shown that phonological awareness in Spanish is closely related to Spanish word recognition. We have also replicated the finding that phonological awareness tests such as segmenting and blending are closely interrelated. However, the critical finding in our study is the cross-language transfer of phonological awareness. We have demonstrated the relationship between phonological awareness in Spanish and word recognition in English. Children who could perform well on Spanish phonological awareness tests were more likely to be able to read English words and English-like pseudowords than were children who performed poorly on phonological awareness tests. This effect was even more salient for those pseudowords that had different pronunciations in Spanish and in English. In short, phonological awareness was a significant predictor of performance on word recognition tests both within and across languages.

Phonological awareness, like other metalinguistic abilities, requires one to reflect on and manipulate the structural features of the spoken language (Tunmer et al., 1988). Unless a child can deliberately focus on the form rather than on the

Aydin Y. Durgunoğlu, William E. Nagy, and Barbara J. Hancin-Bhatt, Center for the Study of Reading, University of Illinois at Urbana-Champaign.

This work was supported in part by the Office of Educational Research and Improvement under Cooperative Agreement No. G0087-C1001-90 with the Reading Research and Education Center and in part by a grant from the Mellon Foundation. The publication does not necessarily reflect the views of the agencies supporting the research. We would like to thank Sofia Ariño-Martí, Kristen Knapp, Jim Kotowski, Montserrat Mir, and Kristen Saunders for their help in testing subjects and scoring the data and Georgia García for her comments. Most of all, we thank the children in our study and their principals and teachers for their cooperation. Portions of this research were presented at the April 1992 American Educational Research Association meetings in San Francisco.

Correspondence concerning this article should be addressed to Aydin Y. Durgunoğlu, who is now at the Department of Psychology and Mental Health, University of Minnesota, Bohannon Hall, Duluth, Minnesota 55812.

content of a word, the components in a word are not readily transparent. For example, a child saying *cat* is normally more interested in its meaning rather than in its structural components. However, once a child is able to reflect on the components of a language, it is likely that this metalinguistic awareness could be applied to an (alphabetic) second language as well.

Just as phonological awareness facilitates word recognition, schooling and learning to read can also facilitate phonological awareness. Because most of our subjects were already reading quite a few words in Spanish, we cannot address this question of directionality. However, regardless of the direction, both phonological awareness and word recognition in Spanish seem to transfer to word recognition in English. Although the two variables have some overlap, both contribute independently to performance on English word and pseudoword recognition.

The pattern of cross-language transfer summarized above indicates that it is possible to build on the strengths that a child already has in his or her first language. A child who already knows how to read in Spanish and who has a high level of phonological awareness in Spanish is more likely to perform well on English word and pseudoword recognition tests. In contrast, a child who has some Spanish word recognition skills but low phonological awareness tends to perform poorly on English transfer tests. Developing phonological awareness and word recognition skills in the first language is likely to help in second-language word recognition.

One could ask whether Spanish phonological awareness affects English word recognition directly or indirectly through its influence on English phonological awareness. We feel that this question incorrectly assumes that phonological awareness is developed specific to a particular language. We hold, on the contrary, that similar types of processing underlie both Spanish and English word recognition. For example, in both of these alphabetic languages, children need to identify the phonological subcomponents of the spoken words and understand how orthographic symbols are mapped onto those phonological subcomponents. Such metalinguistic awareness need not be language specific. When faced with a new language, children may need to acquire new phonemes (e.g., /th/ in English) or new orthographic patterns (e.g., *str-* in English) as well as new matches between phonological segments and orthographic patterns (e.g., pronunciation of *-un* is not like *put* as in Spanish but rather like *nut*).[5] More important, children need to understand which phonological units are salient in orthographic representation (e.g., syllables in Spanish but onset-rime units in English). Given this view of bilingual processing, it is not surprising that children who already have a wide knowledge base (i.e., recognize Spanish words well) and who have high metalinguistic awareness (i.e., exhibit phonological awareness) perform better on the English word and pseudoword reading tasks.

One could then question whether the relationship of phonological awareness measured in Spanish and learning to read English words can be legitimately characterized as cross-language transfer. We would operationalize cross-language transfer in terms of the following, educationally

very relevant, question: Would training students in phonological awareness in Spanish enhance their ability to read in English?

The results of the present study indicate that the answer to this question is yes, given two further points: (a) the results of studies of monolingual children in which training in phonological awareness has produced gains in learning to read, and (b) the assumption that the children in the present study gained their phonological awareness primarily through their first language, through their earlier experiences with spoken Spanish, and in particular, through the process of learning to read in Spanish. We feel that this latter assumption is warranted, given that the children had stronger proficiency in Spanish than in English, as indicated by their placement in the bilingual education program and corroborated by their pre-LAS scores. Moreover, the children had been learning English at school only for a short period of time, and this instruction was aimed (primarily) at developing initial oral proficiency, not at reading. As was pointed out, these children were able to read extremely few English words. In summary, we have supporting data that enable us to assume that these children gained their phonological awareness mainly through Spanish. Within the limits of a correlational study, then, we have found evidence for the cross-language transfer of phonological awareness.

Oral-Language Proficiency

One of the most common criteria used for entering and exiting students to and from bilingual education programs is English oral proficiency. In fact, a survey found that 92–94% of school districts used English oral proficiency (alone or in conjunction with other measures) to make entry/exit decisions (Fradd, 1987). Likewise, the schools in our study made placement decisions on the basis of both English oral proficiency and staff judgments. Our data support the caution expressed by several researchers (e.g., Moll & Diaz, 1985; Saville-Troike, 1984) that oral proficiency by itself is not a very reliable predictor of reading abilities. Performance on our oral proficiency tests did not have any significant correlations with word recognition or phonological awareness measures.

Of course, we were focusing on a very specific component of the reading process. Although word recognition is a crucial component of the reading process, it is not the only component. If we had focused on other components of the reading process or on other reading levels, oral proficiency may have played a more prominent role. For example, Verhoeven (1990) found that oral proficiency of Turkish children in Dutch (as measured by syntax and vocabulary knowledge) showed a higher correlation with Dutch reading comprehension than with word recognition measures. The apparent inconsistency between our results and those of Verhoeven underlines the importance of specifying which components of the reading process are involved, and under which condi-

---

[5] The issue of rimes that have varying pronunciations in English (e.g., *-ut*) that sometimes match the Spanish pronunciations is a topic that needs to be investigated.

tions, when one looks for cross-language transfer effects. We discuss this point further in the next section.

Studying Cross-Language Transfer

Cross-language transfer needs to be investigated under well-specified conditions with well-specified tasks. The question is not whether cross-language transfer occurs or whether oral language proficiency is a good predictor of reading performance. Rather, the question is one of condition-seeking (McLaughlin, 1987): Under what conditions do which components of the reading process reflect cross-language transfer? Under what conditions and for which components of reading is oral proficiency a good predictor? Our results indicate that cross-language transfer can occur in word recognition. Both phonological awareness and word recognition skills in Spanish are predictive of word recognition in English. In contrast, oral language proficiency in Spanish is not related to word recognition processes in English. Further research can elucidate which other skills and knowledge in a reader's first language affect certain components of the reading process in a second language.

Methodologically, another point needs to be highlighted. In our study we have not compared the performance of bilinguals with monolinguals but rather analyzed processing in the two languages of a bilingual (cf. Hakuta, Ferdman, & Diaz, 1987). What a child could do on specific tasks in the first language was used to predict what that child could do on specific tasks in the second language. However, to use this analytic, component-skills approach (cf. Haynes & Carr, 1990), a good model describing the interrelationship of the two sets of tasks is necessary. Monolingual reading research had provided us with a well-supported model that demonstrates the relationship between phonological awareness and word recognition in beginning reading, which we have used to investigate cross-language transfer. The exciting new developments in reading research are beginning to reveal more relationships between different components of the reading process that can be applied to research on bilingual reading.

References

Adams, M. J. (1990). *Beginning to read: Thinking and learning about print.* Cambridge, MA: MIT Press.

Ball, E. W., & Blachman, B. A. (1991). Does phonemic segmentation training in kindergarten make a difference in early word recognition and developmental spelling? *Reading Research Quarterly, 26,* 49–66.

Blachman, B. A. (1987). An alternative classroom reading program for learning disabled and other low-achieving children. In W. Ellis (Ed.), *Intimacy with language: A forgotten basic in teacher education* (pp. 49–55). Baltimore: Orton Dyslexia Society.

Bradley, L., & Bryant, P. (1985). *Rhyme and reason in reading and spelling.* Ann Arbor: University of Michigan Press.

Byrne, B., & Fielding-Barnsley, R. (1991). Evaluation of a program to teach phonemic awareness to young children. *Journal of Educational Psychology, 83,* 451–455.

Calfee, R. C., Lindamood, P., & Lindamood, C. (1973). Acoustic-phonetic skills and reading—Kindergarten through 12th grade. *Journal of Educational Psychology, 64,* 293–298.

Calfee, R. C., & Piontowski, D. C. (1981). The reading diary: Ac-

quisition of decoding. *Reading Research Quarterly, 16,* 346–373.

Carr, T. H., Brown, T. L., Vavrus, L. G., & Evans, M. A. (1990). Cognitive skill maps and cognitive skill profiles: Componential analysis of individual differences in children's reading efficiency. In T. H. Carr & B. A. Levy (Eds.), *Reading and its development* (pp. 1–56). San Diego, CA: Academic Press.

Carrell, P. L., & Eisterhold, J. C. (1983). Schema theory and ESL reading pedagogy. *TESOL Quarterly, 17,* 553–573.

Clay, M. M. (1979). *The early detection of reading difficulties* (3rd ed.). Portsmouth, NH: Heinemann.

Cummins, J. (1981). The role of primary language development in promoting educational success for language minority students. In California Office of Bilingual Bicultural Education (Ed.), *Schooling and language minority students: A theoretical framework* (pp. 3–49). Los Angeles: Evaluation, Dissemination and Assessment Center, California State University.

de Manrique, A. M. B., & Graminga, S. (1984). La segmentación fonológica y silábica en niños de preescolar y primer grado [The phonological and syllabic segmentation in preschool and first-grade children]. *Lectura y Vida, 5,* 4–14.

Devine, J. (1987). General language competence and adult second language reading. In J. Devine, P. L. Carrell, & D. E. Eskey (Eds.), *Research in reading in English as a second language* (pp. 73–85). Washington, DC: TESOL.

Dickinson, D. K., & Snow, C. E. (1987). Interrelationships among prereading and oral language skills in kindergartners from two social classes. *Early Childhood Research Quarterly, 2,* 1–25.

Duncan, S., & De Avila, E. A. (1986). *Pre-LAS.* Monterey, CA: CTB/McGraw-Hill.

Durgunoğlu, A. Y. (1988). Repetition, semantic priming and stimulus quality: Implications for the interactive-compensatory reading model. *Journal of Experimental Psychology: Learning, Memory, and Cognition, 14,* 590–603.

Durgunoğlu, A. Y., & Roediger, H. L. (1987). Test differences in accessing bilingual memory. *Journal of Memory and Language, 26,* 377–391.

Ehri, L. C. (1991). Development of the ability to read words. In R. Barr, M. L. Kamil, P. Mosenthal, & P. D. Pearson (Eds.), *Handbook of reading research* (Vol. 2, pp. 383–417). New York: Longman.

Ehri, L. C., & Wilce, L. S. (1980). The influence of orthography on readers' conceptualization of the phonemic structure of words. *Applied Psycholinguistics, 1,* 371–385.

Faltis, C. (1986). Initial cross-lingual reading transfer in bilingual second-grade classrooms. In E. E. García & B. Flores (Eds.), *Language and literacy research in bilingual education* (pp. 145–157). Tempe: Arizona University Press.

Foorman, B. R., Francis, D. J., Novy, D. M., & Liberman, D. (1991). How letter–sound instruction mediates progress in first-grade reading and spelling. *Journal of Educational Psychology, 83,* 456–469.

Fox, B., & Routh, D. K. (1984). Phonemic analysis and synthesis as word attack skills: Revisited. *Journal of Educational Psychology, 76,* 1059–1064.

Fradd, S. H. (1987). The changing focus of bilingual education. In S. H. Fradd & W. J. Tikunoff (Eds.), *Bilingual and bilingual special education: A guide for administrators* (pp. 1–44). Boston: Little Brown.

García, G. E. (1991). Factors influencing the English reading test performance of Spanish-speaking Hispanic children. *Reading Research Quarterly, 26,* 371–392.

Gass, S., & Selinker, L. (1983). *Language transfer in language learning.* Rowley, MA: Newbury House.

Goswami, U., & Bryant, P. (1990). *Phonological skills and learning to read.* Hillsdale, NJ: Erlbaum.

Gough, P. B., & Juel, C. (1991). The first stages of word recognition. In L. Rieben & C. A. Perfetti (Eds.), *Learning to read* (pp. 47–56). Hillsdale, NJ: Erlbaum.

Goyen, J. D. (1989). Reading methods in Spain: The effect of a regular orthography. *Reading Teacher, 42,* 370–373.

Hakuta, K., Ferdman, B. M., & Diaz, R. (1987). Bilingualism and cognitive development: Three perspectives. In S. Rosenberg (Ed.), *Advances in applied psycholinguistics* (Vol. 2, pp. 284–319). Cambridge, England: Cambridge University Press.

Hakuta, K., & García, E. E. (1989). Bilingualism and education. *American Psychologist, 44,* 374–379.

Haynes, M., & Carr, T. H. (1990). Writing system background and second language reading: A component skills analysis of English reading by native speaker-readers of Chinese. In T. H. Carr & B. A. Levy (Eds.), *Reading and its development: Component skills approaches* (pp. 375–421). San Diego, CA: Academic Press.

Heath, S. B. (1986). Separating "things of imagination" from life: Learning to read and write. In W. H. Teale & E. Sulzby (Eds.), *Emergent literacy: Writing and reading* (pp. 156–172). Norwood, NJ: Ablex.

Hudelson, S. (1984). Kan yu ret an rayt en ingles: Children become literate in English as a second language. *TESOL Quarterly, 18,* 221–238.

Juel, C. (1980). Comparison of word identification strategies with varying context, word type and reader skill. *Reading Research Quarterly, 15,* 358–376.

Juel, C., Griffith, P. L., & Gough, P. B. (1986). Acquisition of literacy: A longitudinal study of children in first and second grade. *Journal of Educational Psychology, 78,* 243–255.

Kellerman, E., & Sharwood Smith, M. (1986). *Crosslinguistic influence in second-language acquisition.* Elmsford, NY: Pergamon Press.

Kendall, J. R., Lajeunesse, G., Chmilar, P., Shapson, L. R., & Shapson, S. M. (1987). English reading skills of French immersion students in kindergarten and Grades 1 and 2. *Reading Research Quarterly, 22,* 135–159.

Liberman, I. Y. (1987). Language and literacy: The obligation of the schools of education. In W. Ellis (Ed.), *Intimacy with language: A forgotten basic in teacher education* (pp. 1–9). Baltimore: Orton Dyslexia Society.

Lomax, R. G., & McGee, L. M. (1987). Young children's concepts about print and reading: Toward a model of word reading acquisition. *Reading Research Quarterly, 22,* 237–256.

Lundberg, I., Frost, J., & Petersen, O. P. (1988). Effects of an extensive program for stimulating phonological awareness in preschool children. *Reading Research Quarterly, 23,* 265–284.

Maclean, M., Bryant, P., & Bradley, L. (1987). Rhymes, nursery rhymes, and reading in early childhood. *Merrill-Palmer Quarterly, 33,* 255–281.

Mann, V. A., Tobin, P., & Wilson, R. (1987). Measuring phonological awareness through the invented spellings of kindergartners. *Merrill-Palmer Quarterly, 33,* 365–391.

Mason, J., & Allen, J. (1986). A review of emergent literacy with implications for research and practice in reading. In E. Rothkopf (Ed.), *Review of research in education* (pp. 205–238). Washington, DC: American Educational Research Association.

McConkie, G. W., & Zola, D. (1981). Language constraints and the functional stimulus in reading. In A. M. Lesgold & C. A. Perfetti (Eds.), *Interactive processes in reading* (pp. 155–175). Hillsdale, NJ: Erlbaum.

McLaughlin, B. (1987). *Theories of second language learning.* London: Arnold.

Moll, L. C., & Diaz, S. (1985). Ethnographic pedagogy: Promoting effective bilingual instruction. In E. E. García & R. V. Padilla (Eds.), *Advances in bilingual education research* (pp. 127–149).

Tucson: University of Arizona Press.

Morais, J., Cary, L., Alegria, J., & Bertelson, P. (1979). Does awareness of speech as a sequence of phones arise spontaneously? *Cognition, 7,* 323–331.

Odlin, T. (1989). *Language transfer.* Cambridge, England: Cambridge University Press.

Perfetti, C. A. (1985). *Reading ability.* New York: Oxford University Press.

Perfetti, C. A., Beck, I., Bell, L., & Hughes, C. (1987). Phonemic knowledge and learning to read are reciprocal: A longitudinal study of first grade children. *Merrill-Palmer Quarterly, 33,* 283–319.

Rayner, K., & Pollatsek, A. (1989). *The psychology of reading.* Englewood Cliffs, NJ: Prentice Hall.

Read, C., Yun-Fei, Z., Hong-Yin, N., & Bao-Qing, D. (1986). The ability to manipulate speech sounds depends on knowing alphabetic writing. *Cognition, 24,* 31–44.

Saville-Troike, M. (1984). What *really* matters in second language learning for academic achievement? *TESOL Quarterly, 18,* 199–219.

Seidenberg, M. S., & McClelland, J. L. (1989). A distributed, developmental model of word recognition and naming. *Psychological Review, 96,* 523–568.

Shanahan, T. (1984). Nature of reading–writing relation: An exploratory multivariate analysis. *Journal of Educational Psychology, 76,* 466–477.

Stanovich, K. E. (1982). Individual differences in the cognitive processes of reading: 1. Word decoding. *Journal of Learning Disabilities, 15,* 485–493.

Stanovich, K. E. (1986). Matthew effects in reading: Some consequences of individual differences in the acquisition of literacy. *Reading Research Quarterly, 21,* 360–406.

Stanovich, K. E. (1991). Word recognition: Changing perspectives. In R. Barr, M. L. Kamil, P. Mosenthal, & P. D. Pearson (Eds.), *Handbook of reading research* (Vol. 2, pp. 418–452). New York: Longman.

Stanovich, K. E., Cunningham, A. E., & Cramer, B. B. (1984). Assessing phonological awareness in kindergarten children: Issues of task comparability. *Journal of Experimental Child Psychology, 38,* 175–190.

Stanovich, K. E., & West, R. F. (1983). On priming by a sentence context. *Journal of Experimental Psychology: General, 112,* 1–36.

Stuart, M., & Coltheart, M. (1988). Does reading develop in a sequence of stages? *Cognition, 30,* 139–181.

Treiman, R. (1985). Phonemic analysis, spelling, and reading. In T. H. Carr (Ed.), *The development of reading skills* (pp. 5–18). San Francisco: Jossey-Bass.

Treiman, R. (1988). The internal structure of the syllable. In G. Carlson & M. Tanenhaus (Eds.), *Linguistic structure in language processing* (pp. 27–52). Dordrecht, Holland: D. Reidel.

Treiman, R., & Baron, J. (1983). Phonemic analysis training helps children benefit from spelling-sound rules. *Memory & Cognition, 11,* 382–389.

Tunmer, W. E., Herriman, M. L., & Nesdale, A. R. (1988). Metalinguistic abilities and beginning reading. *Reading Research Quarterly, 23,* 134–158.

Tunmer, W. E., & Nesdale, A. R. (1985). Phonemic segmentation skill and beginning reading. *Journal of Educational Psychology, 77,* 417–427.

Vellutino, F. R., & Scanlon, D. M. (1987). Phonological coding, phonological awareness, and reading ability: Evidence from a longitudinal and experimental study. *Merrill-Palmer Quarterly, 33,* 321–363.

Verhoeven, L. T. (1990). Acquisition of reading in a second language. *Reading Research Quarterly, 25,* 90–114.

Vygotsky, L. S. (1962). *Thought and language* (E. Hanfmann & G. Vakar, Eds. and Trans.). Cambridge, MA: MIT Press.

Wagner, R. K. (1988). Causal relations between the development of phonological processing abilities and the acquisition of reading skills: A meta-analysis. *Merrill-Palmer Quarterly, 34,* 261–279.

Wagner, R. K., & Torgeson, J. K. (1987). The nature of phonological processing and its causal role in the acquisition of reading skills. *Psychological Bulletin, 101,* 192–212.

Walley, A. C., Smith, L. B., & Jusczyk, P. (1986). The role of phonemes and syllables in the perceived similarity of speech sounds

for children. *Memory & Cognition, 14,* 220–229.

Wells, G. (1987). The learning of literacy. In B. Fillion, C. N. Hedley, & E. C. DiMartino (Eds.), *Home and school: Early language and reading* (pp. 27–46). Norwood, NJ: Ablex.

Williams, J. P. (1980). Teaching decoding with a special emphasis on phoneme analysis and phoneme blending. *Journal of Educational Psychology, 72,* 1–15.

Yopp, H. K. (1988). The validity and reliability of phonemic awareness tests. *Reading Research Quarterly, 23,* 159–177.

Zifcak, M. (1981). Phonological awareness and reading acquisition. *Contemporary Educational Psychology, 6,* 117–126.

Appendix

Words in the Matching Test

Target word	Alternatives		
Initial sounds the same, broken syllable			
*g*anas	luna	*g*ota	bota
*n*ene	base	*n*ota	cana
*c*oche	*c*arta	dedo	misa
*m*ono	lapiz	tiza	*m*adre
*t*oro	malo	arte	*t*ela
*p*era	*p*ino	risa	arbol
Initial two sounds the same, intact syllable			
*ca*pa	leche	*ca*ro	agua
*sa*po	*sa*la	yoyo	curso
*la*ta	pico	zero	*la*do
*bo*ca	casa	torre	*bo*ta
*ar*te	isla	once	*ar*pa
*ba*se	lobo	*ba*ja	pero
*mu*ral	*mu*jer	noche	poder
*va*so	loma	*va*ca	dulce
Initial two sounds the same, broken syllable			
*co*no	*co*rte	rampa	lindo
*la*va	gusto	mundo	*la*rgo
*bo*ta	curva	*bo*lsa	parte
*to*do	*to*rta	campo	busca
*pa*to	mares	color	*pa*rque
*fi*no	gana	*fi*nca	donde

Received November 12, 1991
Revision received December 2, 1992
Accepted January 6, 1993 ■

Excerpted from the *Journal of Educational Psychology,*
Vol. 85, No. 3, September 1993

SECTION IV

Decoding and Word Attack

THE ROLE OF DECODING IN LEARNING TO READ

BY ISABEL L. BECK AND CONNIE JUEL

AS ANYONE knows who has both read to young children and watched them begin learning to read, there is a great difference in the sophistication of their abilities in the two arenas. As an illustration, consider a typical activity in a first-grade classroom.

Twenty-six first graders are sitting on the floor around their teacher, Ms. Jackson. She opens a copy of McCloskey's (1941, 1969) *Make Way for Ducklings* and shows the children a double-page picture of two mallards flying over a pond. Jackson tells them that the birds are mallards, which are a kind of duck, and begins to read.

As the teacher reads, the children's attention, facial expressions, and giggles (for example, when a policeman stops traffic to let the mallards waddle across the road) suggest that they are enjoying the story. Their giggling also provides evidence that they understand the story. Even stronger evidence of their understanding is found in the discussion Jackson initiates. For example,

Isabel L. Beck is professor of education at the School of Education and senior scientist at the Learning, Research, and Development Center, both at the University of Pittsburgh. She has published widely in the area of reading comprehension as well as early reading acquisition. Connie Juel is the Thomas G. Jewell Professor of Education and director of studies in learning to read at the McGuffey Reading Center at the University of Virginia. She has published widely on literacy acquisition, including her recent book, Learning to Read and Write in One Elementary School *(Springer-Verlag: 1994). This article first appeared as a chapter in* What Research Has To Say About Reading Instruction *(1992), edited by S. J. Samuels and A. E. Farstrup, and is reprinted by permission of the International Reading Association.*

Reprinted from *American Educator, Summer 1995*

THE ROLE OF DECODING

one of the questions she asks is why the mallards didn't want to live next to foxes and turtles. The only information given in the story is that "[Mrs. Mallard] was not going to raise a family where there might be foxes or turtles." The reason is not explained, yet the children are able to infer that Mrs. Mallard doesn't want to live next door to foxes and turtles because they might harm the ducklings.

The discussion also provides evidence that the children have control over some sophisticated language structures. Consider such complicated syntax as "But the people on the boat threw peanuts into the water, so the Mallards followed them all round the pond and got another breakfast, better than the first." When the teacher asks several of the children what that sentence means, none has difficulty capturing the notion that the mallards liked the peanuts more than what they had gotten to eat on their own.

Most children entering school have fairly sophisticated knowledge about language and stories. The children described here had enough knowledge of syntax, vocabulary, story elements, and aspects of the world around them to comprehend and enjoy *Make Way for Ducklings*. But no story in any first-grade preprimer can match the literary quality and level of language found in *Make Way for Ducklings*. Why? Because the children will be unable to read many words and therefore have no reliable way to translate the written text into their familiar spoken form of language. Until their word recognition skill catches up to their language skill, they are unable to independently read a story that matches the sophistication of their spoken vocabularies, concepts, and knowledge.

There has been much legitimate criticism of the reading materials used in early reading instruction. Although these materials need improvement, it is important to acknowledge that because children can recog-

nize only a limited number of words, even the most creatively developed materials cannot compete with stories such as *Make Way for Ducklings*. Our goal as educators is to quickly provide children with the tools they need to read some of the marvelous stories gifted writers have created for them. The major tools we can give children are ones that allow them to decode printed words for themselves. To facilitate a discussion of the issues associated with helping children gain control of the code that links the printed word to the spoken word, let us first define some terms.

Defining Reading Terms

Various terms have been used to describe the way children come to recognize printed words. We begin with a discussion intended to sort out a set of easily confused terms: the code, decoding, word attack, word recognition, phonics, and sight words.

One dictionary definition of *code* is "a system of signals used to represent assigned meanings." Signals can be numbers (as in a military code), dots and dashes (Morse code), or letters (as in an alphabetic language like English). In themselves these signals are meaningless. They become meaning-bearing units only when an individual knows what meanings can be assigned to the signals. When an individual can apply meaning to signals, that person has learned to decode.

In written alphabetic languages such as English, the code involves a system of mappings, or correspondences, between letters and sounds. When an individual has learned those mappings, that person is said to have "broken the code." Now the individual can apply his or her knowledge of the mappings to figure out plausible pronunciations of printed words. Most of the time, competent adult readers do not need to apply their knowledge of the mapping system consciously to recognize the words they encounter. If they do encounter a word they have never seen before, however, they are able to bring their knowledge of the code to

bear in a deliberate and purposeful way.

A number of terms are used to describe the application of the code when reading. It may be useful to consider the terms in light of two extremes of attention a reader pays to the code. At one extreme readers apply their knowledge of the code immediately and without any apparent attention. The terms used to describe this immediate phenomenon are *word recognition, word identification,* and *sight word recognition.* At the other extreme, readers consciously and deliberately apply their knowledge of the mapping system to produce a plausible pronunciation of a word they do not instantly recognize, such as the name of a character an English-speaking reader might encounter in a Russian novel. The term associated with this self-aware "figuring out" is *word attack.*

Individuals involved in either extreme are decoding in that they are using symbols to interpret a unit that bears meaning. Hence, word recognition, word identification, word attack, and sight word recognition are all terms applied to decoding, albeit to decoding with different levels of conscious attention.

Two terms that can be confused are sight word *vocabulary* (sometimes called sight word recognition) and sight word *method.* The former is a critical goal of all reading instruction—that children come to respond to most words at a glance, without conscious attention. This goal should not be confused with the instructional strategy called the sight word method (also known as the whole word or look-say approach), in which words are introduced to children as whole units without analysis of their subword parts. By repeated exposure to words, especially in meaningful contexts, it is expected that children will learn to read the words without any conscious attention to subword units. Hence, sight word recognition, or the development of a sight word vocabulary, is a goal of sight word instruction.

The issue of instructional strategies brings us to the terms *phonics* and *word attack.* Phonics embraces a variety of instructional strategies for bringing attention to parts of words. The parts can be syllables, phonograms (such as *an*), other letter strings (such as *ple*), or single letters. The goal of phonics is to provide students with the mappings between letters and sounds but, unlike the goal of the sight word method, phonics is not an end point. Rather, phonics merely provides a tool that enables students to "attack" the pronunciation of words that are not recognizable at a glance; hence the term word attack.

The Importance of Early Decoding Skill

Early attainment of decoding skill is important because this early skill accurately predicts later skill in reading comprehension. There is strong and persuasive evidence that children who get off to a slow start rarely become strong readers (Stanovich, 1986). Early learning of the code leads to wider reading habits both in and out of school (Juel, 1988). Wide reading provides opportunities to grow in vocabulary, concepts, and knowledge of how text is written. Children who do not learn to decode do not have this avenue for growth. This phenomenon, in which the "rich get richer" (i.e., the chil-

dren who learn early to decode continue to improve in reading) and the "poor get poorer" (i.e., children who do not learn to decode early become increasingly distanced from the "rich" in reading ability), has been termed the Matthew effect (Stanovich).

The importance of early decoding skill can be illustrated through the findings of several studies. In a longitudinal study of fifty-four children from first through fourth grades, Juel (1988) found a .88 probability that a child in the bottom quartile on the Iowa Reading Comprehension subtest at the end of first grade will still be a poor reader at the end of fourth grade. Of twenty-four children who remained poor readers through four grades, only two had average decoding skills. By the end of fourth grade, the poor decoders still had not achieved the level of decoding that the average/good readers had reached by the beginning of second grade. The poor decoders also had read considerably less than the average/good readers, both in and out of school. They had gained little vocabulary compared with the good decoders and expressed a real dislike of both reading and the failure associated with reading in school.

Lesgold and Resnick (1982) found that a child's speed of word recognition in first grade was an excellent predictor of that child's reading comprehension in second grade. In a longitudinal study of children learn-

ing to read in Sweden, Lundberg (1984) found a .70 correlation between linguistic awareness of words and phonemes in first grade and reading achievement in sixth grade. Moreover, Lundberg found that of forty-six children with low reading achievement in first grade, forty were still poor readers in sixth grade.

Clay (1979) discusses results of a longitudinal study of children learning to read in New Zealand:

> There is an unbounded optimism among teachers that children who are late in starting will indeed catch up. Given time, something will happen! In particular, there is a belief that the intelligent child who fails to learn to read will catch up to his classmates once he has made a start. Do we have any evidence of accelerated progress in late starters? There may be isolated examples which support this hope, but correlations from a follow-up study of 100 children two and three years after school entry lead me to state rather dogmatically that where a child stood in relation to his age-mates at the end of his first year in school was roughly where one would expect to find him at 7:0 or 8:0 (p. 13).

What Helps Children Learn the Code

The studies reported above all point to the importance of arranging conditions so that children gain reading independence early. The task of learning to decode printed words is made easier when the child has certain prerequisite understandings about print. These include knowing that print is important because it carries a message, that printed words are composed of letters, and that letters correspond to the somewhat distinctive sounds heard in a spoken word. Often these prerequisites develop as a result of a child's having been read to (especially by an adult who has made occasional references to aspects of the print), having attended preschool and kindergarten programs, or having watched instructional television programs like *Sesame Street.* Let us look at these three prerequisites and why children sometimes have difficulty acquiring them.

Printed Words Carry Messages

First, young children need to know that some systematic relationship exists between printed symbols and spoken messages. They need to know that looking at the print itself is important to determine these messages. This idea is not as obvious as it may first appear. Storybooks contain colorful, enticing pictures designed to capture children's interest and attention. In comparison, the black marks at the bottom of the page are rather uninteresting. Likewise, print in the environment is often embedded in rich contexts that are more noticeable and "readable" than the print itself (e.g., for a child, the color and shape of a stop sign has more meaning than the letters forming the word *stop*).

Words Are Composed of Letters

Observations of children's first unguided attempts to use print show that they frequently find some distinctive feature of a word that acts as a cue to identify the word for them (Gates & Boeker, 1923; Gough & Hillinger, 1980). Often this distinctive feature will be tied to a picture or a page location (e.g., *police car* is the last string of letters on the page with a picture of a policeman). Or a child will remember distinctive features of a particular word (e.g., *mallard* is a long string of letters with two straight lines in the middle). Initial letters are frequently used as recall cues (for instance, *duck* starts with a *d*). The problem with this approach is that for each additional word it is harder to find a single, distinctive cue (*d* for *duck* will no longer suffice when *deer* is encountered). At this point, reading can become an increasingly frustrating activity unless a better cue system is developed.

Children often try to combine distinctive features of words (for instance, first letters) with context cues to figure out an unknown word. This hybrid approach is not particularly reliable, however. For example, consider the difficulty a young child would encounter in figuring out an unknown word in the sentence "Mrs. Mallard_____ her eight ducklings." What word fits in the blank? It could be almost any verb. What if the child looked at the first letter (which in this case is *l*), or looked at the first and last letters (*l* and *s*) and approximate length (five letters)? Even with these three feature cues, the word might be *loves, likes, loses,* or *leads,* to list a few. Learning to look at *all* the letters is important.

Letters Correspond to the Sounds in Spoken Words

Once children know that words are composed of letters, they need to be able to map, or translate, the printed letters into sounds. In order to do that, children first need to be able to "hear" the sounds in spoken words—that is, to hear the /at/ sound in *cat* and *fat,* for example, and perceive that the difference between the two words lies in the first sound. (In this article slashes // indicate a speech sound.) If children cannot perceive these sound segments, they will encounter difficulty when trying to sound out words, in both reading and writing. This understanding has been termed phonemic awareness.

Phonemic awareness is not a single insight or ability. Rather, there are various phonemic insights, such as being able to rhyme words as in the cat/fat example above, or knowing that *fat* has three distinctive, yet overlapping and abstract, sounds. The last insight is particularly difficult because phonemes often overlap in speech (e.g., we begin saying the /a/ sound in fat while still uttering the /f/).

Although it is not clear how children gain phonemic awareness, certain activities do appear to foster it. Home factors such as time spent on word play, nursery or Dr. Seuss rhymes, and general exposure to storybooks appear to contribute to phonemic awareness. In a fifteen-month longitudinal study of British children from age three years, four months, Maclean, Bryant, and Bradley (1987) found a strong relationship between children's early knowledge of nursery rhymes and the later development of phonemic awareness. In addition, phonemic awareness predicted early reading ability. Both relationships were found after controlling for the effects of IQ and socioeconomic status.

There is growing evidence that phonemic awareness can be taught to young children and that such teaching can occur in a playful, interactive way. Lundberg, Frost, and Petersen (1988) showed that preschool children can be trained to manipulate the phonological elements in words. Their eight-month training program involved a variety of games, nursery rhymes, and rhymed stories. A typical game designed to foster syllable synthesis included a troll who told children what they would get as presents through the peculiar method of producing the words syllable by syllable. Each child had to synthesize the syllables in order to figure out what the troll was offering. Children who participated in the training showed considerable gains in some phonemic awareness skills—such as phoneme segmentation—compared with children who did not participate in the program. Positive effects of the preschool training were still evident in children's reading and spelling performance through second grade.

Clay (1979) found that many six-year-olds who were not making adequate progress learning to read could not "hear" the sound sequences in words. She adopted a phonemic awareness training program developed by the Russian psychologist Elkonin (1973) to train these children. Clay found that the children could learn and apply the strategy of analyzing the sound sequence of words. This strategy improved both their reading and their writing.

Unfortunately, many children come to school without phonemic awareness, and some fail to gain it from their school experiences. Juel, Griffith, and Gough (1985) found that well into first grade the spelling errors of many children were not even in the domain of what has come to be known as invented spellings (such as using the sounds captured in letter names to spell *light* as *lt* or *rain* as *ran*). These researchers found that many children entered first grade with little phonemic awareness and had difficulty learning spelling-sound relationships. For example, these children's misspellings of *rain* used in a sentence included such things as *yes, wetn, wnishire, rur,* and drawings of raindrops. The course of learning the code for these children will be different and more difficult than for children who are able to hear the sounds in spoken words and who know that these sounds can be mapped to letters.

Instructional Approaches

Given that letters and sounds have systematic relationships in an alphabetic language such as English, it stands to reason that those responsible for teaching initial reading would consider telling beginners directly what those relationships are. Indeed, until about 60 years ago this is what most teachers in the United States did. The techniques used, however, left much to be desired.

Phonics: The Past

It is important to recognize that phonics is not a single procedure. Under the label phonics can be found a variety of instructional strategies for teaching the relationship between letters and sounds. It appears that the kind of phonics practiced in the first decades of this century was an elaborated "drill and more drill" method. Diederich (1973) describes the scene:

> Initial instruction in letter-sound relationships and pronunciation rules was done to death ... children had

to learn so much abstract material by rote before doing any significant amount of reading (p. 7).

To illustrate more concretely what Diederich was describing, picture the following: It is October 1921, and forty first graders are seated at rows of desks. The teacher stands at the front of the class and points with a long wooden pointer to a wall chart that contains columns of letters and letter combinations. As she points to a column of short vowel and consonant *b* combinations, the class responds with the sound of each combination: /ab/, /eb/, /ib/, /ob/, /ub/. She goes to the next column and the class responds, /bab/, /beb/, /bib/, /bob/, /bub/. Then the teacher asks, "What's the rule?" The children respond in unison, "In a one-syllable word, in which there is a single vowel followed by a consonant...." So it went day after day, with "letter-sound relationships and pronunciation rules ... done to death."

It is no wonder that educators as prominent as William S. Gray described this kind of phonics as "heartless drudgery" and urged that it be replaced with what initially was termed the look-say approach and subsequently called the sight word or whole word method. The relief from extended drill with letter sounds, their synthesis into often meaningless syllables, and the recitation of rules of pronunciation is evident in Diederich's (1973) own response to the look-say method:

When [this] writer began his graduate study of education in 1928 ... no less an authority than Walter Dearborn had to send his students to observe several classes that were learning to read by the new "look-say" method before they would believe that it was possible. When prospective teachers like the students of Walter Dearborn discovered what a relatively painless process the teaching of reading could be, using the ... whole word approach, they were not disposed to demand evidence of superior results. It was enough to know that the new method worked about as well as the old and with far less agony (p. 7).

Look-Say

By the 1930s, the look-say method prevailed. The idea behind this approach was that children could learn to recognize words through repeated exposure without direct attention to subword parts. The existence of ideographic writing systems (like Chinese or Japanese Kanji, which is based on Chinese characters) shows that this type of visual learning can occur, but it is difficult. The characters are learned slowly. A child in Japan is expected to learn only seventy-six Kanji in first grade and 996 by the end of sixth grade. In contrast, many Japanese children enter school already reading Kana, which is based on phonetic segments. Most ideographic writing systems have been (or are in the process of being) replaced by alphabetic ones.

English is not an ideographic written language. To teach it as if it were ignores the systematic relationships between letters and the sounds that underlie them. Proponents of the look-say method have been quick to point out the imperfections of these relationships, which are most apparent in some high frequency words (e.g., *come, said*). It should not be overlooked, however, that the pronunciations of even these irregular words do not deviate widely from their spellings. We do not pronounce *come* as *umbrella*, or *said* as *frog*.

The look-say method continued virtually unchallenged until 1955, when Flesch, in his book *Why Johnny Can't Read,* vehemently attacked the approach and demanded a return to phonics. Although the general public and press reacted favorably to Flesch's book, it was rejected by reviewers in educational journals—chiefly because it took the form of a propagandistic argument that presented conclusions beyond what research evidence allowed. A decade later, Chall's (1967) *Learning to Read: The Great Debate* provided a reasoned presentation of the research with the conclusion that the evidence points to benefit from those programs that include early and systematic phonics. Subsequent researchers confirmed this advantage (e.g., Barr, 1972, 1974, 1975; DeLawter, 1970; Elder, 1971; Evans & Carr, 1983; Guthrie et al., 1976; Johnson & Baumann, 1984; Resnick, 1979; Williams, 1979).

Phonics: The Present

Several years ago, the National Commission on Reading, comprising a range of representatives from the research community (and sponsored in part by the National Institute of Education), developed a report that synthesized and interpreted the existing body of research on reading. The report, entitled *Becoming a Nation of Readers* (Anderson et al., 1985), observes in its discussion of early reading that "most educators" view phonics instruction as "one of the essential ingredients." It goes on to note: "Thus, the issue is no longer ... whether children should be taught phonics. The issues now are specific ones of just how it should be done" (pp. 36-37). Approaches to phonics instruction generally can be described by one of two terms—explicit phonics and implicit phonics, referring to the explicitness with which letter sounds (phonemes) are taught in a given approach.

In explicit phonics, children are directly told the sounds of individual letters (the letter *m* represents the /m/ in *man*). In implicit phonics, children are expected to induce the sounds that correspond to letters from accumulated auditory and visual exposure to words containing those letters (for instance, they would induce /m/ from hearing the teacher read *man, make,* and *mother* as she or he points to the words on the chalkboard). In terms of the effectiveness of one approach over the other, *Becoming a Nation of Readers* observes that "available research does not permit a decisive answer, although the trend of the data favors explicit phonics" (p. 42). Let us look more closely at both approaches, beginning with implicit phonics.

As noted above, in implicit phonics the sounds of individual letters are never pronounced in isolation. Instead, the child is expected to induce these sounds from reading words in stories and lists that contain similar spelling-sound patterns. Continuing with the *m* example, a child who encountered the new word *met* and who had seen and heard *man* and *make* would be instructed to think of other words that begin with the letter *m* in order to identify the sound at the beginning of the new word. In order to comply with the instructions, the child needs to be able to identify distinct sounds in spoken words to make a connection between the sound and the target letter. To be able to induce the sound of the letter *m* or the sound of the *et* phonogram, the child must be able to distinguish between the sound of the initial consonant and the rest of the word. This is a difficult task because in speech the sounds of individual letters actually overlap and blend as a word is pronounced. Thus, in actuality, the ability to extract the sound of a letter from a spoken word is more "in the mind" than "in the mouth."

A problem with implicit phonics is that many children fail to induce the sounds because they are unable to segment a word into distinctive sounds. It takes very sophisticated phonemic awareness to do so. Many children do not come to school with such awareness, yet implicit phonics requires this ability right from the start.

Explicit phonics requires less sophisticated phonemic awareness because the sounds associated with letters are directly provided. Explicit phonics, however, has its own potential problem; the sounds of some consonant letters cannot be said in isolation without adding a schwa, or /uh/ (e.g., the isolated sound of the letter *b* in *but* is distorted to /buh/). Do we harm children by telling them these distortions? Not if instruction in how to blend letter sounds is provided. In reviewing the research associated with this question, Johnson and Baumann (1984) noted that "there is no substance to the long-held belief that pronouncing sounds in isolation is detrimental" (p. 592). Similarly, the

THE ROLE OF DECODING

commission that developed *Becoming a Nation of Readers* concluded that "isolating the sounds ... and teaching children to blend the sounds of letters together to try to identify words are useful instructional strategies" (p. 42). Thus, the prevailing conclusion seems to be that isolating sounds offers an advantage when it is done in moderation and when it includes good blending instruction.

Explicit phonics is helpful because it provides children with the real relationships between letters and sounds, or at least approximations of them. But knowledge of letter-sound relationships is of little value unless the child can use that knowledge to figure out words. Whether children have learned the sounds of letters through implicit or explicit phonics, figuring out a new word still requires that the sounds of the letters be merged or blended.

We will return to the topic of blending in considering instructional issues. First we address another major issue associated with phonics—the relationship between what children learn in phonics and the stories they read.

Phonics and Reading Materials

We begin this section by recalling that among the serious problems Diederich (1973) pointed to about the way phonics was presented in the past was that "children had to learn so much abstract material [i.e., letter-sound relationships] by rote before doing any significant amount of reading" (p. 7). This "abstractness" problem can be eliminated by recognizing that adequate instruction gives students opportunities to apply what they are learning. Children need a lot of early experience reading meaningful material that includes many words that exemplify the sound-spelling patterns being introduced.

Current beginning reading programs tend to fall into two groups: (1) those in which there is a strong relationship between the sound-spelling patterns children are learning in their phonics lessons and the words in the stories they read, and (2) those in which this relationship is weak. To illustrate the differences, *Becoming a Nation of Readers* presented excerpts from two representative programs. Both excerpts came from material that would be read some time in or near November of first grade, when both programs would have introduced about thirty letter-sound relationships. A twenty-six-word passage from the weak-relationship program contained seventeen different words, out of which "only three (or 17 percent) could be decoded entirely on the basis of letter-sound relationships that [had] been introduced in the program's phonics lessons" (p. 45). In contrast, out of eighteen different words in the passage from the strong-relationship program, seventeen (or 94 percent) "could be decoded entirely on the basis of letter-sound relationships that students should know from the program's phonics lessons" (p. 46).

This gap in the percentage of decodable words results from the word selection process for the stories of each program. The first program selected high-frequency words that are likely to be in a young child's vocabulary. Word choice was not constrained by the letter-sound relationships or letter patterns introduced in the program's phonics lessons. In the second program, word choice was, to a large extent, constrained by the letter patterns introduced.

These two excerpts reflect the findings of Beck's (1981) analysis of eight beginning reading programs. The analysis included all the material students would read in the first third of each program. The percentage of decodable words in the four programs that based word selection on the letter-sound relationships introduced in their phonics lessons was 100 percent, 93 percent, 79 percent, and 69 percent, respectively. In contrast, the percentage of decodable words in the programs that selected their words from high-frequency lists was 0 percent for two programs, 3 percent for the third, and 13 percent for the fourth.

Problems arise when the relationship between what children learn in phonics and the stories they read is either too low or too high. When too few of the words are decodable it is questionable whether what is taught in phonics is of any use. On the other hand, when all but one or two of the words in a selection are constrained by the letter sounds introduced, it is virtually impossible to write interesting selections in natural sounding language. This is, in part, a result of exclusion of such high-frequency but irregular words as *said, come, have,* and *you.* At its extreme, excluding such words and overemphasizing the last few letter sounds introduced results in sentences of the "Dan had a tan can" variety.

Is there an optimal relationship between the letter sounds children are learning in phonics and the words in their readers? Clearly, the answer is no. *Becoming a Nation of Readers* makes the point that establishing a rigid guideline is a poor idea: "What the field of reading does not need is another index that gets applied rigidly. What the field does need is an understanding of the concepts at work" (p. 47). The concept at work is that a "high proportion of the words in the earliest selections children read should conform to the phonics that they have already been taught." However, "requiring that, say, 90 percent of the words ... conform to letter-sound relationships already introduced would destroy the flexibility needed to write interesting, meaningful stories" (p. 47).

The issues we have raised in the last two sections concern instructional strategies for teaching phonics and the relationship between what is learned in phonics and the selections children read. Having raised these issues in terms of existing instructional materials, let us turn to the teacher's role.

What Teachers Can Do

It is well established that basal reading programs are the most widely used resources for teaching reading in the elementary school. Although program implementation undoubtedly varies with individual teachers, there is strong evidence that the program teachers use heavily influences their classroom teaching (Diederich, 1973). Hence, we will frame our discussion of what teachers can do in relationship to the kinds of programs in use.

Since the most widely used reading programs employ implicit phonics, this seems to be the most prevalent approach. In implicit phonics, individual sounds are not produced in isolation. However, we would encourage teachers to make the individual sounds available. As teachers told Durkin (1984), who observed them producing sounds in isolation even though their manuals did not recommend it, "Children need to hear the sounds" (p. 740).

Although we recommend making individual sounds explicitly available, we caution against using them in isolation. Specifically, we recommend that teachers start with a word the children already know from oral language, extract the sound from that word, and then place it back into the word. For example, in preparation for learning the sound of the letter *d,* the teacher can draw students' attention to a word like *duck* from a recent story or use a line from a nursery rhyme, such as "diddle, diddle, dumpling." Then the teacher should explain that the first letter of these words, called a *d,* represents the /d/ sound.

This strategy not only overcomes the problem in implicit phonics of requiring children to extract a sound from a spoken word, but it also reduces a potential problem in explicit phonics—the difficulty of saying the sounds of some of the consonant letters in isolation. By starting with strong words, extracting the sound from those words, and placing the sound right back into words, teachers can avoid the pitfalls of explicit phonics approaches in which a string of isolated letter sounds is accumulated.

As noted earlier, an important issue associated with phonics is blending. *Becoming a Nation of Readers* makes two important points that can be applied to this topic. The first is that blending "is a difficult step for many children. Until a child gets over this hurdle, learning the sound of individual letters … will have diminished value" (p. 39). The second point is that when children attempt to figure out a word by blending sounds, it is not necessary for them to produce a perfect pronunciation. Rather, they need to be able to "come up with approximate pronunciations—candidates that have to be checked to see whether they match words known from spoken language" (p. 38).

We have two suggestions for promoting children's blending ability. In one the teacher models decoding of unknown words by slowly blending their component letter sounds. A model of blending involves stretching out each component sound until it merges with the next sound and then collapsing the sounds together so the word can be heard more clearly. For example, the teacher could select a new word that will be encountered in an upcoming selection, let's say *met,* write it on the board, and demonstrate how one might go about sounding it out. She or he would note that the first letter, the *m,* represents the /m/ sound, like at the beginning of *mittens.* Next the teacher would produce /m/ and add the short *e,* first elongating the sounds, /mmee/, then collapsing them, /me/. Then the teacher would add the /t/, at first giving a slightly exaggerated, then a more natural, pronunciation of *met.*

It is not difficult to involve the children in practicing this strategy. For example, the teacher can write a word on the board and tell the children to think of the sound of the first letter and keep saying it until he or she points to the next letter, and keep saying the sound of the two letters until they add on the sound of the last letter.

Resnick and Beck (1976) note that an important feature of blending instruction is merging different sounds successively—that is, /m/, /me/, /met/. Teachers should avoid using sequences in which the merging does not occur until each sound has been produced, such as /m/, /e/, /t/, /met/. Among the reasons that successive blending is preferable is that it avoids the need to keep a string of isolated sounds in memory.

Blending instruction does not have to be tedious. Teachers can choose from a variety of active and fun possibilities. For example, the teacher might give large cardboard letters to some children and start a word by telling the child who has the card that says /m/ to stand up. Then the child whose card makes /m/ say /me/ can go up and stand next to the /m/ child, followed by the /t/ bearer, who can complete the word *met.* The teacher might then ask the child who can make *met* say *bet* to go up and change places with the /m/ child.

This last example brings us to the second instructional strategy that promotes blending. Here children are involved with many opportunities to make words and to experiment with and observe the results of a letter change. A traditional implementation of this strategy involves a variety of letter substitution techniques. For example, the teacher places a phonogram such as *an* on a flannel board and then puts various consonants in front of the pattern, having the children read the resulting words (e.g., *can, man*). Or the teacher places the letters *s, a, t* on a flannel board and after the children read *sat,* she or he changes the vowel so the word reads *sit,* then changes it again to read *set.* This technique can be extended so that children use their own letter cards (which they can make or get from the teacher) to create words by changing letters in all positions—for instance, *sat* to *sit* to *bit* to *bot* to *bop* to *mop* to *map.* By deleting, adding, or substituting letters, more complex sequences, such as *black* to *back* to *tack* to *tick* to *trick,* can be developed.

Building words in this fashion externalizes the blending process. It makes the process readily accessible to children by making it very concrete. Children physically handle the letter cards, attach sounds to them, and manipulate the cards to produce new words.

Now let us turn to instructional issues associated with the relationship between what children are learning in phonics and the words in the stories they read and consider what the teacher can do if the relationship is either too low or too high. First, if the selections do not use words that allow the children to practice what has been taught in phonics, the teacher will need to write or find materials that do.

One teacher developed a way to write stories that incorporated the sound spelling patterns introduced in the program she was using. Essentially, she made "little books" by revising some of the stories in the basal. She started with a selection and inserted new words whose letter-sound relationships had already been taught. She

found she was able to develop meaningful stories by adding and deleting various sentences, phrases, and words. Most often, her revised stories were longer than the original ones. Sometimes they were elaborated versions of the original stories, but frequently the deletion and addition of words allowed her to vary the plots of these stories.

The teacher reported that she enjoyed revising the selections, but found it very time consuming. Since all teachers cannot be expected to have the time or knack for making such little books, published materials are needed. Some published children's stories (such as Dr. Seuss's *The Cat in the Hat, Hop on Pop, Fox in Socks,* and *There's a Wocket in My Pocket*) can be used. If a book contains too many unknown words, the teacher could use it in a shared reading situation in which she reads some of the story to the children and the children read the parts (perhaps from a "Big Book") that contain the words with learned sound spelling patterns. Other sources of material that may be useful are nursery rhymes ("How now brown cow") and tongue twisters ("How many cans can a canner can…"). In addition, teachers can give children opportunities to write their own tongue twisters.

If the program being followed is too constrained in using only phonics-related words (the "Dan had a tan can" variety), the teacher needs to incorporate into the selections some high-frequency words that have lots of utility for future readings. The teacher also should include words of interest to the children and words that have appeared in the children's writings. So we might get "Dan had a big can full of tan monsters." Or the teacher can leave blanks in a story where the children can fill in words:"Dan had a _____ can full of _____. A _____ man took the can." Basically the teacher leaves blanks where adverbs, adjectives, and prepositional phrases could go. The children might copy and illustrate these stories, collecting them into storybooks that can be taken home and read to others.The teacher also can use these types of text in chart stories or Big Books.

Children's writing can be used to foster phonic skill. For this strategy to work, children must have the prerequisite understandings discussed earlier in the sec-

tion on phonemic awareness. Bissex (1980) gives an example of how a child who could analyze words into spoken sounds gained knowledge of the code through writing. Bissex's five-year-old son, Paul, advanced by asking his mother questions concerning letter-sound relationships as he wrote. For example, Paul asked what made the "ch" sound in *teach,* to which his mother responded "c-h" (p. 12). Or this dialogue:

Paul: What makes the "uh" sound?
Mother: In what word?
Paul: Mumps.
Mother: u (p. 13).

To ask such questions, Paul had to have rather sophisticated phonemic awareness (for instance, he could segment the /uh/ sound in *mumps*). Likewise, teachers of young children may be able to foster such interaction as they respond to their young students' questions about how to write the sounds in certain words.

Just as teachers model blending to decode unknown words, they can model how to sound and blend sounds into written words. For example, "If I wanted to write the word *met* in a story, I'd first say the word to myself very slowly, /mmeett/. Then I'd think of the letter that makes the /m/ sound at the beginning of met and write it [writing the letter *m* on the board]. Then I'd think of what letter needs to be added to make it say /meee/ [adding the letter *e*]. Then I'd think of what letter needs to be added to make it say *met* [adding the letter *t*]." The teacher can encourage children to sound out and write the words in their stories in a similar manner.

As teachers can help children induce the code by repeatedly answering the question "What's this word?" they also can help them by answering "What letter stands for this sound in this word?" With either reading or writing, successful induction of the code will depend both on whether the child has the prerequisite understandings (i.e., phonemic awareness) and whether someone is around to answer these questions frequently. The fortunate child who has both of these conditions in place can learn the code even more quickly by being directly informed about the alphabetic code (e.g., through explicit phonics). The child who has little prerequisite knowledge about print and who lacks an informed partner in learning may need to *depend* on systematic and explicit phonics instruction. This child has fewer opportunities to induce the code through exposure to print and is thus more dependent on instruction to lay bare the alphabetic system.

The course of acquiring the code for a child like Paul, who at age five wrote above his workbench DO NAT DSTRB GNYS AT WRK (Bissex, 1980, p. 23), will be very different from that of the child who in the middle of first grade is spelling *rain* as *yes* or *wnishire*. Paul already had a good understanding of the alphabetic system and knew a fair amount about the code prior to first grade. He would have learned to read in first grade no matter what the instruction. Many children are not as fortunate as Paul. They depend almost exclusively on the instruction they receive in school to learn to read and write.

We have discussed the extreme importance of learning the code in first grade because early decoding reliably predicts reading comprehension in subsequent grades. Failure to teach the code in the most straightforward manner (e.g., through good, explicit phonics instruction coupled with reasonably constrained texts) would leave many children without the key to unlock the printed message. Children without this key cannot independently enter the world of quality literature; some may learn to dislike reading entirely. Each day that goes by without the child being able to read a book like *Make Way for Ducklings* is a day in which the knowledge and joy that can come from such reading are lost.

References

Anderson, R.C., Hiebert, E.H., Scott, J.A., & Wilkinson, I.A.G. (1985). *Becoming a nation of readers: The report of the Commission on Reading*. Washington, DC: National Institute of Education.

Barr, R. (1972). The influence of instructional conditions on word recognition errors. *Reading Research Quarterly, 7*, 509-529.

Barr, R. (1974). Influence of instruction on early reading. *Interchange*. 5(4). 13-21.

Barr, R. (1975). The effect of instruction on pupil reading strategies. *Reading Research Quarterly, 4*, 555-582.

Beck, I.L. (1981). Reading problems and instructional practices. In G.E. MacKinnon & T.G. Waller (Eds.), *Reading research: Advances in theory and practice* (vol. 2, pp. 53-95). New York: Academic.

Bissex, G.L. (1980). *GNYS AT WRK: A child learns to read and write*. Cambridge, MA: Harvard University Press.

Chall, J.S. (1967). *Learning to read: The great debate*. New York: McGraw-Hill.

Clay, M.M. (1979). *Reading: The patterning of complex behavior*. Portsmouth, NH: Heinemann.

DeLawter, J. (1970). *Oral reading errors of second grade children exposed to two different reading approaches*. Unpublished doctoral dissertation. Teachers College, Columbia University, New York.

Diederich, P.B. (1973). *Research 1960-1970 on methods and materials in reading* (TM Report 22), Princeton, NJ: Educational Testing Service.

Durkin, D. (1984). Is there a match between what elementary teachers do and what basal reader manuals recommend? *The Reading Teacher, 37*, 734-744.

Elder, R.D. (1971). Oral reading achievement of Scottish and American children. *Elementary School Journal, 71*, 216-230.

Elkonin, D.B. (1973). U.S.S.R. In J. Downing (Ed.). *Comparative reading* (pp. 551-579). New York: Macmillan.

Evans, M.A., & Carr, T.H. (1983). *Curricular emphasis and reading development: Focus on language or focus on script*. Symposium conducted at the biennial meeting of the Society for Research on Child Development, Detroit, MI.

Flesch, R. (1955). *Why Johnny can't read*. New York: Harper & Row.

Gates, A.I. & Boeker, E. (1923). A study of initial stages in reading by preschool children. *Teachers College Record, 24*, 469-488.

Gough, P.B. & Hillinger, M.L. (1980). Learning to read: An unnatural act. *Bulletin of the Orton Society*, 30, 179-196.

Guthrie, J.T., Samuels, S.J., Martuza, V., Seifert, M., Tyler, S.J. & Edwall, G.A. (1976). *A study of the focus and nature of reading problems in the elementary school*. Washington, D.C.: National Institute of Education.

Johnson, D.D. & Baumann, J.F. (1984). Word identification. In P.D. Pearson (Ed). *Handbook of reading research* (pp. 583-608). White Plains, NY: Longman.

Juel, C. (1988). Learning to read and write: A longitudinal study of fifty-four children from first through fourth grade. *Journal of Educational Psychology, 80*, 437-447.

Juel, C., Griffith, P.L. & Gough, P.B. (1985). Reading and spelling strategies of first grade children. In J.A. Niles & R. Lalik (Eds.). *Issues in literacy: A research perspective* (pp. 306-309). Rochester, NY: National Reading Conference.

Lesgold, A.M., & Resnick, L.B. (1982). How reading disabilities develop: Perspectives from a longitudinal study. In J.P. Das, R. Mulcahy, & A.E. Wall (Eds.). *Theory and research in learning disability*. New York: Plenum.

Lundberg, I. (1984, August). Learning to read. *School Research Newsletter*. Sweden: National Board of Education.

Lundberg, I., Frost, J., & Petersen, O. (1988). Effects of an extensive program for stimulating phonological awareness in preschool children. *Reading Research Quarterly, 23*, 263-284.

Maclean, M., Bryant, P., & Bradley, L. (1987). Rhymes, nursery rhymes, and reading in early childhood. *Merrill-Palmer Quarterly, 33*, 255-281.

McCloskey, R. (1941/1969). *Make way for ducklings*. New York: Viking.

Resnick, L.B. (1979). Theories and prescriptions for early reading instruction. In L. B. Resnick & P.A. Weaver (Eds.), *Theory and practice of early reading* (vol. 2, pp. 321-338). Hillsdale, NJ: Erlbaum.

Resnick, L., & Beck, I.L. (1976). Designing instruction in reading: Interaction of theory and practice. In J.T. Guthrie (Ed.), *Aspects of reading acquisition*. Baltimore, MD: Johns Hopkins University Press.

Stanovich, K.E. (1986). Matthew effects in reading: Some consequences of individual differences in the acquisition of literacy. *Reading Research Quarterly, 21*, 360-406.

Williams, J.P. (1984). Reading instruction today. *American Psychologist, 34*, 917-922.

Irene H. Blum
Patricia S. Koskinen

Repeated Reading: A Strategy for Enhancing Fluency and Fostering Expertise

Reflect on something you do well, something at which you are an expert. It may be cooking, playing tennis, teaching children to read, or a range of other activities. When asked to do this activity, you probably approach the task with confidence, knowing what you need to do and how you are going to do it. You can assess your own success and if you run into difficulty, you competently find a solution. In addition, you probably can tell others what they are doing right or wrong in relation to this task. It is likely you gained this expertise because, for some reason, you were motivated to practice repeatedly over a long period of time.

In our work with teachers and students, we have been focusing on developing an instructional setting that fosters expertise. In such an environment, students understand what they read, learn strategies to improve their reading, feel successful, and are motivated to practice. We have been especially interested in using repeated reading as an instructional strategy to develop fluency (i.e., smooth, accurate, natural, expressive reading) with beginning readers as well as with less proficient readers. This deceptively simple rehearsal strategy involves multiple readings and provides substantial practice in reading connected discourse. It enables novices to feel like experts as they acquire fluency.

Irene H. Blum is a Chapter 1 reading specialist at Fairfax County Public Schools, Fairfax, VA; Patricia S. Koskinen is a member of the graduate faculty of the Reading Center at the University of Maryland.

Fluency and Repeated Reading

While fluency has traditionally been a neglected goal in instruction, Allington (1983) stimulated an interest in examining the role of fluency in skilled reading. He reviewed a variety of sources that support the view that oral fluency should be regarded as a necessary feature of defining good reading, that readers can be helped to acquire fluency through training, and that fluency training improves overall reading ability.

In an effort to explore these ideas, researchers, using a variety of repeated reading strategies, have documented evidence of improved fluency as a result of training. Studies provide impressive evidence of improvement in both reading rate and accuracy (Chomsky, 1976; Dahl, 1974; Dowhower, 1987; Samuels, 1979). A growing body of work also adds support to the view that fluency training is linked to improving overall reading ability. There is considerable evidence that rereading improves reading comprehension (Dowhower, 1987; O'Shea, Sindelar, & O'Shea, 1985;), increases vocabulary (Elley, 1989; Koskinen & Blum, 1984), and helps students understand and remember more concepts (Bromage & Mayer, 1986; Taylor, Wade, & Yekovich, 1985). In addition, there are indications that repeated reading helps students feel more confident about their reading and is an activity in which they want to participate (Koskinen & Blum, 1984; Topping, 1987; Trachtenberg & Ferruggia, 1989).

Characteristics of Experts

While substantial support for the use of repeated reading can be found in the literature, a conceptual framework is needed in which to interpret some of its success and to support its wider use in instruction. The theory of automatic information processing as developed by LaBerge and Samuels (1974) emphasizes the importance of practice. According to this theory, practice enables beginning readers to achieve a level of automaticity in decoding so that they can focus attention on comprehension. Recent literature on expertise broadens our understanding of the nature of effective practice, noting the influence of task difficulty on comprehension monitoring behavior. In addition, this research clarifies the relationship between motivation and practice.

A review of the literature on expertise indicates common elements among experts: (a) They have extensive knowledge about their topic, (b) they have a variety of strategies for learning, and (c) they are highly motivated to practice (Meichenbaum & Biemiller, 1990). Not only is the knowledge of experts coherently organized and easily accessed (Bereiter & Scarmadalia, 1986), but these experts also employ a range of metacognitive skills. They efficiently select strategies to advance their learning and monitor their comprehension. When they encounter difficulties, they call upon fix-up strategies (Ericsson & Smith, 1989, cited in Meichenbaum & Biemiller, 1990). In addition, experts' high level of motivation leads to extensive practice over an extended period of time and in a range of settings (Ericsson, Tesch-Romer, & Krampe, 1989, cited in Meichenbaum & Biemiller, 1990). It appears that success begets success. Not only does practice enhance knowledge, but knowledge enhances interest, thereby stimulating continued motivation to practice.

Research by Meichenbaum and Biemiller (1990) with self-directed elementary students reveals that these child "experts" exhibit behavior that is similar to other experts in specific disciplines. Not only do these children have enhanced knowledge and motivation, they have a repertoire of effective learning strategies. These child "experts" engage in considerable metacognitive behavior, monitoring their own activities as well as those of others. In addition, they design new situations in which to develop their metacognitive abilities and extend their personal knowledge.

Of particular interest in this research with self-directed children is the relationship between task difficulty and behavior as an expert. The research results indicate that behavior as an expert is a function of setting. Children who were self-directed and "experts" in one setting did not necessarily behave in this self-directed "expert" way in another setting (e.g., going from the academic setting of the classroom to the creative setting of the art room). Meichenbaum and Biemiller (1990) suggest a need to view expertise "*not* as a characteristic of an individual . . . but rather as a reflection of the *fit* between the level of task demands (e.g. difficulty and interest levels) and the child's abilities (knowledge strategy and motivation)" (p. 33). They observed that self-directed children typically selected tasks at a moderate level of difficulty and were able to monitor their task behavior.

While some students develop expertise on their own, the research by Meichenbaum and Biemiller (1990) highlights the need to provide a classroom environment that allows less spontaneous learners to behave like experts. They propose that one way to create this environment is to provide activities that offer a wide range of difficulty levels so that each student can participate in activities where the cognitive demands of the task are not overwhelming, thus allowing the student to reflect on and monitor the task.

Repeated Reading and Expertise

In our efforts to design a learning environment that fosters literacy, helping students develop expertise has been an important component. We have been particularly interested in providing instructional opportunities where students are exposed to interesting and important content knowledge, where they acquire strategies for learning, and where they are motivated to extend and use their knowledge. Providing meaningful activities that students can complete successfully is a critical feature of this instruction.

Teachers have successfully used repeated reading in a variety of ways. Typically it has been used as an adjunct to regular instruction, providing repeated practice for fluency. More recently, however, teachers have begun to integrate it into the fabric of literacy instruction. Research on the use of successful methods includes repeated reading of passages (Dowhower, 1987; Herman, 1985; Samuels, 1979) and assisted repeated reading, where a live or audiotaped model of the passage is provided (Carbo, 1978; Chomsky, 1976). Another variation is paired repeated reading (Koskinen & Blum, 1984) where students work together reading short passages of text and evaluate both their own improvement and that of their partners.

Repeated reading appears to provide opportunities for learners to develop expertise by contributing to increases in knowledge of both content and strategy. In addition, increased knowledge and awareness of improvement provides considerable motivation for continued practice. Because it allows students at many different instructional levels to participate in the same activity and improve at their own pace, repeated reading responds to Meichenbaum and Biemiller's (1990) recommendation to provide activities at a wide range of difficulty levels.

The following is an example of one teacher's use of paired repeated reading as a fluency strategy that encourages the development of expertise (Blum & Koskinen, 1990):

> In a unit on monkeys, Mrs. B. read a group of second grade beginning readers the book *Curious George* (Rey, 1969) while the children read along with their own text. An audiotape of this story was then put in the listening center as part of the class audio library. During the students' independent practice time, students were asked to work in pairs, selecting a short 50 word or less segment from the book to read to a partner. This segment was to focus on something interesting they learned about George. Each student read the segment three times to their partner. After each reading, the reader rated his/her improvement on a five point Likert scale ranging from "fantastic" to "terrible," and then the listener commented on how their partner's reading improved.

This repeated reading activity fostered expertise in a variety of ways, described in the following sections.

Increasing Content Knowledge

Students reread specific story content at least four or five different times. They heard the whole text initially and interacted with it again when selecting the segment for repeated reading. This selection process often required students to reread larger portions of text to find an interesting segment upon which to focus.

Following the paired repeated reading activity, which involved reading and listening to a segment three times, the students became quite comfortable with this text. Not only were all students able to respond with at least one important idea they remembered about George, the repeated reading further expanded students' knowledge about George's actions and adventures. In addition, children demonstrated they had learned factual information about monkeys (e.g., that George came from Africa).

Increasing Strategy Knowledge

All the students were able to participate in the activity, both as readers and listeners. As readers, each was able to select a segment, reread the segment to a partner, and rate the reading. As partners, each was able to listen to the partner's reading and then identify a way the reading had improved. Through independent practice, students gained skill in rereading as a strategy for acquiring information.

In addition, the cooperative learning setting of repeated reading provided an opportunity for students to reflect on their reading improvement. By evaluating each of their successive readings, they practiced monitoring their success. The listener provided monitoring guidance by offering compliments on improvement (e.g., the reader knew more words, read more smoothly). This role of listener provided important support for the reader and developed the listener's metacognitive awareness of the critical features of fluent reading.

Increasing Motivation

By using literature as an introductory activity, Mrs. B. engaged students with inviting material. The expressive oral reading by the teacher not only stimulated interest, but also provided background knowledge and word identification support so students could confidently begin individual text reading. In Mrs. B.'s class, students' motivation to practice was provided initially by external teacher purposes and evaluation directions. However, internal motivation began to develop from students' observations of increased fluency, partners' compliments, and increased familiarity with content information.

Providing for Different Ability Levels

Although students in Mrs. B.'s group were functioning at very different levels (from pre-primer to first grade), her repeated reading activity was structured so that everyone was able to experience success. The initial reading of the text by the teacher provided a chance for students to hear smooth fluent reading. While most students could understand the story concepts, they could not decode many of the words. The teacher's oral reading greatly increased students' familiarity with the text, thereby decreasing the complexity of subsequent reading tasks.

Individual reading was conducted within a paired learning paradigm where students were encouraged to support each other. This meant students could ask their partners for information or help with difficult words. In other words, they were not facing this task alone.

By varying the length of the passage selected for rereading, students could also adjust the task's difficulty. Some readers selected 50-word passages while others were encouraged to select short passages. Some less proficient readers selected only one or two sentences for rereading after going to the listening center to get extra assistance in identifying an interesting part. Because of the inherent flexibility of repeated reading procedures, these students were able to work at a pace that was comfortable for their individual skill level.

Integrating Repeated Reading

As we found and as research shows, there are considerable benefits to using repeated reading as a strategy for fostering expertise while enhancing fluency and comprehension (Dowhower, 1987; Koskinen & Blum, 1984; Yaden, 1988). Repeated reading is a powerful strategy that is flexible and adaptable for classroom use. Thus, teachers and researchers have been exploring ways to integrate repeated reading practice more extensively into classroom instruction. Educators who have used shared book experiences and focused on whole language instruction have suggested procedures for using repeated reading as an integral part of instruction (Baskwill & Whitman, 1987; Butler, 1988; Butler & Turbill, 1985; Holdaway, 1979; Trachtenberg & Ferruggia, 1989).

An illustration of the integration of repeated reading into instruction is provided by the experience of a teacher working with second grade less proficient readers in a unit on monkeys (Blum & Koskinen, 1990). This teacher, Mrs. B., began by introducing literature selections to motivate interest in the theme. These included poems, such as "Five Little Monkeys" (Richards, 1972), and books, such as *The Monkey and the Crocodile* (Galdone, 1969).

These materials were repeatedly read as part of shared reading time, with an emphasis on appreciation of the various readings' language, content, and humor. Where applicable, character development was discussed. As the units proceeded, new materials were introduced and students participated in paired repeated readings, read-along activities, and research on related topics. In a writing component, the students worked individually and as a group to generate ideas and put together a child-authored text. The activities involved with creating this text—revising, editing, illustrating, etc.—created further opportunities for meaningful repeated reading.

This sequence of repeated reading activities within a theme based unit helped students feel like experts as they became fluent, comprehending readers. It provided a new depth of understanding that enhanced content and strategy knowledge as well as motivation. Concepts were expanded and reviewed in informational texts and child-authored materials. Children read and then restructured information both orally and in writing.

Presenting the same information in a variety of ways provides such a range of levels that all students can be assured some degree of success. The following section elaborates further on ways to vary the use of repeated reading so that it can be integrated more extensively into classroom instruction.

Variations

From our work with teachers over a period of years, we have found that they use repeated readings in a variety of creative ways. The example of theme based instruction in Mrs. B.'s classroom presents a number of these successful variations in both direct instruction and independent practice settings. Within each of these settings, motivation to practice was provided by adjusting the purposes for repeated reading and by using different types of materials and modalities.

Vary the Instructional Setting

Mrs. B. used repeated reading in both teacher-directed and independent-practice settings. During teacher-directed instruction, Mrs. B. guided students through repeated reading, modeling important features (e.g., fluent reading and active listening) during an activity where the group listened to an audiotape. She then helped students monitor their use of the strategy.

During independent practice, students had opportunities to use the information they gained about content (monkeys) and strategy (repeated reading and related monitoring behavior). By practicing repeatedly, students developed facility both in learning new information and refining the information they already possessed.

Vary Purposes for Rereading

During teacher-directed instruction, Mrs. B. used a variety of purposes to reinforce content knowledge and monitor comprehension. With narrative text, the purpose of the initial reading was enjoyment. Subsequent readings focused on such purposes as identifying motivations of characters and learning characteristics of monkeys. With informational text, the initial reading focused on finding out about monkeys. A second reading was done to identify one important idea. Purposes for reading child-authored text varied from checking to see if all important ideas were included to performing editing functions.

In addition, students practiced repeated reading as performance opportunities to share knowledge with others (e.g., a parent, visitors to the classroom, another group). By using different purposes, Mrs. B. was reinforcing and providing motivation to obtain both content and strategy knowledge. During independent practice time, she included rereading activities with a variety of purposes, such as planning an illustration or preparing to read to others.

Vary Materials

Mrs. B. provided many different materials for repeated reading. During directed instruction, she began with examples of narrative texts and then introduced a variety of expository materials. In addition, students used both group and individual child-authored materials. Independent practice included the use of all the variety of materials used in teacher directed instruction, including narrative and expository material on monkeys as well as group and individual writing that related to ideas about monkeys.

By using this variety of material, children had many opportunities to practice vocabulary and concepts, thereby increasing their knowledge base and decreasing the concept demands of the task. Interaction with each successive text enabled students to work with an expanded base of prior knowledge and to increase their familiarity with new words.

Vary Modalities

By varying modalities, Mrs. B. was able to add another dimension of richness to the repeated reading process. Children had the opportunity to read silently with a fluent model or a tape. In other activities, they read aloud with the model. Sometimes children reread a piece of text, either narrative or expository, that had been introduced earlier. Children participated in restructuring information both orally and in their writing. During independent practice, students reread orally and listened to others read aloud. Varying modalities not only enhances interest and motivation, but it also helps to moderate levels of difficulty by adjusting the cognitive demands of the task.

Conclusion

Repeated reading offers considerable benefits as a strategy for enhancing fluency and comprehension while fostering expertise. This approach seems to contribute to an increase in content and strategy knowledge as well as motivation. In addition, repeated reading procedures allow students to work at a level of difficulty where they can be successful. The unique features of this fluency strategy suggest a need for continued exploration of its use, particularly when it is integrated into instruction. Although considerable research supports repeated reading as an adjunct to instruction, there is limited controlled research on integrating repeated reading into literacy instruction. However, repeated reading is currently being used as an important part of whole language classrooms.

Certainly the conceptual base for integrating repeated reading into literacy instruction is sound. The need now is to look at it systematically. Research should investigate its effectiveness by varying purposes, materials, and modalities in both direct instruction and independent practice settings.

References

Allington, R. (1983). Fluency: The neglected goal. *The Reading Teacher, 36,* 556-561.

Baskwill, J., & Whitman, P. (1987). *Whole language sourcebook.* Richmond Hill, Canada: Scholastic-TAB Publications.

Bereiter, C., & Scarmadalia, C. (1986). Educational relevance of the study of expertise. *Interchange, 17,* 10-19.

Blum, I.H., & Koskinen, P.S. (1990). [Integrating writing and repeated reading.] Unpublished raw data.

Bromage, B.K., & Mayer, R.E. (1986). Quantitative and qualitative effects of repetition on learning from technical text. *Journal of Educational Psychology, 78,* 271-278.

Butler, A. (1988). Shared book experience. Crystal Lake, IL: Rigby.

Butler, A., & Turbill, J. (1985). *Towards a reading-writing classroom.* Portsmouth, NH: Heinemann.

Carbo, M. (1978). Teaching reading with talking books. *The Reading Teacher, 32,* 267-273.

Chomsky, C. (1976). After decoding: What? *Language Arts, 53,* 288-296.

Dahl, P.J. (1974). *An experimental program for teaching high speed word recognition and comprehension skills.* (Final Report of Project No. 3-1154). Washington, DC: National Institute of Education, Office of Research. (ERIC Document Reproduction Service No. ED 099 812).

Dowhower, S.L. (1987). Effects of repeated reading on second-grade transitional readers' fluency and comprehension. *Reading Research Quarterly, 22,* 389-406.

Elley, W.B. (1989). Vocabulary acquisition from listening to stories. *Reading Research Quarterly, 24,* 174-187.

Galdone, P. (1969). *The monkey and the crocodile.* New York: Houghton Mifflin/Clarion Books.

Herman, P.A. (1985). The effect of repeated readings on reading rate, speech pauses, and word recognition accuracy. *Reading Research Quarterly, 20,* 553-564.

Holdaway, R. (1979). Foundations of literacy. Portsmouth, NH: Heinemann.

Koskinen, P.S., & Blum, I.H. (1984). Repeated oral reading and the acquisition of fluency. In J. Niles & L. Harris (Eds.), *Changing perspectives on research in reading/language processing and instruction.* Thirty-third yearbook of the National Reading Conference (pp. 183-187). Rochester, NY: National Reading Conference.

LaBerge, D., & Samuels, S.J. (1974). Toward a theory of automatic information processing in reading. *Cognitive Psychology, 6,* 293-323.

Meichenbaum, D., & Biemiller, A. (1990, May). *In search of student expertise in the classroom: A metacognitive analysis.* Paper presented at the Conference on Cognitive Research for Instructional Innovation, University of Maryland, College Park, MD.

O'Shea, L.J., Sindelar, P.T., & O'Shea, D.J. (1985). The effects of repeated readings and attentional cues on reading fluency and comprehension. *Journal of Reading Behavior, 17,* 129-142.

Rey, H.A. (1969). *Curious George.* Boston: Houghton Mifflin.

Richards, L.E. (1972). Five little monkeys. In B. Martin & P. Brogan (Eds.), *Sounds around the clock* (pp. 108-109). New York: Holt, Rinehart & Winston.

Samuels, S.J. (1979). The method of repeated reading. *The Reading Teacher, 32,* 403-408.

Taylor, N.E., Wade, M.R., & Yekovich, F.R. (1985). The effects of text manipulation and multiple reading strategies on the reading performance of good and poor readers. *Reading Research Quarterly, 20,* 566-574.

Topping, K. (1987). Paired reading: A powerful technique for parent use. *The Reading Teacher, 40,* 608-614.

Trachtenberg, P., & Ferruggia, A. (1989). Big books from little voices: Reaching high risk beginning readers. *The Reading Teacher, 42,* 284-289.

Yaden, D. (1988). Understanding stories through repeated read-alouds: How many does it take? *The Reading Teacher, 41,* 556-560.

 From *Theory Into Practice, Vol. 30, No. 3, Summer 1991*

Developing Syntactic Sensitivity in Reading Through Phrase-cued Texts

Highlights the benefits of developing students' skills in grouping text into syntactically appropriate units as a way of addressing reading problems and increasing proficiency

By Timothy V. Rasinski

For Bryan, reading is a frustrating experience that he suffers through every day in his regular and remedial reading classes. A third grader, he's still receiving intensive instruction in word recognition even though he appears to have the basic abilities to decode or "sound out" words. Bryan's teachers share his frustration. They recognize that he can, as one teacher put it, "figure words out." Nevertheless, his reading seems laborious, with lack of expression, poor phrasing, and inadequate comprehension.

Bryan's special reading teacher decides to try something new. She copies a section of a story that he has been plodding through without much success and lightly pencils in slash marks within the sentences to highlight where phrase breaks occur. The teacher hypothesizes that perhaps Bryan's reading problem is not so much in word recognition as it is in putting words together in naturally occurring and meaningful phrases. The teacher recognizes that Bryan really has received little, if any, instruction in this area. Perhaps a little support or guidance in reading in phrases would help his reading.

Did it ever! Almost immediately, Bryan and his special teacher noted improvement in his reading. Although his rate did not improve at first, he began to move away from word-by-word reading to reading in meaningful chunks or phrases. His comprehension improved noticeably as well. Bryan's teacher is now working on ways to continue this assistance while helping him to transfer this more proficient reading to conventional, unmarked passages.

Difficulties in Reading

Children experiencing significant reading problems in the elementary grades often manifest difficulties in word recognition. Adeptness in word recognition is generally viewed as a necessary but insufficient condition for proficient reading (Harris & Sipay, 1990). Recent research suggests that good and poor readers can be distinguished by their context-free word recognition abilities (Perfetti, 1986; Stanovich, 1986).

Instructional efforts aimed at correcting student reading difficulties in the elementary grades are often characterized by a strong, and sometimes exclusive, emphasis on word recognition skills and strategies. Although many students benefit from corrective instruction in word recognition, a significant number of students fail to demonstrate improvements in overall reading and reading comprehension as a result of such efforts (Fleisher, Jenkins, & Pany, 1979). It may be that students who fail to demonstrate generalized improvements in reading from word recognition instruction are experiencing problems in other facets of reading, such as difficulties in vocabulary, motivation, attention, background information, and phrasing.

Syntactic Processing

According to current models of the reading process, readers segment incoming textual information into syntactically appropriate units or phrases (Gough, 1985; Just & Carpenter, 1987; LaBerge & Samuels, 1985; Rumelhart, 1985). These models imply that proficient reading is characterized not only by fast and accurate word recognition, but also by readers' word chunking or phrasing behavior while reading connected discourse. Thus, it is possible that readers whose general reading performance fails to improve significantly after being given word recognition instruction may have poorly developed skills in parsing text into syntactically appropriate units for semantic processing, which limits their ability to read fluently and comprehend text (Schreiber, 1980, 1991).

Schreiber (1980) argued that in oral speech, listeners use the prosodic cues embedded in utterances to segment the utterances into syntactically appropriate and meaningful units. Children appear to rely more heavily than adults on prosodic features for parsing (Schreiber & Read, 1980). In written discourse, however, prosodic cues are largely absent. Readers must rely on the morphologic and syntactic cues in texts rather than prosodic cues in order to phrase and make sense out of the text. Schreiber argued that another primary source of difficulty in reading for many less proficient readers, then, is a less well-developed ability to phrase written text into syntactically appropriate units. Poor readers may encounter more difficulty in switching from prosodic to other cues in order to parse written texts into appropriate phrases.

Oral reading behavior of children who are less able to phrase text is often characterized as slow, choppy, or word-by-word, and as read in a monotone or expressionless voice. Because they have difficulty phrasing text, these readers tend not to mark phrase boundaries with pauses or with the prosodic features that normally accompany syntactic units.

Kleiman, Winograd, and Humphrey (1979) had fourth-grade above- and below-average readers parse sentences into meaningful phrases under two conditions: with prosodic cues (fluent oral reading heard with a written version of the text) and without prosody (written version only). Although the good readers performed equally well under both conditions, the poor readers were significantly less able to identify phrase boundaries in the no-prosody condition. This supports Schreiber's assertion that the nature of poor readers' difficulty may be attributed in part to difficulty in parsing the text into appropriate syntactic units.

Rasinski (1989) found that difficulties in syntactic sensitivity may even extend to adult readers. College students who were identified as having difficulty in reading were less able to identify phrase boundaries in written texts than college students whose reading abilities fell within more normal ranges.

If an ability to phrase written texts into syntactically appropriate units is necessary for fluent and proficient

reading, and if good and poor readers exhibit different levels of ability to phrase text appropriately, then corrective instruction to help students learn to phrase text may be needed. One approach to help students develop sensitivity to syntactic units in texts and proficiency in using those units to aid overall reading is the use of phrase-cued texts.

". . . perhaps Bryan's reading problem is not so much in word recognition as it is in putting words together in naturally occurring and meaningful phrases."

Phrase-cued Texts

A phrase-cued text is a written passage in which intrasentential phrase boundaries are explicitly marked or cued for the reader. This cueing is normally done by placing a vertical line or diagonal slash at the appropriate phrase breaks, adding additional blank spaces between phrases, or writing the text so that only one phrase appears on a line of print. Proficient readers can determine phrase boundaries through reliance on grammatical rules related to sentence structure or through instinctive identification. Although most proficient readers cannot specify the appropriate linguistic rule for segmenting text, they display a strong ability for identifying conventional phrase breaks based upon their own developed sense of good, fluent reading (Rasinski, 1989).

A considerable amount of research conducted over an extended period of time has investigated the effect of phrase-cued texts on reading performance (Rasinski, 1990). Although this corpus of research has demonstrated the effectiveness of phrase-cued efforts in improving reading performance, reading scholars and curriculum developers have largely ignored the potential of phrase-cued texts as an instructional method for reading pedagogy or as an intervention technique for re-

medial and corrective instruction in reading.

In his review of research related to phrase-cued texts, Rasinski (1990) found that over 75% of the 20 studies reviewed reported positive effects for the use of phrase-cued texts. For example, Mason and Kendall (1979) found that the comprehension performance of fourth-grade students improved when they read texts in which phrases were explicitly cued. Weiss (1983) reported similar results for students at all reading ability levels in Grades 4 through 7. Gerell and Mason (1983) had fifth graders read conventional and phrase-cued versions of texts. Significant improvements in comprehension were found when students read the phrase-cued texts. O'Shea and Sindelar (1983) had first- through third-grade students read conventional and phrase-cued texts. The phrase-cued texts resulted in higher levels of comprehension for students at all grade and ability levels. Moreover, O'Shea and Sindelar found that the facilitative effect was particularly strong for students identified as having good word recognition skills but who were less proficient in reading rate. Finally, Stevens (1981) reported that the performance of 10th-grade students was facilitated by having them read phrase-cued versions of standardized reading comprehension tests. Low-and middle-ability readers found the phrased texts particularly helpful in improving comprehension.

The studies reported here, as well as others reviewed by Rasinski (1990), suggest that the phrase-cued texts may facilitate reading performance, especially for students experiencing some difficulty in reading. Thus, remedial and corrective reading teachers, as well as teachers of students with learning disabilities, may be able to use phrase-cued texts to improve students' phrasing, fluency, and comprehension in reading. The remainder of this article will explore how teachers can use phrase-cued texts to help less able readers.

Phrased-cued Text Lesson

The first issue in using phrase-cued texts is developing such texts. Because there are very few commercially produced texts that contain phrase markings, teachers will have to create phrase-cued texts on their own. Perhaps the easiest way to create a phrase-

Implementing Phrase-cued Text Lessons

1. Find a short passage (100 to 250 words) written at the student's instructional or independent reading level.

2. Run a copy of the passage.

3. With a pencil, lightly mark phrase breaks (naturally occurring pause points) within sentences with a slash mark (/). You may wish to mark sentence boundaries and other major boundaries within sentences with double slashes (//). Ask a colleague to check your work to make sure you didn't leave out any important phrase breaks.

4. Explain the passage format to the student. Emphasize the importance of reading in phrases in order to comprehend efficiently.

5. The teacher should model reading the phrased text as the student follows along silently.

6. Ask the student to read the text two or three times. Observe for any differences in reading. Ask how he or she liked reading the formatted passage. (Many students at first feel that the phrased text is difficult to read. With practice, however, most students become comfortable with it.) Discuss the student's reading and the content of the passage.

7. Finally, return to the original version of the passage and ask the student to read the same passage without the phrase marks. Observe the student's reading and ask the student if he or she was better able to read the passage.

The lesson takes about 10 minutes to accomplish. Try to do it three or four times a week with students having difficulty in reading in phrases and in comprehension.

---

cued text is to lightly mark the phrase boundaries of conventional texts with penciled vertical lines or slash marks. Teachers should use their intuitive sense of phrasing to identify appropriate phrase breaks. The penciled cues can later be erased as readers become more adept in their phrase reading. An example of such a text is shown below.

> In the winter I like to ski in Stowe. Although it may be cold, I like the idea of speeding down a mountain at top speed. Winter truly is my favorite time of the year.

With the advent of computer word processing programs, teachers can also re-type texts with embedded slashes or with exaggerated spaces between phrases.

> In the winter/ I like/to ski/ in Stowe.// Although it may be cold/ I like the idea/ of speeding down a mountain/ at top speed.// Winter truly is/ my favorite time/ of the year.//

Phrase-cued passages are meant to be practiced orally. Thus, relatively brief passages of 100 to 250 words seem most appropriate. Narrative prose selections, poems, and speeches would be good choices for phrase-cued texts. The passages should be well within students' instructional or independent reading levels.

When presenting phrase-cued texts to students, the teacher should explain the nature of the text and the purpose of the activity. The teacher can explain that good readers read in phrases or chunks of text. Moreover, when good readers read, they embed intonation and expression in their oral reading that corresponds to the phrases. The phrase cues are placed into the text to aid the reader in identifying phrase boundaries. Students should attempt to read so that the phrases or text chunks are read as units. The teacher should also explain that although students may find the phrase cues distracting at first, they will find them helpful with continued oral reading practice.

Modeling is a useful teaching strategy in reading. Once students have been provided copies of the phrased text to be read, the teacher should read the text aloud in an expressive voice while students follow along in their text. After a couple of readings, the teacher can explore with the class how his or her reading matched the phrase cues. Students can be invited to comment on the teacher's use of expression and pause in the reading.

After the teacher models reading the text, students should be invited to practice reading the text chorally, in pairs, or individually. Ask students to practice reading the text several times. This can be followed by opportunities for individuals or groups of students to perform reading the text to the class or to other audiences such as to another class, the principal, or other teachers or adults. Students should receive positive feedback for their oral reading.

Teachers can also ask parents to practice the passages with their children. Such activities should require minimal amounts of time and should be well within the ability of parents to implement effectively. Teachers should stress to parents the importance of positive reading experiences for their children.

The ultimate goal of the phrase-cued text is to help students develop sensitivity and proficiency in reading conventional texts. Thus, following the practice with the phrase-cued texts, students should be given conventional versions of the same passages. This can occur immediately after the phrase-cued text lesson or on a following day. As with the previous lesson, modeling, discussion, practice, and performance should be important parts. Teachers may wish to come back to previously encountered texts throughout the school year.

There are many variations and elaborations possible with the phrase-cued text strategy. For example, a transparent overlay could be placed over a text and appropriate phrase breaks could be marked on the overlay. After the student has practiced the text with the phrase markings, the overlay could be lifted to reveal a conventional text. In providing group instruction, the teacher may use a copy of a text on an overhead transparency with an overlay transparency marking the phrase markings. Again, once the overlay is removed, students will see the conventionally formatted text. This procedure may help students see more closely the connection between conventional and phrased texts. Tape recorders could be used to provide students with model readings of a passage. Students could also develop greater self-awareness by audio-recording and analyzing their own reading of a passage. They could be given a conventionally formatted passage and asked, individually or in groups, to mark appropriate phrase breaks. Students could work in groups to analyze and read their phrase-cued texts.

The phrase-cued text lesson should take no more than 10 to 15 minutes. Teachers can use it as a warm-up for other reading activities.

Developing sensitivity to phrases in students' reading may not occur quickly. The phrase-cued text lesson will have the greatest impact when used on a daily or alternate day schedule. Teachers should closely monitor students' oral reading to detect growth. Teachers should attend to phrasing, use of pause at appropriate points in the text, expression while reading, reading rate, and general ease and enjoyment while reading in order to determine if students are improving in their reading.

Allington (1983) has called fluency the "neglected goal" of reading instruction. Many teachers fail to recognize the importance of fluency to overall reading proficiency and fail to foster it through instruction. A recent study of elementary students referred for remedial instruction in reading found that an overwhelming majority manifested significant difficulties in fluency (Rasinski, Padak, & Dallinga, 1991). Moreover, fluency problems were more apparent than difficulties in word recognition or comprehension, two typical foci of compensatory and remedial reading instruction.

The ability to read in syntactically appropriate phrases is an important aspect of fluency. Poor readers' lack of ability to phrase text while reading may significantly contribute to their overall reading difficulties (Schreiber, 1980). The use of text in which phrase boundaries are explicitly cued for readers is no panacea for reading problems. However, it provides remedial teachers with a viable, proven, and easily implemented approach for helping students in an area of reading that has encountered a substantial amount of instructional neglect and indifference. Teachers in classrooms and clinics who work with children exhibiting disfluent, choppy reading should explore the systematic use of phrase-cued texts with

their students. The potential exists for it to be a key element of instruction for many readers. ▰

Timothy V. Rasinski, PhD, is currently an associate professor at Kent State University and is interested in effective instruction for children experiencing difficulties in learning to read. He is also a co-editor of *The Reading Teacher*. Address: Timothy Rasinski, Department of Teacher Development and Curriculum Studies, 404 White Hall, Kent State University, Kent, OH 44242.

References

Allington, R. L. (1983). Fluency: The neglected reading goal. *The Reading Teacher, 36,* 556–561.

Fleisher, L. S., Jenkins, J. R., & Pany, D. (1979). Effects on poor readers' comprehension of training in rapid decoding. *Reading Research Quarterly, 15,* 30–48.

Gerell, H. R., & Mason, G. E. (1983). Computer-chunked and traditional text. *Reading World, 22,* 241–246.

Gough, P. B. (1985). One second of reading. In H. Singer & R. B. Ruddell (Eds.), *Theoretical models and processes of reading* (3rd ed., pp. 661–686). Newark, DE: International Reading Association.

Harris, A. J., & Sipay, E. R. (1990). *How to increase reading ability* (9th ed.). New York: Longman.

Just, M. A., & Carpenter, P. A. (1987). *The psychology of reading and language comprehension.* Boston: Allyn & Bacon.

Kleiman, G. M., Winograd, P. N., & Humphrey, M. H. (1979). *Prosody and children's parsing of sentences* (Tech. Rep. No. 123). Urbana: University of Illinois, Center for the Study of Reading.

LaBerge, D., & Samuels, S. J. (1985). Toward a theory of automatic information processing in reading. In H. Singer & R. B. Ruddell (Eds.), *Theoretical models and processes of reading* (3rd ed., pp. 689–718). Newark, DE: International Reading Association.

Mason, J. M., & Kendall, J. R. (1979). Facilitating reading comprehension through text structure manipulation. *The Alberta Journal of Educational Research, 25,* 68–76.

O'Shea, L. J., & Sindelar, P. T. (1983). The effects of segmenting discourse on the reading comprehension of low- and high-performance readers. *Reading Research Quarterly, 18,* 458–465.

Perfetti, C. A. (1986). Continuities in reading acquisition, reading skill, and reading disability. *Remedial and Special Education, 7*(1), 11–21.

Rasinski, T. V. (1989). Adult readers' sensitivity to phrase boundaries in texts. *Journal of Experimental Education, 58,* 29–40.

Rasinski, T. V. (1990). *The effects of cued phrase boundaries in texts.* Bloomington, IN: ERIC Clearinghouse on Reading and Communication Skills. (ED 313–689)

Rasinski, T. V., Padak, N. D., & Dallinga, G. (1991). *Incidences of difficulty in reading fluency.* Paper presented at the annual meeting of the College Reading Association, Crystal City, VA.

Rumelhart, D. E. (1985). Toward an interactive model of reading. In H. Singer & R. Ruddell (Eds.), *Theoretical models and processes of reading* (3rd ed., pp. 722–750). Newark, DE: International Reading Association.

Schreiber, P. A. (1980). On the acquisition of reading fluency. *Journal of Reading Behavior, 12,* 177–186.

Schreiber, P. A. (1991). Understanding prosody's role in reading acquisition. *Theory into Practice, 30,* 158–164.

Schreiber, P. A., & Read, C. (1980). Children's use of phonetic cues in spelling, parsing, and—maybe—reading. *Bulletin of the Orton Society, 30,* 209–224.

Stanovich, K. E. (1986). Matthew effects in reading: Some consequences of individual differences in the acquisition of literacy. *Reading Research Quarterly, 21,* 360–407.

Stevens, K. C. (1981). Chunking material as an aid to reading comprehension. *Journal of Reading, 25,* 126–129.

Weiss, D. S. (1983). The effects of text segmentation on children's reading comprehension. *Discourse Processes, 6,* 77–89.

From *Intervention in School and Clinic, Vol. 29, No. 3, January 1994*

Kathryn Button
Margaret J. Johnson
Paige Furgerson

Interactive writing in a primary classroom

Interactive writing provides a means for teachers to engage in effective literacy instruction, not through isolated skills lessons, but within the framework of constructing texts filled with personal and collective meaning.

"We're going to finish up our list for our story map," Paige Furgerson explains to her kindergarten students. "Let's read what we have so far."

As Ali points to the words written on the paper attached to the easel, her classmates read along with her: "Trees, 3 bowls, 3 spoons, 3 chairs, house, 3 beds, 3 bears."

"I know that there are some other things that we need. Can you think about the story of 'Goldilocks and the Three Bears'? What else do we need to write on our list?" Miss Furgerson asks.

Brody suggests, "A window."

Joey requests, "Three bathrooms. One for each bear."

Katelin volunteers, "Goldilocks."

"Oh, you know what?" Furgerson says. "I think we really do need her. Did you hear what Katelin said, that we needed Goldilocks?"

"Goldilocks," the children repeat in unison.

"Goldilocks," Furgerson replies. "We need a Goldilocks. We're almost out of room right here." Furgerson points to the bottom of the list of items needed for the class story map. "So where should we write *Goldilocks*?" After the children decide that a new column needs to be started, they help Furgerson hear the sounds in the word *Goldilocks* and proceed to write the word.

"Let's say the word together, slowly," Furgerson reminds the children.

"Goldilocks. *O*, I hear an *o*," Adam states.

"I hear a *d*," Quang suggests.

"A *g*, a *g*," repeats Katelin.

After observing her children and listening to them encode *Goldilocks*, Furgerson explains. "There is an *o* and a *d* and a *g*. The *g* is at the beginning, Katelin. You come up and write the *g*, and then we'll let Adam write the *o* that he heard. Do you know what? This is a person's name, *Goldilocks*. Do you know what kind of a *g* we have to use?

Rosa replies, "A capital."

"A capital *g* because it's somebody's name." Furgerson then leads the class forward in their task. "That's a good capital *g*. Now, Adam, you come up and write the *o*. Class, let's say the word again to see if we hear any other sounds. Help me."

This scene took place in a kindergarten classroom at Ramirez Elementary School in Lubbock, Texas, USA. Of the 17 students in the class, 2 were Asian, 8 Hispanic, 6 non-Hispanic White, and one African American. Fifteen of the children received free or reduced-price lunch, and 6 had attended a prekindergarten program. The teacher, Paige Furgerson, and the children spent their days engaged in a variety of literacy activities, including interactive writing lessons like the one described above.

Roots of interactive writing

Interactive writing has its roots in the language experience approach developed by Ashton-Warner (1963) in which children dictated a text and the teacher acted as scribe. The text was then used as reading material for the youngsters. McKenzie (1985), working with British teachers, developed a process she called "shared writing" in which the teacher and children collaborated on a text to be written. The focus of the writing could come from a children's literature selection, an event experienced by the children in the class, or a topic under study in social studies or science. In McKenzie's model, the teacher served as scribe and usually used chart paper to create a text that then served as the students' reading text. As the charts accumulated, they were displayed around the room, surrounding the children with meaningful print.

Interactive writing, a form of shared writing, is part of the early literacy lesson framework (see Figure 1) developed by educators at The Ohio State University (Pinnell & McCarrier, 1994) to provide rich, educative experiences for young children, particularly those considered to be educationally at risk. The framework draws on the concept of emergent literacy, a term coined by Clay (1966), and is explicated by other early childhood educators (see Strickland & Morrow, 1989; Teale & Sulzby, 1986).

In the early literacy framework, the use of quality literature (Huck & Kerstetter, 1987) scaffolds the development and integration of all literacy processes (reading, writing, speaking, listening, thinking). Three to five trade books, which represent various genres, are read aloud to children each day. Prior to the construction of the students' list for their story map of "Goldilocks and the Three Bears," Miss Furgerson had read aloud Galdone's (1972) version several times. The repeated readings helped students reconstruct the story line and recall characters and story sequence, the information necessary to generate their lists and construct the actual map. Often the focus of the daily interactive writing lesson was an extension of a book read aloud to the class.

Clay (1991) explained that children are active constructors of their own language and literacy. Their competence grows as they gain inner control over constructing meaning from print. This growth does not take place without environmental support. Rather, with supportive instruction, children develop in language and literacy competence (Vygotsky, 1962). The early literacy framework is a balanced program of instruction and independent exploration. Interactive writing provides opportunities for teachers to engage in instruction precisely at the point of student need.

Interactive writing provides opportunities for teachers to engage in instruction precisely at the point of student need.

Interactive writing differs from shared writing in two important ways. First, children take an active role in the writing process by actually holding the pen and doing the writing. Second, the teacher's role changes as she scaffolds and explicates the children's emerging knowledge about print (Button, 1992). Through questioning and direct instruction, the teacher focuses the children's attention on the conventions of print such as spaces between words, left-to-right and top-to-bottom directionality, capital letters, and punctuation. Clay (1979) reminds teachers to utilize the child's strengths and not to do for the child "anything that she can teach him to do for himself" (p. 4).

Interactive writing in practice

To guide the interactive writing process and make children's knowledge about print explicit, the teacher might ask questions such as these:

"How many words are there in our sentence?"

"Where do we begin writing?"

Figure 1
The Ohio State University Early Literacy Learning Initiative
A framework for early literacy lessons

Element	Values
1. Reading aloud to children (rereading favorite selections)	Motivates children to read (shows purpose). Provides an adult demonstration. Develops sense of story. Develops knowledge of written language syntax and of how texts are structured. Increases vocabulary and linguistic repertoire. Supports intertextual ties through enjoyment and shared knowledge; creates community of readers.
2. Shared reading Rereading big books Rereading retellings Rereading alternative texts Rereading the products of interactive writing	Demonstrates early strategies. Builds sense of story and ability to predict. Demonstrates process of reading. Provides social support from the group. Provides opportunity to participate, behave like a reader.
3. Guided reading	Provides opportunity to problem solve while reading for meaning. Provides opportunity to use strategies on extended text. Challenges the reader and creates context for successful processing on novel texts. Provides opportunity for teacher guidance, demonstration, and explanation.
4. Independent reading	Children read on their own or with partners from a wide range of materials.
5. Shared writing	Children compose messages and stories; teacher supports process as scribe. Demonstrates how writing works.
6. Interactive writing	Demonstrates concepts of print, early strategies, and how words work. Provides opportunities to hear sounds in words and connect with letters. Helps children understand "building up" and "breaking down" processes in reading and writing. Provides opportunities to plan and construct texts.
7. Guided writing and writers' workshop Teacher guides the process and provides instruction	Demonstrates the process of writing. Provides opportunity for explicit teaching of various aspects of writing. Gives students the guidance they need to learn writing processes and produce high-quality products.
8. Independent writing Individual retellings Labeling "Speech balloons" Books and other pieces	Provides opportunity for independence. Provides chance to write for different purposes. Increases writers' ability to use different forms. Builds ability to write words and use punctuation. Fosters creativity and the ability to compose.
9. Letters, words, and how they work	Helps children learn to use visual aspects of print.

Extensions and themes: Drama, murals, story maps, innovations on text, surveys, science experiments, and others.
• Provides opportunities to interpret texts in different ways.
• Provides a way of revisiting a story.
• Fosters collaboration and enjoyment.
• Creates a community of readers.
• Provides efficient instruction through integration of content areas.

(continued)

"After writing one word, what do we have to remember to do? Why?"

"What word are we writing next?"

"Say the word slowly. What sounds do you hear?"

"Can you write the letter that stands for that sound?"

"Can you find the letter on our alphabet chart that we need to write?"

"What comes at the end of the sentence?"

"Would that make sense?"

"Does that look right?"

"Would you point and read what we have written so far?"

These questions and the instruction they represent vary according to the knowledge and needs of the children (see Figure 2). For children beginning the process, the teacher may need to attend more to letter formation. At times the teacher may show a child a model or assist the child with the formation of the needed letter. As children gain competence, attention may shift to punctuation, capitalization, prefixes, suffixes, and phonetic structures such as digraphs, consonant blends, and vowel patterns.

An interactive writing lesson need not be lengthy. On the first day of kindergarten, Furgerson and her students engaged in interactive writing for 15 minutes. As the year progressed, lessons lasted from 20 to 30 minutes. The power of the lesson lies not in the length of the text constructed but in the quality of the interaction. Typically the children are seated on a carpet facing an easel holding unlined chart paper, a marking pen, correction tape, and a pointer. The teacher usually sits within easy reach of the easel, facing the children. Teachers have found interactive writing to be successful with classes that range in size from 15 to 32 children.

The environment the teacher creates during this process should support risk taking. Children are encouraged to take an active role in negotiating the text. The teacher assumes that the children are in the process of learning about print and that some of their responses will be approximations. The teacher explains to the children that because they and other people will be reading the story, it is important that the words be conventionally constructed. The teacher uses correction tape to mask preconventional attempts (the child's approximations) and helps the child to write the word, letter, or punctuation mark conventionally. Teacher sensitivity is needed to value the knowledge reflected in the attempt yet also to teach the standard conventions of print used in books such as the ones the children read.

For example, during the construction of a class big book about the incubation of eggs, a classroom experience that occurred late in the school year, the children decided to write the sentence: "When the chicks get bigger, we will send the chicks to the farm." After everyone repeated the sentence aloud, Furgerson asked the class what word needed to be written first. They agreed that the first word should be *when*. Rosa stepped up to the easel and wrote *wen*. Furgerson said, "It does sound like *w-e-n*, but we need an *h* before the *e*." She then cov-

Figure 2
Interactive writing expectations and guidelines in primary classrooms over a school year

Beginning of the year ————————————➤ Later in the year ———————————➤

Establish routine
Negotiate simple text (a label)
Construction of text may be completed in one day (news)
Repeat orally word or line to be written

The teacher will
Model hearing sounds in words
Model sound/symbol relationships
Support letter recognition (using alphabet chart or chart listing class members' names)
Model and question for Concepts About Print (CAP): spacing, left-to-right directionality, top-to-bottom directionality, word-by-word matching during shared reading
Link words to be written with names of children in the class

The teacher may
Write more of the text
Write challenging parts of word/text
Assist with letter formation

Routine established
Negotiate a more complex text
Construction of text continues over several days
Count the words to be written before starting to write

Students will
Hear dominant sounds in words
Represent sounds with symbols (letters)
Write letters without copy
Have control of core words
Begin linking known words to unknown words
Leave spaces between words
Use familiar chunks (-ed; -ing)
Control word-by-word matching during shared reading
Punctuate sentences on the run
Write text with little support
Make generalizations about print

ered the letters *en* with a piece of correction tape and asked Rosa to write an *h* and then the *en* that she initially had written. During the writing of the word *the* Simon wrote *teh*. For some of the children *the* was a known word, but Simon could not yet spell it conventionally. Xuchen responded, "You have the right letters but in *the* the *h* comes before the *e*." One of the children tore off a piece of correction tape and handed it to Simon to place over the letters *eh*. He then wrote *he*. Jane asked Furgerson, "What did it say?" After the teacher pronounced *teh*, Jane commented that it didn't make sense. The children agreed that *the* looked right and that *teh* neither made sense nor looked like a word they knew. This information confirmed for Furgerson that some of her students knew that what they wrote needed to make sense (semantics).

Texts for interactive writing represent many forms of writing. Children might want to create a list of characters from a story as part of the process of forming a story map. Survey questions might be used as a basis for interactive writing. For example, after reading the books written by their visiting author, Rafe

Martin, the children created a survey chart to display their favorite book title. Children might retell a story they have read or write an alternative text. After students read *The Farm Concert* (Cowley, 1990), they wrote their own variant entitled "The Classroom Concert." Children might compose an invitation to a class party or write a letter to pen pals in another city. Recipes, a review of a trip, class news, and many other forms of communication can also serve as topics for interactive writing.

What interactive writing looks like in one classroom

At the beginning of the school year, Furgerson used informal assessments, including Clay's Observation Survey (Clay, 1993a), to determine the strengths and knowledge of her students. She found about half her children could write their names. Only two of the children could name all the letters of the alphabet. All of the children could identify the front of a book, distinguish between illustrations and print, and indicate where they would begin to read. They all knew print carried a message.

On the first day of kindergarten, Furgerson began with an interactive writing experience based on the focus book of their first thematic unit. After reading Galdone's (1975) *The Gingerbread Boy*, the class took a walking tour of the school to find gingerbread boys hidden in certain spots throughout the building. When they returned to the classroom, they created a list of the spots where the gingerbread boys were found. After explaining the purpose of the writing, Furgerson asked the students what word they wanted to write first on their list.

They decided to begin with the word *lab*. She asked the children where they should start writing. One child stepped forward to point to the upper left-hand corner of the chart paper. Furgerson asked the students to say the word aloud—*lab*—listening for the sounds they heard. Some of the students heard a *b* and some an *l*. At this initial point in the process, Furgerson took the responsibility of seriating the sounds. "Yes," she told the children, "we do hear a *b* and an *l*. When we write the word *lab*, the *l* comes first."

Furgerson knew Larry could write his name. "Larry," she said, "you come and write the *l*. You have an *l* in your name." After Larry wrote the letter *l*, the children said the word again, listening for additional sounds. Brody heard the sound represented by the letter *b*. While Brody came up to write the *b*, Furgerson explained to the class that Brody's name began with a *b*. Before he wrote the *b*, however, she explained that the letter *a* came before the *b* although it was hard to hear. Brody wrote the *a* and then the *b*.

Furgerson then called another child to come up to the chart and, using the pointer, point under the word they had just written for the class to read. She then asked where else they found gingerbread boys. They followed a similar process with other items on their list. Furgerson chose to write three words at this sitting and to add to the list on subsequent days. Interactive writing was a daily event in her classroom.

Furgerson built on the knowledge students had about the sounds represented by letters in their names. She used everything the children appeared to know at the time of the lesson and then, through demonstration and explanation, extended their knowledge by providing the letters representing unfamiliar sounds. Clay

(1993b) states, "At the beginning of the school year what the child can write is a good indicator of what the child knows in detail about written language" (p. 11). As the children finished writing a word, a list, or a sentence, they read it. One child pointed under each word to help the others to track the print while reading. This process demonstrates in a powerful and immediate way the reciprocal nature of reading and writing.

Later in the year, the children were thoroughly familiar with the routine of interactive writing and much more sophisticated in their knowledge about the conventions of print. They were able to analyze the phonological features of the message to be written (hear sounds in words), sequence the sounds heard, represent the sounds they heard with letters, and discern many different patterns. The children were also aware that their purpose for writing dictated the type of writing they would undertake. When the class decided to reply to their Ohio pen pals, they knew their letter would begin with the line, "Dear Miss Patacca's Class," and what followed would be written from left to right across the page.

On the first day of kindergarten, Furgerson began with an interactive writing experience based on the focus book of their first thematic unit.

In the spring the children decided to retell the story of Michael Rosen's (1989) *We're Going on a Bear Hunt*. They had spent several days listening to repeated readings of the book. Using interactive writing, they had made lists of the characters and the different settings from the story, which then served as references for an elaborate story map. To accompany the map, the children spent several days writing a retelling of the story.

Furgerson and the children negotiated the first line of the retelling. Borrowing in part from the text of the story, they decided to write: "The children walked through the forest, stumble trip, stumble trip." They repeated the sentence several times to fix the message clearly in their minds and to give them something against which to monitor their writing. Furgerson then asked the children to count the words as they said the sentence. She asked them what word they would write first. At this point in the school year, *the* was a known word for all the children in the room. Miss Furgerson asked the children what they needed to remember. Most knew that they start writing in the upper left-hand corner of the page, begin the first word of the sentence with a capital letter, and leave a "hand space" between the words.

Although the focus of Furgerson's curriculum was not to teach her children to read, but to immerse them in meaningful print rich activities, most of them were reading by spring of their kindergarten year.

After writing and reading *the*, the children told Furgerson that the next word they needed to work on was *children*. This was not a known word for most of them. Following a routine well established at this point, the students said the word together slowly, yet naturally, thinking about the order of the sounds in the spoken word. One child commented that the word had two parts—*chil* and *dren*. Furgerson turned the child's observation into a teaching moment, explaining that, indeed, *children* had two syllables and showing the class how to clap as they said the word, one clap for each syllable. Capitalizing further on the observation, she told the students they would be listening for the sounds in the first syllable. They heard the first sound easily and all knew the digraph *ch*. Furgerson asked Chaz to come up to the easel and write the first two letters while the class said the first syllable again, listening for additional sounds.

Rosa said she heard an *i* like in *him*. At this point, most of the children were beginning to connect known words and new words. Rosa came up, took the marker from Chaz, and wrote the *i*. As Rosa repeated the word aloud while writing, she said she also could hear an *l*. Furgerson said, "You are right. You may write the *l*." She then asked the children to say the word again, listening for the sounds in the last syllable. Quang said he heard a *tr*. Furgerson said, "Yes. It does sound like a *tr*, but in this word it is a *dr*. TR and *dr* do sound almost alike." Quang came up to the easel and wrote the *dr*. After saying the word one more time, Joshua said he heard an *n*. Furgerson said, "Yes, you are right, there is an *n*. But before the *n*, there is an *e* which is harder to hear. Would you like to come up and write *en* for us?"

Throughout the school year the children also had 20 to 30 minutes every day to write independently either in their journals or at the writing center. This gave students time to use the knowledge gained from interactive writing instruction and time to take further risks as writers. They made independent choices about what to write about and how to organize their texts. They were encouraged to use invented spelling, copy from environmental print, and make use of their growing core of known words. Furgerson's observations of what the students wrote and how they wrote independently informed her teaching for future interactive writing sessions.

Literacy assessment

Assessment in the early literacy framework is ongoing as the teacher documents the children's growth over time. Furgerson used a checklist she developed to monitor the growth children exhibited through their journal writing. Although the children varied in their control of the conventions of print, they all thought of themselves as readers and writers. Although the focus of Furgerson's curriculum was not to teach her children to read but to immerse them in meaningful print-rich activities, most of them were reading by spring of their kindergarten year.

To document the growth her students made during the year and to provide information for next year's first-grade teacher, Furgerson and a class of trained undergraduate language/literacy students administered the Observation Survey (Clay, 1993a) in May to all of the children. She analyzed the children's scores on each of the six tasks assessed and then compared the May scores with the September scores.

The children exhibited growth in all areas measured by the Observation Survey. In the spring of the year, 13 of 17 children were able to read with 90% or better accuracy books like *The Chick and the Duckling* (Ginsburg, 1972) and *Mary Wore Her Red Dress and Henry Wore His Green Sneakers* (Peek, 1985). These books have illustrations that provide moderate support for the reader and stories that tell about familiar objects. The stories contain varied, often repetitive, simple sentence patterns that include action such as, "'I am taking a walk,' said the Duckling." (See Peterson, 1991, for characteristics of texts to support beginning readers.)

The children improved the most in their ability to hear sounds in words as measured by the Dictation Task. In this task, children are asked to record a dictated sentence containing a possible 37 phonemes. Each child's attempt is scored by counting the number of letters (graphemes) written by the child that represent the sounds (phonemes) analyzed by the child. In the fall the children had a mean dictation score of 9.8 (maximum score = 37). The children represented primarily initial consonants. In the spring, the children's mean dictation score was 29 (almost three times higher than in the fall). The children's ability to hear sounds in words, practiced daily during interactive writing, enabled them to represent initial and final sounds heard in each word. In addition, they could accurately spell high-frequency words like *the*, *is*, and *it*. This growth in the Dictation Task is particularly significant given the importance of phonemic awareness as a predictor of success in learning to read (see Adams, 1990).

On the Writing Vocabulary Task of the Observation Survey children were asked to write as many words as they could in a 10-minute period. In the fall, the children's scores ranged from 0 to 20 with a mean score of 4.8. Many children were able to write their first name and names of family members like *mom* and *dad*. In the spring, the Writing Vocabulary scores ranged from 1 to 56 words written in a 10-minute period with a mean score of 23.9. In addition to writing names of family members and friends, the children wrote high-frequency words like *on*, *the*, *in*, *go*, and *to* and favorite words like *pizza* and *dog*.

Meeting individual students' needs

Furgerson used information from the Observation Survey, anecdotal notes, and writing checklists to help her meet the needs of each of her students. Valerie's fall Observation Survey summary indicated that she could recognize 14 of 54 letters, no high-frequency words, and 7 out of 24 concepts about print; could represent no phonemes on the Dictation Task; and could write no words during the Writing Vocabulary Task. During the interactive writing lesson, Furgerson built on Valerie's strengths, asking her to write the *l* and *a* when they were needed in words the class was writing, as these were 2 of the 14 letters Valerie knew. Valerie delighted everyone one day when she announced that the particular sentence the class was writing needed a question mark at the end. She quickly became in charge of question marks. As the year progressed, Furgerson also worked individually with Valerie at the teacher table during center time and guided her during journal writing. At the end of kindergarten Valerie recognized 46 of the 54 letters, no high-frequency words, and 14 of the 24 concepts about print; she could represent 3 phonemes on the Dictation Task, and on the Writing Vocabulary Task she could write her name. Furgerson stated that Valerie's spring scores exhibited growth even though the growth was atypical for children her age. Valerie also showed marked growth in other areas such as art and oral language. Even with the most supportive literacy framework, some children require more intensive instruction. Valerie would be a prime candidate for Reading Recovery (see Pinnell, Fried, & Estice, 1990).

Concluding remarks

Interactive writing provides an authentic means for instruction in phonics and other linguistic patterns within the context of meaningful text. Children learn the conventions of spelling, syntax, and semantics as they engage in the construction of letters, lists, and stories. Interactive writing is a tool that puts reading and learning about conventions into a dynamic relationship. As children attend to meaningful text, they develop their knowledge of the conventions embedded in that text. As they gain more knowledge of conventions, they are able to construct and interpret more sophisticated messages.

Interactive writing is an important part of the early literacy lesson framework (see Figure 1) because it provides so many opportunities to teach directly about language conventions, sense of story, types of writing, and concepts about print. These teaching moments do not follow a specified sequence but evolve from the teacher's understanding of the students' needs. The early literacy lesson framework blends independent problem solving, shared literacy experiences, and teacher instruction within a literacy-rich classroom.

Too often teachers feel they must choose between using holistic literacy experiences and teaching basic skills. In interactive writing sessions, teachers do both at the same time. Interactive writing provides a means for teachers to engage in effective literacy instruction, not through isolated skills lessons, but within the framework of constructing texts filled with personal and collective meaning.

Button teaches early literacy courses and Johnson teaches language and literacy courses at Texas Tech University. Furgerson teaches kindergarten in the Lubbock Independent School District. Button may be contacted at Texas Tech University, Box 41071, Lubbock, TX 79409-1071, USA.

References

Adams, M.J. (1990). *Beginning to read: Thinking and learning about print.* Cambridge, MA: MIT Press.

Ashton-Warner, S. (1963). *Teacher.* New York: Simon & Schuster.

Button, K.A. (1992). *A longitudinal case study examination of the theoretical and practical changes made by three urban kindergarten teachers during participation in early literacy training.* Unpublished doctoral dissertation, The Ohio State University, Columbus.

Clay, M.M. (1966). *Emergent reading behavior.* Unpublished doctoral dissertation, University of Aukland, New Zealand.

Clay, M.M. (1979). *The early detection of reading difficulties: A diagnostic survey with recovery procedures.* Portsmouth, NH: Heinemann.

Clay, M.M. (1991). *Becoming literate: The construction of inner control.* Portsmouth, NH: Heinemann.

Clay, M.M. (1993a). *An observation survey of early literacy achievement.* Portsmouth, NH: Heinemann.

Clay, M.M. (1993b). *Reading Recovery: A guidebook for teachers in training.* Portsmouth, NH: Heinemann.

Huck, C.S., & Kerstetter, K.J. (1987). Developing readers. In B. Cullinan (Ed.), *Children's literature in the reading program* (pp. 30-40). Newark, DE: International Reading Association.

McKenzie, M.G., (1985). Shared writing: Apprenticeship in writing. *Language Matters, 1-2,* 1-5.

Peterson, B. (1991). Selecting books for beginning readers. In D.E. DeFord, C.A. Lyons, & G.S. Pinnell (Eds.), *Bridges to literacy: Learning from Reading Recovery* (pp. 119-147). Portsmouth, NH: Heinemann.

Pinnell, G.S., Fried, M.D., & Estice, R.M. (1990). Reading Recovery: Learning how to make a difference. *The Reading Teacher, 43,* 282-295.

Pinnell, G.S., & McCarrier, A. (1994). Interactive writing: A transition tool for assisting children in learning to read and write. In E. Hiebert & B. Taylor (Eds.), *Getting reading right from the start: Effective early literacy interventions* (pp. 149-170). Needham, MA: Allyn & Bacon.

Strickland, D.S., & Morrow, L.M. (1989). *Emerging literacy: Young children learn to read and write.* Newark, DE: International Reading Association.

Teale, W.H., & Sulzby, E. (Eds.). (1986). *Emergent literacy: Writing and reading.* Norwood, NJ: Ablex.

Vygotsky, L. (1962). *Thought and language.* Cambridge, MA: MIT Press.

Children's books cited

Cowley, J. (1990). *The farm concert.* Bothell, WA: The Wright Group.

Galdone, P. (1972). *The three bears.* New York: Clarion.

Galdone, P. (1975). *The gingerbread boy.* New York: Clarion.

Ginsburg, M. (1972). *The chick and the duckling.* New York: Macmillan.

Peek, M. (1985). *Mary wore her red dress and Henry wore his green sneakers.* New York: Clarion.

Rosen, M. (1989). *We're going on a bear hunt.* New York: McElderry.

From *The Reading Teacher, Vol. 49, No. 6, March 1996*

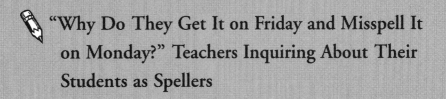
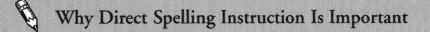

"WHY DO THEY GET IT ON FRIDAY AND MISSPELL IT ON MONDAY?" TEACHERS INQUIRING ABOUT THEIR STUDENTS AS SPELLERS

CHARLENE HILLAL GILL AND PATRICIA L. SCHARER

Spelling remains a big question mark for many teachers. In this study a group of teachers examined their children's spelling patterns and errors and made changes in their instructional strategies based on what they saw.

They [students] are still missing those words in their writing that they get right on a spelling test. That is when you think, "All that time that you are spending on spelling and all the time the parents are spending at home just isn't really worth it."

The first-grade teacher quoted above summed up the frustrations of her colleagues about spelling instruction during our first meeting in a series of six inservice sessions. The building principal had invited us to meet monthly with 15 teachers from her two elementary buildings to discuss language arts instruction and assessment techniques that could inform teachers' instructional decision making. Topics requested by the teachers (Grades 1–5) at the initial meeting included spelling, literature-based reading, and the writing process. Spelling was an area of concern for all the teachers and, thus, was selected as the focus for the inservice program.

We wanted to know the questions teachers had about spelling to help us plan for the meetings, so we asked all 15 teachers to complete a survey we developed. Nine of the 15 teachers subsequently volunteered to have inter-

We appreciate the efforts of the principal and teaching staff at Hardin Central and Eastcrest Elementary Schools, Kenton, Ohio, who inquired about their students as spellers.

views with us tape recorded. The interviews had a dual purpose: (a) to provide additional insight into teachers' current practices, concerns, and questions, which would aid us in planning appropriate inservice sessions, and (b) to begin to identify and explore issues of teacher change in relation to spelling instruction.

All 9 teachers expressed discomfort about their current spelling instruction and were anxious to discuss issues related to teaching spelling in their classrooms. For example, a second-grade teacher (see Teacher E in Table 1) had experimented with her weekly schedule of spelling assignments by requiring her students to use the spelling words in sentences with correct punctuation. She soon abandoned the practice, observing that "it was too much torture." She was anxious to change her spelling program and explained that "I have a lot of questions. I think it goes back to not knowing any better, so you just do it that way."

As we talked with the teachers, we began to wonder about the ways teachers would respond to the developmental perspective and assessment tools we would share in the inservice sessions. Would there be certain questions all teachers ask about their students as spellers? How would they respond as they learn to analyze spelling errors within a developmental perspective? What difficulties might they experience as they examine student errors? Would there be instructional changes—from a traditional program of spelling instruction to one informed by the research on developmental spelling—as they learn more about analyzing students' spellings?

We gained insight into these questions by analyzing data from the survey instrument; transcripts of initial and final interviews with the 9 volunteer teachers; and data from the three informal, small-group forum discussions scheduled at the request of teachers during the third and fourth inservice sessions. Although recommendations for spelling instruction are found in various professional journals, researchers have not yet examined the ways recent spelling research affects teachers' decisions regarding spelling instruction in their classrooms. According to Schlagal and Schlagal (1992), "The instructional implications of this research on developmental word knowledge are interesting and varied, but they remain largely untapped" (p. 419).

This article describes how teachers inquired about their students as spellers, how their learning about students by analyzing spelling errors affected their instruction, and how their inquiry led to instructional changes in their classrooms. The stories of their inquiries about spelling are a modest beginning to understanding how teachers can discover the individual needs of their students and create instructional methods supporting spelling achievement in elementary classrooms.

Theoretical Background

Since the early 1970s, a growing body of research has revealed that orthographic knowledge develops as a process in children and that this development is reflected in their errors or invented spelling (Chomsky, 1970; Henderson & Beers, 1980; Read, 1971). This process has been described as a continuum of increasingly complex inferences of sound-symbol relationships made by children. As such, the development of orthographic knowledge has been compared to the development of oral language. Parallel research of children's development in spelling in other languages has revealed a similar sequence of approximations in spelling and thus suggests that this may be a universal linguistic process (Gill, 1980).

Henderson (1990) and his colleagues have described this development across five stages: *preliterate, letter name, within word, syllable juncture,* and *derivational constancy.* The preliterate stage of spelling development is characterized by scribbles, drawings, and random letters or letter-like forms that the child intends to represent words, names, or a message. The letter-name stage is identified by the child's achieving control over letter names and forms and using a discernable code to create or invent spellings to represent words. This code is an extraction of the sound of the letter name to represent salient sounds in words. For example *KAK* is a typical letter-name spelling for *cake; JGN* is a frequent spelling of *dragon;* and *BOP* often spells *bump.* Letter-name spellers generally do not represent silent letters or nasals before a consonant, as is the case with *M* in

bump. Letter-name spellers substitute standard spellings for short vowels with the long vowel letter name that "feels" most similar as it is formed in the vocal tract (where articulation occurs)—for example *NAT* for *net, FES* for *fish.* The within-word stage of spelling development is characterized by correct representation of short vowels and variations in representing the marking system of long vowels—*RANE* for *rain, FEIDE* for *feed.* During the syllable-juncture stage, students begin to correct errors in multisyllable words at the point where the syllables join—*HOPPING* for *hoping, DIRECTSION* for *direction.* The derivational-constancy stage begins as students honor the preservation of meaning through spelling patterns in related words such as *sign, signal,* and *signature.* Errors often result when the writer spells the word as it sounds, as in *COMPATITION* for *competition.*

Based on these studies, researchers began to question existing approaches to spelling instruction in favor of practices supporting the child's naturally developing awareness of orthography (Bloodgood, 1991; Henderson, 1981, 1990; Schlagal & Schlagal, 1992; Templeton, 1991). Typical basal spelling lessons are characterized by weekly lists of words for the whole class to learn, written exercises emphasizing memorization, and two weekly tests (trial and final). In contrast, spelling instruction informed by recent research involves adapting the scope and sequence of basal spelling materials to reflect the unique developmental level of each student. This type of instruction also uses wide reading and writing, as opposed to unitary placement in the grade-level basal spelling book (Scharer, 1992a; Wilde, 1990).

Learning About Teachers' Questions

During the first inservice meeting, all 15 teachers completed a survey instrument with questions about knowledge of current spelling research; descriptions of their present instructional approach, including materials, activities, and schedule; students' current achievement levels; and methods of determining student achievement. Nine of the teachers then volunteered to participate in follow-up interviews to clarify and extend the survey data before our second meeting. Survey data relevant to spelling program organization in the 9 classrooms at the beginning of the study are displayed in Table 1.

We wanted to document the questions teachers were asking initially as well as any changes that might occur over the course of our meetings; therefore, the initial interviews, three forum discussions, and a second round of nine interviews at the end of the 6-month inservice

Table 1
Spelling Program at the Beginning of the Study

Teacher	Grade	Minutes Each Week (Teacher Directed)	Source of Weekly List	Use of Weekly List	Weekly Trial & Final Tests	Materials	Activities
A	Transitional First	100	Teacher-selected words	Single list for whole class	Yes	Magic slates, letters & chart, overhead projector	Sing letters in order, write words using magic slates or shaving cream
B	First	50	Teacher-selected, high-frequency words	Multiple lists for small groups	Yes	Paper & pencil, magnetic letters, magic slates	Write words 4x each, solve scrambled word list, put words in sentences
C	First	150	Teacher-selected CVC patterns	Single list for whole class	Yes	Paper & pencil	Write words and illustrate
D	First	30	Teacher-selected words misspelled in student writing, high-frequency words, student-selected challenge words	Individual lists	Yes	Individual spelling notebooks, paper & pencil	Write words 4x each, practice with a partner, add words to individual dictionaries
E	Second	105	Basal speller	Single list for whole class	Yes	Paper & pencil, flashcards	Discuss patterns, write words for handwriting grade, play spelling games
F	Second	95	Basal speller and teacher-selected words	Single list for whole class	Yes	Paper & pencil	Write words 4x each, use words in sentences, alphabetize in small groups
G	Fourth	115	Basal speller	Single list for whole class	Yes	Textbook, paper & pencil	Write words in sentences, practice in teams, work with dictionary, play games, conduct board drill, alphabetize, unscramble
H	Fifth	15	Teacher-selected words from reading books or themes	Single pretest. Students select 10 words to learn from errors	Yes	Paper & pencil, spelling dictionaries	Choose 10 words missed on pretest to practice with spelling monitors (students with perfect pretest papers); monitors give final tests
I	LD	30	Student-selected words from reading book	Individual lists	Yes	Paper & pencil, spelling dictionaries	Write in dictionary, write words 4x each, alphabetize, write in sentences, practice with partners

period were audiotaped, transcribed, and entered into a computer program—the Ethnograph (Seidel, Kjolseth, & Seymour, 1988)—to facilitate coding, analysis, and retrieval. Twenty-four coding categories (Bogdan & Biklen, 1982) emerged during multiple readings of the data. After coding all interviews and forums, we used the Ethnograph to generate printouts of each category across the data. These categories were then clustered to further examine patterns of teacher questions, concerns, and changes over time. For example, categories QIWK, TESTING (general assessment), TESTWK (weekly tests), and ERRORS (student errors in writing) were clustered to discern patterns of responses informing the question: How do teachers respond as they learn to analyze spelling errors using a developmental perspective?

Learning Together About Developmental Spelling

Initially, we reflected on the survey data and first round of interviews to plan the series of inservice sessions and decided to begin with assessment tools. Later, we used teachers' analysis of their students' achievement as spellers to raise instructional issues. During our final sessions, we posed ways to respond instructionally to classrooms of diverse learners.

The first inservice session focused on learning to administer and analyze the Qualitative Inventory of Word Knowledge (QIWK) to help teachers learn about the individual capabilities of their students as spellers (see Schlagal [1989] for procedural details). The QIWK consists of graded word lists containing increasingly complex spelling patterns related to developmental stages. Together, during subsequent inservice sessions, we analyzed students' accuracy scores and error patterns on the QIWK to determine grade level achievement and stage of development. In addition to the monthly inservice programs, we held three informal, after-school forum discussions where teachers shared both struggles and successes experienced as they implemented new spelling strategies. The final inservice sessions focused on using assessment information to make instructional decisions, including the selection of words for study and appropriate word study activities.

At the request of the teachers, we also provided classroom demonstrations of the word study activities discussed during inservice sessions. One type of activity demonstrated was the use of word sorts (see Barnes, 1989; Zutell, 1993). A word sort is a manipulative activity in which individual words are printed on small cards and are then grouped or categorized according to a specified feature. For example, *train, cake, made, gate,* and *pain* may be categorized as long-*A* words and contrasted with short-*A* words such as *dad, hat, cat,*

pan, and *ran.* Later, long-*A* words can be further analyzed and categorized into spelling patterns such as *aCe* (*cake, made, gate*); *-ai-* (*train, rain, pain*); and *-ay* (*may, say, play*). After students have conducted a word sort, they may record their lists of words under the labels they have used to categorize them in a word study notebook. This notebook serves as a student reference book for use during writing and is also useful to document instruction and student progress. Such instructional activities helped teachers in this study explore a variety of ways to work with individuals and small groups to best meet their students' individual needs as spellers.

Teachers' Questions About Current Practice

At the beginning of this project, most of the teachers' questions centered on issues of time, instructional organization, classroom management, and grading. A fourth-grade teacher (Teacher G in Table 1) asked, "How do I organize this so that I don't feel like I am losing control of what they are learning as far as spelling is concerned?" The teachers also questioned how to assign grades on the report card and how to communicate students' development to their parents. Regarding grades, for example, Teacher E said, "My only way of [giving grades] was to give a test." Due to a strong tradition of spelling grades based on weekly tests over a single word list, teachers were concerned about parents' responses to changes in spelling assessment that did not rely exclusively on a weekly test score.

> *At the beginning of this project, most of the teachers' questions centered on issues of time, instructional organization, classroom management, and grading. . . . At the end of the inservice, teacher's questions shifted to express concern for how to refine newly adopted teaching strategies.*

At the end of the inservice, teacher's questions shifted to express concern for how to refine newly adopted teaching strategies. For example, they wanted to know specifically how to get words for the word sorts, what to do with word cards after instructional activities, whether students should keep individual sets of word cards from their word sorts, and how word study notebooks should be utilized. Teachers still had questions about management issues, but these questions became more specific, such as how to manage individual and small-group spelling lessons in contrast to whole-class assignments and tests.

Teachers' Responses During Analysis of Spelling Errors

During analysis of the 18 pre- and post-interviews and forum discussions, we saw three patterns of teacher responses as they analyzed student spelling errors using the QIWK. First, as they scored the test, teachers were surprised by their students' instructional levels as well as the range of student's scores in their class. The teacher of learning disabled students (Teacher I in Table 1), for example, had previously tested her students using the Brigance Diagnostic Inventory of Basic Skills. She reported, "My kids were pretty close to the same [scores]. . . at a third- and fourth-grade level." Consequently, she established two instructional groups using third- and fourth-grade materials and "saw in the first several weeks that it wasn't going to work. There were some kids who weren't getting the spelling test." As she used the QIWK, she learned that these students were functioning at a much lower level, and this caused her to reconsider the level of difficulty for instruction. After using the QIWK, another teacher (Teacher H) of a fifth-grade class expressed her surprise that the ability range in her class spanned from Level 2 to Level 8. Similarly, Teacher E concluded:

> I need to get better at recognizing what levels they are at. It only makes sense that if kids are at different reading levels, they will also be at different levels in their spelling. I don't know why I didn't recognize this before.

Thus, using the QIWK encouraged teachers to reexamine how grouping decisions were made and to reconsider their practice of posing a single word list for their class.

A second way the QIWK increased teachers' knowledge about spelling resulted from analyzing the QIWK in two steps. First, the accuracy percentage of individual students for each list of the QIWK was generally used to identify students' instructional level. Next, teachers closely examined student errors within each list for insight into qualitative changes in student's errors, which demonstrated achievement over time. A first-grade teacher (Teacher B) expressed concern that the accuracy percentage scores for her students in May did not reflect an upward movement in levels when compared to January scores. However, when she com-

pared characteristics of the errors students made on the two tests, she concluded that over half of her students were, indeed, moving from letter-name stage to within-word stage. Analyzing student spellings beyond accuracy percentages provided evidence of achievement in spelling otherwise masked by superficial numerical comparisons.

Third, as teachers learned to administer and interpret the QIWK, they noticed changes in the ways they examined students' spelling errors in written assignments and stories. Rather than circling spelling mistakes, they began to document patterns of errors in students' writing assignments in a systematic way that was informed by their work in analyzing errors from the QIWK. Consequently, teachers learned about their students as spellers and documented their achievement during the completion of various written assignments as well as within more formal spelling assessments.

Difficulties

Although the close analysis of student errors both in the QIWK and in their writing enabled teachers to better understand students' spelling achievement, they expressed frustration about the amount of time it took to conduct the analysis. Teachers recognized the benefits of analyzing spelling errors but clearly identified the need for more practice analyzing errors, additional inservice opportunities, more time to talk with their colleagues about their observations of student errors, and more time to plan instruction based on those observations. Teacher E, for example, shared the following: "What scares me is the diagnostic part of this. Making sure that I know enough so I do a good job at this." In addition, as teachers increased their recognition of individual differences, this awareness heightened feelings of inadequacy about their ability to provide appropriate instruction to support the multiple needs of their classes.

Instructional Changes

Teachers varied in the amount of change they instituted during the course of this study. One first-grade teacher (Teacher C) reported that she had made few changes during the 6-month inservice period, explaining that, "I am going to do it differently next year, but I didn't want to change in the middle." Other teachers began to make a variety of changes in their approach to spelling. One change involved rethinking the criteria for choosing words for weekly lists. Teachers who were using teacher-selected lists at the beginning of the study began selecting words misspelled in their students' writing that were appropriate developmentally rather than using vocabulary from books the students were reading. Spelling instruction also began to be linked to writing through mini-lessons based on observed errors in students' writing and coaching in self-editing and peer-editing strategies. Teachers began moving away from activities that supported memorization to activities that involved the children in comparing and contrasting word features in both large- and small-group settings. Word hunts and word study notebooks were also being used to extend and record students' developing word knowledge.

Concerns about grading and reporting to parents led to the development of a rubric to inform grading decisions. The rubric included: participating in instructional activities, recognizing relationships among words, increasing grapho-phonetic knowledge, applying skills in purposeful writing, engaging in self- and peer editing, and using available resources to spell conventionally in final drafts (see Figure 1). Using the rubric reduced teachers' concerns about how to assign grades in spelling without using weekly test scores. Teachers reported that parents responded favorably to the rubric and agreed that it was more informative than a single letter grade on a report card.

Discussion, Limitations, and Future Research

The instructional activities teachers used at the beginning of this inservice emphasized writing words many times and having students practice with partners in preparation for weekly spelling tests. Such activities were easy to plan and organize but encouraged memorization and short-term learning. Although teachers found comfort in this type of classroom organization, they were frustrated as they observed students who correctly spelled words during a test on Friday and misspelled the same words as they wrote stories on Monday.

Their use of the QIWK did enable teachers to look at students' spelling in a more informed manner, but it also increased teachers' discomfort with their former practice in teaching spelling as well as their frustration in not being facile in providing developmentally appropriate instruction in spelling for their students. Was it worth it? One first-grade teacher (Teacher A) stated:

I am glad that I had the opportunity to change because I would have done it like it had always been done. I would have felt in my heart that it wasn't right. This is

Primary Grades

	Always	Sometimes		Never	
	A	B	C	D	E
Participates in group instructional activities					
Identifies relationships among and between words					
Demonstrates expanding knowledge of grapho-phonetic relationships when uncertain of correct spelling in written discourse					
Correctly spells high-frequency words in purposeful writing activities					
Participates in self-editing and peer editing					
Uses available resources to use conventional spelling					

Upper Grades

	Always	Sometimes		Never	
	A	B	C	D	E
Participates in group instructional activities					
Identifies relationships among and between words					
Demonstrates expanding knowledge of grapho-phonetic relationships when uncertain of correct spelling in written discourse					
Correctly spells high-frequency words in purposeful writing activities					
Participates in self-editing and peer editing					
Uses available resources to use conventional spelling					
Spells conventionally in final drafts					

Figure 1. Spelling Assessment Matrix Developed by Teachers to Supplement Student's Grade Card

so much more pleasant. You can see growth. What more could you ask for?

Guskey (1986) argues that changes in teachers' beliefs and attitudes are facilitated by observations of changes in student learning outcomes. The use of the QIWK and the efforts spent in analyzing spelling errors enabled the teachers in this study to see their students in deeper,

> *Teachers began moving away from activities that supported memorization to activities that involved the children in comparing and contrasting word features in both large- and small-group settings.*

more complex ways. On one hand, this new knowledge seemed to overwhelm teachers at times when they began to perceive the implications of understanding their students' development beyond percentages on final tests. On the other hand, learning about the individual needs of their students, ways to respond to those needs, and ways to document spelling growth supported their efforts to value the complexity of the knowledge children brought to their classrooms and to respond by moving away from simplistic spelling instruction.

As we worked with these teachers and talked with them about their progress, questions, and concerns, it was clear that the instructional shifts they were attempting were facilitated by their personal discomfort with past practices, their participation in the inservice sessions, their interactions with each other, and the support provided by their principal. However, we were also struck by the pressures they identified that worked against their attempts to change, which included lingering concerns about parents' reactions, perceptions of colleagues who were not implementing changes, and personal feelings of inadequate expertise. In a sense, these teachers traded one set of frustrations for another as they changed from being passive administrators of word lists and tests to active decision makers. These teachers became involved in learning about their students and using such knowledge to make instructional decisions because of the needs of their students, not the demands of a list. Although the path to understanding developmental spelling was littered with doubts, discomfort, and frustration, we still believe that educators should not ignore current spelling research. They should embrace the difficult task of translating that research into appropriate classroom practice.

We offer two areas of concern as efforts begin to adjust spelling instruction as informed by recent research. First, we celebrate current efforts to integrate instruction using thematic approaches as well as to use children's literature to make connections across curricular areas and to organize classrooms in complex ways (Pappas, Kiefer, & Levstik, 1990; Vacca & Rasinski, 1992). It is tempting to teach spelling by creating word lists from the thematic readings as a way to integrate spelling with other content areas. Research has demonstrated, however, that children can often read, for accurate spelling, texts that are 2 years beyond their capability (Zutell & Fresch, 1991). Word selection, then, must be informed by knowledge of student's developmental level rather than dictated by the theme of the month. Secondly, as publishers of spelling programs begin to develop word lists and teaching manuals based on recent research, we encourage the development of inservice programs that will strengthen teachers' understanding of students' errors and movement toward accurate spellings at various levels. Such programs might include diagnostic tools such as the QIWK, recommendations for classroom instruction involving multiple lists, and teacher-directed lessons created by matching the developmental needs of students with appropriate activities. Spelling programs should also encourage instruction to go beyond 15 minutes each day on a single list to include wide writing on self-selected topics, peer editing, the use of multiple reference tools, and the development of final drafts with accurate spellings before publication.

At the final inservice, all of the participants indicated their intent to continue exploring innovations in their spelling programs. Although the focus of the sessions was spelling, the teachers recognized the value of integrating spelling with writing, reading, vocabulary, and other content areas. They celebrated the interconnections between subject areas and used their observations of students to expand their definitions of spelling instruction. Six months of support, however, was not enough. During final interviews, teachers expressed a strong desire for continued support, including inservice opportunities, provision of professional reading materials, and opportunities to observe and meet with other teachers. Teacher G said,

> I am not sure exactly where I am going to go yet.... It is going to take a lot more reading and development on my part. I am just headed in that direction somewhere. I don't want to let it drop by the wayside.

Such concerns point to the limitations of the one-shot inservices that are commonly organized in school districts. Needed instead are long-term contacts between educators as they explore spelling in depth over time.

The data we collected were not intended to be part of a carefully orchestrated and extensive research project. Rather, we used the survey and interview data to help us better understand the questions and concerns of teachers inquiring about their students as spellers and themselves as teachers. Our goal was to support teachers' efforts in response to their needs in much the same way that QIWK provided the knowledge of their students that informed instructional decisions.

Although recognizing the limitations of this exploratory study, we believe that the questions, struggles, and successes of these teachers add to our current understanding of the change process in elementary classrooms in a new and unique way. There has been some documentation of the change process during implementation of literature-based reading programs (Scharer, 1992b) and extensive reporting of transitions from traditional writing instruction to a process writing approach (Calkins, 1986; Graves, 1983). None, however, have reported on the pedagogical shift that occurs when teachers explore recent research about developmental spelling and related assessment techniques and use that knowledge to inquire about their students as spellers.

Future studies might focus on questions similar to these: What are the long-range implications of changes in teachers' pedagogical decisions that have been informed by a knowledge of developmental spelling? What are the effects on students' attitudes and achievement during the change process? Is there any evidence of a ripple effect or impact on other areas of instruction, such as reading and writing, when teachers move away from a traditional spelling program? Classroom-based investigations of such questions will enable educators to understand better the ways developmental spelling research can be used to benefit students as spellers.

References

Barnes, W. G. (1989). Word sorting: The cultivation of rules for spelling in English. *Reading Psychology, 10*, 293–307.

Bloodgood, J. W. (1991). A new approach to spelling instruction in language arts programs. *The Elementary School Journal, 92*, 203–212.

Bogdan, R. C., & Biklen, S. K. (1982). *Qualitative research for education.* Boston: Allyn and Bacon.

Calkins, L. M. (1986). *The art of teaching writing.* Portsmouth, NH: Heinemann.

Chomsky, C. (1970). Reading, writing, and phonology. *Harvard Education Review, 40*, 287–309.

Graves, D. (1983). *Writing: Teachers and children at work.* Exeter, NH: Heinemann.

Gill, C. (1980). An analysis of spelling errors in French. (Doctoral dissertation, University of Virginia, 1980). *Dissertation Abstracts International, 41*, 3924A.

Guskey, T. R. (1986). Staff development and the process of teacher change. *Educational Researcher, 15*(5), 5–12.

Henderson, E. H. (1981). *Learning to read and spell: The child's knowledge of words.* DeKalb, IL: Northern Illinois University Press.

Henderson, E. H. (1990). *Teaching spelling* (2nd ed.). Boston: Houghton Mifflin.

Henderson, E. H., & Beers, J. W. (Eds.). (1980). *Developmental and cognitive aspects of learning to spell.* Newark, DE: International Reading Association.

Pappas, C. C., Kiefer, B. Z., & Levstik, L. S. (1990). *An integrated language perspective in the elementary school: Theory into action.* New York: Longman.

Read, C. (1971). Pre-school children's knowledge of English phonology. *Harvard Educational Review, 41*, 1–34.

Scharer, P. L. (1992a). From memorization to conceptualization: History informing the teaching and learning of spelling. *Journal of Language Experience, 11*, 43–58.

Scharer, P. L. (1992b). Teachers in transition: An exploration of changes in teachers and classrooms during implementation of literature-based reading instruction. *Research in the Teaching of English, 26*, 408–445.

Schlagal, R. C. (1989). Constancy and change in spelling development. *Reading Psychology, 10*, 207–232.

Schlagal, R. C., & Schlagal, J. H. (1992). The integral character of spelling: Teaching strategies for multiple purposes. *Language Arts, 69*, 418–424.

Seidel, J. V., Kjolseth, R., & Seymour, E. (1988). The ethnograph [Computer program]. Littleton, CO: Qualis Research Associates.

Templeton, S. (1991). Teaching and learning the English spelling system: Reconceptualizing method and purpose. *The Elementary School Journal, 92*, 185–202.

Vacca, R. T., & Rasinski, T. V. (1992). *Case studies in whole language.* Fort Worth, TX: Harcourt Brace Jovanovich.

Wilde, S. (1990). A proposal for a new spelling curriculum. *The Elementary School Journal, 90*, 275–289.

Zutell, J. (1993). The directed spelling thinking activity (DSTA): A developmental, conceptual approach to advancing students' word knowledge. In *Literacy for the new millenium* (pp. 184–191). Melbourne, Australia: Australian Reading Association.

Zutell, J., & Fresch, M. J. (1991, May). *A longitudinal study of reading and spelling connections for third- and fifth-grade students.* Paper presented at the annual meeting of the International Reading Assocation, Las Vegas, NV.

Charlene Hillal Gill is Associate Professor of Education and Chair of the Department of Teacher Education at Randolph-Macon Woman's College in Lynchburg, Virginia. Patricia L. Scharer is Associate Professor of Education at The Ohio State University at Lima, where she teaches preservice and inservice courses in literacy methods and children's literature.

From *Language Arts, Vol. 73, February 1996*

SCHOLASTIC

Spelling™

RESEARCH PAPER

VOLUME 2

Why Direct Spelling Instruction Is Important

Barbara Foorman

Should spelling occupy its own place in the curriculum? Recent research indicates that it should. For a decade, teachers have been advised that spelling instruction should be integrated into a reading and writing curriculum. Yet new studies show that the management of spelling integration has proven unwieldy and the results ineffective. Other studies clearly indicate that formal spelling instruction improves students' proficiency, and perhaps more important, helps them become more powerful readers and writers.
Barbara Foorman, researcher and **Scholastic Spelling** *Senior Author, makes the case for explicit spelling instruction.*

S pelling deserves to be taught in its own right, not just as an adjunct to reading and writing. In fact, one can argue for the primacy of spelling knowledge in learning to read and write. If a child can spell a word, he or she can usually read the word, although being able to read a word does not necessarily predict accurate spelling.

Why does spelling knowledge relate so well to good reading, but not the reverse? The answer is at once simple and complex. The simple answer is that correct spelling requires a complete representation of the sound-letter connections in the word, whereas correct reading of words often can be based on a partial representation of letter-sound connections — partial because only the beginning and ending letters may be fully considered.

The complex answer is that spelling knowledge is an amalgam of orthographic knowledge (an understanding of how one's writing system works) and phonological awareness (an understanding of the sound structure of one's language). Ehri (1992) explains the interdependence of spelling and reading in the following way:

> Visual-phonological connections are made when letters in spelling are processed as symbols for phonemes in the pronunciations of specific words. As a result, spellings become amalgamated to pronunciations and are retained in memory as orthographic "images" of the words, that is, visual letter-analyzed representations. These representations

also become amalgamated to meanings in memory. It is this amalgam that is accessed directly when sight words are read and recognized via this connection (p.120).

Let me provide an explanation of how this amalgamation comes about and then turn to answering the questions of why spelling needs to be taught directly and deserves its own place in a teacher's planbook.

Phonology and Orthography

The orthography of English is an alphabet. The 26 letters of the English alphabet represent from 44 to 52 speech sounds called phonemes. The number of phonemes varies because vowels, in particular, are subject to regional, dialectical, and individual differences in speech production.

Take, for example, the words *pin* and *pen*. For some people these two words are pronounced differently with distinct medial phonemes. For other people, however, these words share the same three phonemes, with context as the clue to meaning. In addition to the fact that phonemes can have several spoken forms, phonemes are not spoken as separate units. We say that the word *park* has four sounds, but when we pronounce *park,* the initial consonant /p/ is influenced by the medial vowel /a/, and the medial vowel is influenced by the consonants before and after it. Thus, in speech, phonemes are co-articulated into a syllabic unit that is difficult to separate into discrete parts. Moreover, some vowels become assimilated into the following consonant in speech, as in the "r-controlled" vowel in *park* or the nasalized vowels in the words *and, went,* and *gym.* These assimilations result in spellings of "p-r-k" for park and "w-e-t" for *went.*

> *"The majority of students must be explicitly taught that letters of the alphabet relate to sounds in speech."*

Consonants as well as vowels are affected by co-articulation. Consider the words *let* and *lad.* The *t* and *d* sound distinct in these two words. However, in the words *letter* and *ladder,* the medial /t/ and /d/ phonemes are reduced to a common phoneme called a "tongue flap." Not surprisingly, students are likely to spell *letter* as "l-e-d-r." Moreover, /t/ and /d/ are affected by /r/ in consonant blends.

Children listen for sounds and proceed to phonetically represent a word with a spelling such as "c-h-r-a-n" for *train.* Spelling errors can sometimes help you diagnose problems with phonemic awareness — problems that need to be addressed instructionally (Moats, 1995).

How Patterns, Principles, and Rules Help Organize Instruction

When Glenda Bissex (1980) described her four-year-old son's writing of DO NAT DTRB GYNS AT WRK ("Do not disturb, genius at work"), we celebrated the precocious use of letter-name and letter-sound knowledge demonstrated by this temporary spelling. For children like Bissex's son, alphabetic knowledge may become so well constructed that even the unpredictable sound-spellings of highly frequent Anglo-Saxon words such as *the, of,* and *they* are learned. But the majority of students must be explicitly taught that letters of the alphabet relate to sounds in speech.

Many people think that spelling is memorizing all the words in a dictionary. That would truly be a daunting task! However, we have a useful and efficient alphabet. In English, there are patterns, principles, and rules for organizing spelling words. Students can use these rules as an aid in spelling unknown words.

Let's put spelling in perspective. There are about 400,000 words in the average dictionary. Only about 13 percent of words in the dictionary are truly exceptional. (Hanna, Hanna, Hodges, & Rudorf, 1966). These have to be memorized by sight. In about 50 percent of the words, sound and symbol connect perfectly. The connection is one to

one, so those words don't have to be memorized. The remaining 37 percent are easily learned through instruction of letter-sound correspondences. It is learning these last two categories of words — nearly 90 percent of English — where students learn to understand spelling principles and patterns and benefit most from explicit spelling instruction using organized lists.

How Should Spelling Instruction Progress?

It is best to start with the words that have one-to-one correspondence. By mastering these easily, students feel comfortable, confident, and successful. And they are developing the knowledge with which to spell nearly half of the words they'll encounter in English.

Then students can be introduced to words with slightly more complex sound-symbol correspondences from that 37 percent for which we learn rules and patterns. That's the bulk of spelling work. The remaining 13 percent of words are sight words that must be memorized and can be sprinkled throughout the program.

Students should progress from knowing highly reliable sound-spelling correspondences to knowing something about the slightly more complex sound-spelling patterns in which there are many-to-one correspondences. Then they should be introduced to morphology, or the study of roots, prefixes, suffixes, and inflections.

By fifth or sixth grade, students should focus on derivations and etymologies. They should learn how English has borrowed words from other languages, particularly Latin and Greek, which are very systematic. Through study of derivations and etymologies, students get a sense of the history of the English language.

Focusing on word meaning is an important part of spelling instruction in the upper elementary grades. The way to unlock word meaning is by knowing a word's spelling. By knowing its spelling, students know its pronunciation, how to read the word, and its meaning. To be good readers,

students must first unlock the meanings of words because that unlocks the meaning of sentences, paragraphs, and the whole text. So through spelling instruction, teachers are helping students become independent readers by providing word study that enables them to venture independently into a broad variety of text reading.

What Should Be Taught in a Spelling Program?

My colleague Louisa Moats, co-author of *Scholastic Spelling,* suggests useful instructional elements and sequence in her research. I include it here as a handy guide for educators who want to give spelling its own place in the language arts curriculum.

- Starting in the middle of first grade and continuing until third grade, students need to be taught single correspondence units such as consonants, short vowels, consonant digraphs, consonant blends, long vowel silent-e, vowel combinations for long vowels, diphthongs, and silent-letter graphemes.

- In second and third grades, students need to be taught inflectional morphology (e.g., plurals and past tense) and conditional orthographic patterns and rules (e.g., *qu;* double *f, l, s, z;* simple consonant doubling; drop *e;* change *y* to *i; ge-dge* alternation; *ch-tch; c, k, ck;* hard and soft *c* and *g*). In addition, students should learn such spelling oddities as homophones, contractions, homographs, compounds, and unusual word forms.

- In grades 3 through 5, students need to be taught about syllable constructions such as closed, open, consonant *-le,* and *r*-controlled vowels. They also need to be instructed in how syllable juncture patterns explain doubled letters (e.g., why *writing* has one *t* but *written* has two).

- In upper elementary school, students need to be introduced to etymology and taught derivational morphology (e.g., Latin roots, suffixes, and prefixes).

- In middle school, students should study

etymology, such as Greek and Latin-based morphology and foreign–language influences on English.

Spelling Instruction Should Be Fun!

Although instruction needs to be explicit about these sound-spelling principles, instruction need not be dull. Students can become word-pattern sleuths, investigating samples of words to form hypotheses about orthographic rules. They can develop knowledge through word sorts and spelling games. *Scholastic Spelling* author Richard Hodges describes the effectiveness of word sort activities on pages 3-4. Students can master rigorous spelling rules and patterns through engaging activities that really make learning stick.

There is another factor that motivates students. The knowledge they gain through explicit instruction enhances their reading and writing. By knowing how to fully represent the phonemes in speech with the correct ortho-graphic symbols, students are able to automatically recognize words in text and effortlessly produce their spellings in writing. Spelling instruction makes for better readers and writers. When students understand this, it reinforces their desire to learn more. It helps construct that all-important learning cycle in which success breeds success. ■

References

Bissex, G. (1980). *Gyns at Wrk: A Child Learns to Write and Read.* Cambridge, MA: Harvard University Press.

Ehri, L.C. (1992). Reconceptualizing the development of sight word reading and its relationship to recoding. In P.B. Gough, L.C. Ehri, and R. Treiman, eds., *Reading Acquisition*, 107–144. Hillsdale, NJ: Erlbaum.

Foorman, B.R., and Francis, D.J. (1994). Exploring connections among reading, spelling, and phonemic segmentation during first grade. *Reading and Writing*, 6, 65–91.

Hanna, P.R., Hanna, J.S., Hodges, R.E., and Rudorf, E.H. (1996). Phoneme–grapheme correspondences as cues to spelling improvement. Washington, D.C.: U.S. Government Printing Office, U.S. Office of Education.

Moats, L.C. (1995). *Spelling: Development, Disability, and Instruction.* Baltimore, MD: York Press.

From *Scholastic Spelling: Research Paper, Vol. 2, 1997*

A Cognitive Theory of Orthographic Transitioning: Predictable Errors in How Spanish-Speaking Children Spell English Words

Olatokunbo S. Fashola, Priscilla A. Drum, Richard E. Mayer, and Sang-Jin Kang
University of California, Santa Barbara

Schools in the United States serve a large and increasing number of Spanish-speaking students who are making the transition to English language literacy. This study examines one aspect of the transition to English literacy, namely, how Spanish-speaking students spell English words. Samples of 38 students who speak Spanish at home (Spanish-speaking group) and 34 students who speak English at home (English-speaking group) listened to a list of 40 common English words dictated to them by the teacher and wrote down each word one at a time. Spanish-speaking students produced more errors that were consistent with the correct application of Spanish phonological and orthographical rules (i.e., predicted errors) than did English-speaking students, and the groups generally did not differ in their production of other kinds of spelling errors (i.e., nonpredicted errors). Theoretical and practical implications for bilingual education are discussed.

OLATOKUNBO S. FASHOLA is an Associate Research Scientist at the Center for Research on Education of Students Placed at Risk, Johns Hopkins University, 3505 North Charles Street, Baltimore, MD 21218. Her specializations are reading, language development, emergent literacy, problem solving, and bilingual education.

PRISCILLA A. DRUM is a Professor Emeritus of Education, University of California, Santa Barbara. She can be contacted at RR2 Box 3940, Pahoa, HI 96778. Her specializations are reading and language development.

RICHARD E. MAYER is a Professor in the Department of Psychology, University of California, Santa Barbara, CA 93106. His specialization is educational psychology.

SANG-JIN KANG is an Assistant Professor in the Department of Education, Yonsei University, Seoul, 120-749, Korea. His specializations are statistics and measurement and multilevel modeling.

A pressing issue facing American education today is how to address the instructional needs of language-minority students. The demographics of the American public school population are changing such that more students are now coming from homes in which languages other than English are the primary languages spoken (National Center for Education Statistics, 1995; National Commission on Migrant Education, 1992). In the United States, there are more than 3.5 million non-English-speaking students in kindergarten through Grade 12. In California alone, there are 1.2 million K–12 non-English-speaking students, and that number has more than doubled over the past decade (California State Department of Education, 1992). The largest component of this group is students who speak Spanish at home.

As the demographics of the American public school population change, educators must develop methods of instruction that are sensitive to student needs. This study focuses on one segment of the changing school population, namely students who speak Spanish as their first language. The topic of interest is their orthographic transitioning as they change from learning to spell in Spanish to learning to spell in English. In particular, this research study examines differences in how Spanish-speaking students who are making the transition to English and English-speaking students learn to spell in English.

In this study, we hypothesized that transitioning children whose first language is Spanish may initially operate in English spelling according to a systematic and predictable set of rules. In short, we hypothesized that, when they make errors, transitioning children are likely to use the rules of spelling in Spanish to spell words in English. With experience and proper instruction, their spelling will eventually change from transitional orthography to fully acquired bilingual orthography in both languages.

Examples of Phonetic and Orthographic Sources of Error in Spelling

Given the central role of basic language skills in the development of literacy, we focused on the process of spelling by elementary school students who are transitioning from Spanish to English language use in school. When a transitioning student makes a spelling error, the source may be a lack of knowledge of spelling rules. In this case, the child will make random spelling errors, which we call nonpredicted errors. Alternatively, a student may be correctly applying spelling rules from Spanish that are inappropriate for English. In this case, the child will produce errors that can be predicted on the basis of Spanish phonology and orthography, which we call predicted errors.

For example, consider a writing assignment in which an elementary school student who is transitioning from Spanish to English writes "I tok a lok on cavul." From the point of view of English spelling rules, this student produced three misspelled words, namely, "tok," "lok," and "cavul." However, from the point of view of Spanish spelling rules, the three words represent the closest approximation to sounds in Spanish for the words *took, look*, and *cable*, respectively. Because the "oo" and middle "b" sounds in English do not have identically corresponding sounds in Spanish, Spanish-speaking students may hear them as the closest Spanish sounds ("o" and "v," respectively). In this case, the student is producing the correct spelling of words as they would be pronounced using Spanish phonemes. In short, some spelling errors may result from adjusting English phonology to fit within the Spanish phonological system.

Consider another writing assignment in which a student produces the following sentence: "I was driming of a triqui jero." From the point of view of English spelling rules, there are three spelling errors: "driming," "triqui," and "jero." From the point of view of Spanish spelling rules, however, these three words represent correct applications of Spanish phonological and orthographic rules to the sounds for "dreaming," "tricky," and "hero," respectively, as they are pronounced in English. In short, some spelling errors may result from correct application of Spanish orthographic rules to the sounds of English words, such as using "i" for the /ee/ sound, "qu" for the /k/ sound, and "j" for the /h/ sound.

A Componential Analysis of a Word Dictation Task

In a word dictation task, a word is presented orally and the student writes the word. According to a componential analysis of the cognitive processes involved in the word dictation task, when an English word is presented orally, the following cognitive processes occur:

(a) *construction of a sensory representation*—the student receives the sensory information aurally and holds the input in sensory memory,

(b) *construction of a phonetic representation*—the student converts the sensory information into a phonetic representation in working memory (i.e., a series of phonemes) by matching it with known sounds from long-term memory, and

(c) *construction of an orthographic representation*—the student converts the phonetic representation into an orthographic representation (i.e., a series of letters) in working memory by matching each phoneme with a known letter or letter string from long-term memory.

The student then translates the orthographic representation into a written response.

What are the sources of spelling errors? According to this cognitive model of the word dictation task, errors in the written response can be attributed to errors in the construction of a sensory representation, a phonetic representation, or an orthographic representation. A sensory error occurs when the student has a hearing disorder that prevents the sounds from being heard properly. In this case, the student is unable to produce a sensible written response. Our focus is not on physically based hearing disorders, so we do not explore the role of sensory errors in this study.

A phonetic error occurs when the sensory representation (i.e., the received sound) does not correspond to a known phoneme in long-term memory, so the student is most likely to represent the sound as a known phoneme that is similar to the received sound. For example, for a word containing "sh," a Spanish-speaking student who does not possess the "sh" sound in long-term memory may perceive the sound as "ch." A spelling error will occur if the student then converts the "ch" phoneme into the "ch" digraph orthographically. We refer to this process as a phonetic processing bug.

An orthographic error occurs when the phonetic representation corresponds to a letter or letter string in long-term memory that is different from the English letter or letter string. For example, for a word containing the /h/ phoneme, a Spanish-speaking student may correctly map the "h" sound as a phonetic representation but convert that sound into the *j* grapheme as an orthographic representation. This results in a spelling error if the English spelling is based on the "h" sound being represented orthographically as *h*. We refer to this process as an orthographic processing bug.

Predicted Errors Based on a Cognitive Theory of Transitional Spelling

In this study, we examined phonetic and orthographic sources of spelling errors for Spanish-speaking children who were transitioning to literacy in English. In particular, we examined spelling errors for eight English allophones that could be predicted on the basis of the application of correct Spanish phonological and orthographical rules to English words.

Table 1 lists the actual and predicted spellings for each of five words in each of eight categories. The following subsections present phonological and orthographic descriptions of the eight categories, including explanations for the predicted spelling errors.

Category 1: /k/ Allophone

Velar voiceless stops are represented by the same sound, namely the /k/ phoneme, in both languages. In English, the medial orthographic spelling forms are written as *ck* or *cc*, whereas, in Spanish, the corresponding orthographic forms are *c, k,* and *qu*. The model predicts that Spanish transitional spellers will tend to use the *c* or *k* consonant or the *qu* digraph to spell the /k/ sound.

Category 2: /h/ Allophone

The English voiceless glottal fricative /h/ exists in both languages. The orthographic representation of the sound in English is *h*, whereas, in Spanish, the orthographic representation is *j*. The model predicts that Spanish transitional spellers will tend to substitute the *j* grapheme for the *h* grapheme.

Table 1
Actual and Predicted Spelling for Words in 8 Categories

Actual spelling	Predicted spelling
Category 1 (cc and ck become c, k, qu)	
soccer	socer, soker, soquer
locker	locer, loker, loquer
packet	pacet, paket, paquet
ticket	ticet, tiket, tiquet
tricky	tricy, triky, triqui
Category 2 (h becomes j)	
handball	jandball
happy	japi
hero	jero (giro)
handbag	janbag
handle	jandul
Category 3 (sk becomes sc, squ)	
basket	bascet, basquet
risky	risci, risqui
asking	ascing, asquing
masking	mascing, masquing
frisky	frisci, frisqui
Category 4 (b becomes v)	
cable	cavul
habit	havit
treble	trevul
rebel	revul
fabric	favric
Category 5 (all becomes oll, ol, o, al)	
football	futboll, futbol, futbo, futbal
wall	woll, wol, wo, wal
tall	toll, tol, to, tal
stall	stoll, stol, sto, stal
tall	foll, fol, fo, fal
Category 6 (a becomes ei, ell, ey)	
baby	beibi, bellbi, beybi
case	ceis, cells, ceys
baseball	beisbol, bellsbol, beysbol
flame	fleim, flellm, fleym
vase	veis, vells, veys
Category 7 (oo becomes o, u)	
took	tok, toke
book	bok, boke
looking	loking
soot	sot, sote
rooster	ruster
Category 8 (ea and ee become i)	
dreaming	driming
beanbag	binbag
meaning	mining
beetle	bitul
seam	sim

Category 3: "sk" Blend

The word-internal consonant cluster written as *sk* in English does not exist in Spanish orthography. The closest orthographic sequence in Spanish for the sound of this consonant cluster is *sc* or *squ*, whereas it is represented in English orthography using *sk*. Therefore, the predicted error of the Spanish-speaking students is to replace *sk* with *sc* or *squ*, whereas a person using Spanish orthography would not be expected to represent the "sk" blend using *k*.

Category 4: /b/ Allophone

The English-voiced bilabial stop /b/ exists in both languages and is orthographically represented as *b* in English. In Spanish, when this sound exists in an intervocalic position, it is pronounced as a voiced bilabial fricative and is represented orthographically as *b* or *v*. The Spanish-speaking students are thus expected to process the medial preconsonantal voiced bilabial stop phonetically as a voiced bilabial fricative and to represent it orthographically as *v*.

Category 5: "all" Cluster

First, the /a/ vowel is pronounced as an /a/ sound in English and an /o/ sound in Spanish; the corresponding orthography is *a* in English and *o* in Spanish. Second, the alveolar lateral /l/ is a phoneme in both languages; in English, however, it is orthographically represented as *l* or *ll*, while in Spanish it is orthographically represented only as *l*. When the alveolar lateral /l/ appears at the end of a word as part of the /al/ phoneme, Spanish-speaking students tend to either write it as one letter or eliminate the letters altogether. The predicted errors—*al, o, ol,* and *oll*—can be attributed to both phonetic and orthographic differences between English and Spanish.

Category 6: /e/ Vowel

Some English words containing "a" involve the tense midfrontal vowel represented by /e/. Because the Spanish vowel system involves only central vowels, the /e/ vowel may be perceived by Spanish-speaking students as a diphthong. The closest phonetic representation of this sound in Spanish is [ey], which is represented in Spanish orthography by the digraph *ey, ei,* or *ell*. The *ll* digraph could be used because it represents a voiced palatal fricative /y/, which is part of the [ey] diphthong. Therefore, Spanish-speaking children are expected to spell the words in this category using *ey, ei,* or *ell*.

Category 7: /u/ and /U/ Phonemes

Some English words containing *oo* involve the high back tense vowel /U/, which exists only in the English language. The closest Spanish sound is the midback vowel /u/, represented orthographically in both languages as *o*. Therefore, the predicted error of the Spanish-speaking children is to replace *oo* with *o*, whereas a person using Spanish orthographic rules would not be expected to represent the "o" phoneme using the geminated vowel digraph *oo*. Sometimes Spanish-speaking children may perceive the sound as the high back vowel /u/, represented in Spanish orthography as *u*. When this happens, Spanish-speaking children are also expected to spell this phoneme using the letter *u*.

Category 8: /i/ Phoneme

English words containing *ee* or *ea* involve the same phoneme in English and Spanish, namely the high frontal vowel /i/. In Spanish, this vowel phoneme is written orthographically as *i*. The Spanish-speaking children are expected to spell words in this category using the letter *i* instead of the vowel digraph *ee* or *ea*.

Literature Review

Phonetic Factors Affecting Communicative Competence

Knowledge of phonics constitutes an important component underlying communicative competence. To be communicatively competent in English, a student needs to hear and produce sounds in the same way as the native speakers of the language. Even acknowledging that there are different dialects, accents, and idiolects, native speakers of the language still sound more alike than different. In the process of learning to read, write, and spell, the phonetic qualities of a language represent one of the qualities that contribute to a child's ability to spell words correctly (Adams, 1990; Ehri, 1989).

Although an analysis of the phonological similarities and differences between Mexican Spanish and American English is beyond the scope of this article, there are important differences in the two languages. In particular, some sounds exist in English but not in Spanish (like "sh" in "shoe"), some sounds exist in Spanish but not in English (like "rr" in "correo"), and some sounds exist in both languages (such as "a" in "baby"). For example, if a Spanish-speaking child is attempting to spell an English word such as *shoe*, the child has to first learn to hear the "sh" phoneme, which exists only in English, and then later write it using the correct grapheme.

Another factor that influences transitioning is the relationship between the two orthographic systems that the children are using to spell. In this case, both the English and the Spanish orthographic systems use an alphabetic system. Sometimes the systems have the same letters; as is the case with the phonemes, however, there are symbols that exist in one language but not the other (e.g., *ñ* in Spanish). As a further complication, there are symbols that exist in both languages (such as *v*) but that represent two different sounds, or two sounds that exist in both languages but are represented using two different symbols (like /h/, represented by *h* in English and *j* in Spanish).

Orthographic Factors Affecting Communicative Competence

Knowledge of orthography constitutes a second major component of communicative competence. The English orthography system is written in an alphabetic form that identifies its smallest units phonetically. This orthographic system consists of 26 alphabetic letters (21 consonants and 5 vowels) that can be used to orthographically represent at least 44 phonemes (Stockwell, Bowen, & Martin, 1965). The English orthographic system does not have a strong letter-to-phoneme relationship, and this lack of consistency can be a troubling aspect of English orthography for novices (Bradley, 1969). According to Bradley (1969), when the spoken form of the language changed from Old English, the spelling did not; as a result, many inconsistencies arose between the written and spoken forms of English.

The Spanish alphabet has 30 graphemes, 5 of which are vowels, 22 of which are single letters, and 3 of which are digraphs (Cressey, 1978). In learning the Spanish alphabet, one learns the digraphs as part of the regular alphabet. In the Spanish orthographic system, the 30 graphemes generally represent the 30 sounds that exist in the Spanish phonology system. This relatively lawful correspondence between letters and sounds is not generally true in English. The expectation of a one-to-one sound-to-grapheme correspondence is a major issue when discussing transitional orthography issues because Spanish has a much more phonetically consistent orthographic system than English. Spanish-speaking spellers are at a disadvantage because they have not had much experience dealing with the exceptions to the rules of spelling.

The English system has three vowel systems, one that consists of tense vowels, one that consists of lax vowels, and one that consists of diphthongs. On the other hand, Spanish-speaking spellers are taught to write and read using only one vowel system (i.e., the full vowel system), and, when they encounter other types of vowels, they are at a disadvantage because they do not know how to represent them. An example of this is that the Spanish-speaking spellers would be apt to substitute the two Spanish vowel graphemes for a perceived English diphthong. Rather than write the word *b(a)seball*, the student would be more apt to write the word *b(ei)sball*, *b(ai)sball*, *b(eis)b(ol)*, or *b(ais)b(ol)*. Also, if any two or more vowels appear side by side in the Spanish system, they are usually pronounced in their original forms (as full vowels) and not altered depending on letters preceding or following them.

Understanding Students' Spelling Errors

A Spanish-speaking child who has fully transitioned to English language literacy understands, consciously or unconsciously, the orthographic and phonemic systems in both languages. A thesis of this study is that the "errors" made as a result of the interaction between these two languages should be further examined not just according to the standards of the rules of one language (English) but according to the standards of the rules of both languages. The end result is that transition should be evaluated as a developmental process. Children who make these errors are capable of "getting their message across," and eventually, when full transition is acquired, the frequency of these "errors" will diminish.

Several studies have examined the systematic nature of spelling errors among second-language spellers and have concluded that differences between the two languages are the sources of the spelling errors (Luelsdorff, 1986; Temple, 1979; Zutell & Allen, 1988). Luelsdorff's (1986) project was similar to this one in that he made specific predictions for the spelling errors, but there were two major differences. The first difference was that he used the Slavic languages instead of Spanish, and the second difference was that he did not have a control group to serve as a contrast for his predictions. Temple (1979) examined the English spelling errors of Spanish-speaking students, but his study lacked some of the methodological and theoretical features of our study. He did not have a control group of English speakers with which to compare the spelling results of his population and to affirm that the findings were indeed a result of the spelling systems. Also, he did not administer a controlled spelling test but instead described the errors that the children made, and he did not provide a theoretical analysis of phonetic aspects or the properties of the two languages.

The closest study to the one described in this report was conducted by Zutell and Allen (1988), who investigated the effect of Spanish pronunciation and spelling rules on children's English spelling strategies. Specifically, Zutell and Allen proposed that the students in their study would "generate unique patterns of errors based on their own pronunciation of English words and on the possible interference from their knowledge of Spanish letter-name-sound relationships" (p. 334). One hundred eight bilingual students in Grades 2, 3, and 4 were given a list of 20 words, with five categories of errors and four words per category. The five categories of errors included long "e" vowel (as in *seat*) and long "a" (as in *case*), the initial consonants "y" and "h," and finally the consonant blend "sp." Three of the categories in the Zutell and Allen study were used in this study (long "a," long "e," and "h"). Because there was no English-speaking control group, there was no way to ascertain that the errors were indeed Spanish-influenced errors. Another difference between the two studies is that Zutell and Allen (1988) predicted only one misspelling for each word, whereas in this study there were sometimes two or three predicted spellings based on a cognitive analysis of transitional spelling. Furthermore, in the study reported here, the predictions were based on phonological and orthographic rules for differences in spelling between the two languages, but Zutell and Allen (1988) discussed orthographic differences only from a letter name perspective.

Conclusion

This study has both theoretical and practical implications. On the theoretical side, the results show that students who are transitioning from Spanish to English may misspell English words by systematically applying the phonological and orthographical rules of Spanish. In our study, differences in the pattern of spelling errors of Spanish-speaking and English-speaking students can be understood by recognizing that Spanish-speaking students sometimes apply correct Spanish phonologic and orthographic rules to the spelling of English words. Aside from these kinds of errors (which we call predicted errors), Spanish-speaking and English-speaking students do not generally differ in how they misspell English words (which we call nonpredicted errors). Overall, the pattern of results provides support for a cognitive model of transitional spelling based on phonological and orthographic processes.

On the practical side, these results provide implications for fostering English language literacy in Spanish-speaking students. Our study of spelling errors provides evidence for the idea that acquiring literacy in a second language is tied to and builds upon literacy in one's first language. Teachers of language-minority students would benefit from recognizing when students' errors in English occur as a result of their applying rules that are correct in their native language. For example, teachers of limited-English-proficient Latino students would benefit from knowing the phonological and orthographic rules of Spanish so that they could better recognize predictable spelling errors. Rather than simply marking a predicted error as incorrect, the teacher could explicitly point out that the phonological or orthographic rule in English is different from the one in Spanish. In conclusion, both teachers and test designers who are working with bilingual and transitioning populations need knowledge of orthographic and phonological transitioning errors so that they can differentiate transitioning errors from random errors.

Overall, as would be expected, children from lower grade levels made more spelling errors than did children from higher grade levels. For some categories of sounds, there was an interaction pattern in which native English-speaking children improved more than Spanish-speaking children or in which English-speaking students produced low error rates at both grade levels. It may take more time for Spanish-speaking children to improve their English spelling than it does for English-speaking children, presumably because Spanish-speaking students must learn how to spell in two languages, whereas English-speaking students can concentrate on learning just one language.

A limitation of this study is that it is based on a relatively small sample taken from a single region in the United States. However, it should also be noted that approximately one third of the Spanish-speaking students in the United States live in California, and, of these, almost half live in Los Angeles County, the site of our sample.

Students who are transitioning from Spanish to English language have a somewhat more difficult task than monolingual English-speaking students. The Spanish-speaking students in this study had at least partial exposure to phonology and orthography in both languages and were transferring these skills to English. The goal for the monolingual spellers is to eventually master the phonological and orthographic rules for just one language. Bilingual spellers, however, have much more to accomplish. They have to understand the functional values of orthographic images in English and Spanish, which means that the spellers should be able to apply these values to the words when encountered in both languages.

Students who are engaged in transitional orthography have had partial exposure to a second language and sometimes are using skills used in their primary language to spell words in their second language. This is the point at which the "errors" are being made. The errors, however, are a part of problem solving and also a part of learning, because the process that leads to these errors is a result of communicative competence in several areas. What the Spanish-to-English transitioning students have not acquired, however, is strategic knowledge that prepares them with a plan about where and/or when to apply these rules correctly. This kind of strategic knowledge results from properly mediated learning. Moreover, Barnitz (1982) stated that, in addition to understanding phonemic differences between the two languages, it is also important to understand more complex structures such as morphemes and the roles that they play in orthography later on.

Many authors have discussed the issue of bilingualism and that of bilingual orthography, but few have addressed how to teach transitional orthography so that bilingual students will maintain their orthographic skills in both languages. For example, Hailer (1976) argued that children should initially be taught in their own languages and then gradually acquire English language skills. The goal of such a program should be to convert gradually from the native language of instruction to the English language medium of instruction, but emphasis is put on the fact that it must be gradual and strategic.

For the most part, the immigrants discussed in this study plan to and usually do retain their own individual cultures through language, literacy, food, and so forth. They are usually in constant contact with their homeland, because it is connected to the United States. Thus, these immigrants cannot be expected to discard their original language for English; both languages are still of use to them, and they are expected to function in both environments. A good transitional orthography program should help to ease the process, because the rules of pronunciation and orthography in both languages are recognized. Assistance at home for literacy is an important issue, especially when parents may be literate in Spanish but not in English

(Ylenalto, 1980). Finally, Hornberger (1989) argued that transitional orthography programs should be voluntary rather than forced, because the eventual results of a program stem from how it is seen by the learner.

In conclusion, if transitional spellers do not learn correctly, they may remain in the transitional stage, and the "orthographic pidgin" will then become a permanent structure, similar to an orthographic Creole. Research such as ours suggests that teachers who are familiar with Spanish phonology and orthography will be able to help Spanish-to-English transitional spellers achieve competence in both languages.

Notes

This study was made possible by a Graduate Research Mentorship Program Fellowship awarded by the Graduate Division of the University of California, Santa Barbara. We wish to thank Almedia Jacqueline Toribio, Guillermo Solano-Flores, and Maria Araceli Ruiz-Primo for their consultations concerning Spanish phonology and orthography. We also are grateful to the principal, teachers, and students of the cooperating elementary school, who must remain anonymous in order to protect student confidentiality.

[1]There were 11 boys and 8 girls in the younger Spanish group, 7 boys and 7 girls in the younger English group, 12 girls and 7 boys in the older Spanish group, and 11 boys and 9 girls in the older English group. A chi-square test revealed that the proportion of boys and girls in the Spanish and English groups did not differ significantly, $\chi^2(1) = 0.421$, *ns*. Students classified as limited English proficient lacked basic communication skills in English, but their level of Spanish proficiency was not assessed. All Spanish-speaking students were Latino; most English-speaking students were Caucasian, some were Asian American, and none were African American.

[2]Welch tests (Howell, 1992) conducted on the data in Table 2 produced results generally consistent with the results of the analyses of variance reported in the text.

References

Adams, M. J. (1990). *Beginning to read: Thinking and learning about print*. Cambridge, MA: MIT Press.

Barnitz, J. (1982). Orthographies, bilingualisms, and learning to read English as a second language. *Reading Teacher, 35*, 560–567.

Bradley, H. (1969). *On the relations between spoken and written language, with a special reference to English*. Folcroft, PA: Folcroft Press.

California State Department of Education. (1992). *Language census report for California public schools*. Sacramento: Author.

Cressey, W. (1978). *The sound patterns of English*. New York: Harper & Row.

Ehri, L. C. (1989). The development of spelling knowledge and its role in reading acquisition and reading disability. *Journal of Learning Disabilities, 22*, 356–365.

Hailer, R. M. (1976). *Meeting the needs of the bilingual child. A historical perspective of the nation's first transitional bilingual education law: Chapter 71A of the Acts of 1971, Commonwealth of Massachusetts*. Boston: Massachusetts State Department of Education.

Hornberger, N. H. (1989). Continua of biliteracy. *Review of Educational Research, 59*, 271–296.

Howell, D. C. (1992). *Statistical methods for psychology* (3rd ed.). Belmont, CA: Duxbury Press.

Luelsdorff, P. (1986). *Constraints of error variables in grammar: Bilingual misspelling orthographies*. Amsterdam: Benjamins.

National Center for Education Statistics. (1995). *A first look: Findings from the

National Assessment of Educational Progress. Washington, DC: Office of Educational Research and Improvement.

National Commission on Migrant Education. (1992). *Invisible children: A portrait of migrant education in the United States.* Washington, DC: Author.

Stockwell, R. P., Bowen, J. D., & Martin, J. W. (1965). *The sounds of English and Spanish.* Chicago: University of Chicago Press.

Temple, C. (1979, November). *Learning to spell in Spanish.* Paper presented at the National Reading Conference, San Antonio, TX.

Ylenalto, O. (1980). Reading ability and differences in the middle and upper primary school. In J. Kavanagh & R. Venezky (Eds.), *Orthography, reading, and dyslexia.* Baltimore: University Park Press.

Zutell, J., & Allen, J. (1988). The English spelling strategies of Spanish-speaking bilingual children. *TESOL Quarterly, 22,* 333–340.

Manuscript received March 16, 1996
Revision received June 16, 1996
Accepted June 24, 1996

Excerpted from *American Educational Research Journal,
Vol. 33, No. 4, Winter 1996*

Vocabulary

 Vocabulary Teaching and Learning in a
Seventh-Grade Literature-Based Classroom

Janis M. Harmon

Vocabulary teaching and learning in a seventh-grade literature-based classroom

This program supported vocabulary teaching and learning both explicitly and implicitly. Varying classroom configurations expanded learners' word knowledge and enhanced their word learning abilities.

Vocabulary is an important area of concern for teachers, because children who know many words are more likely to be competent readers than those with limited vocabularies. As children approach the middle grades and become more proficient in decoding and recognizing known words, vocabulary acquisition focuses more on meaning than recognition (Chall, 1987). From then on, children learn new words for known concepts and new words for new concepts in various content areas and in more sophisticated literature books. The need for a rich vocabulary base becomes even more important during the ensuing middle and secondary school years.

Word learning is a complex task that occurs in many settings. These settings range from incidental occurrences in oral and written contexts to direct instruction. Nagy and Anderson (1984) estimated that the average student in the middle grades and beyond must acquire approximately 3,000 new words yearly in order to stay current with each succeeding grade level. As a result, many vocabulary experts assert that learning from context plays a significant part in the student's yearly acquisition of such a large volume of words. Incidental word learning from oral and written contexts seems to occur incrementally over a long period of time with multiple exposures to words (Jenkins, Stein, & Wysocki, 1984; Nagy, 1988; Nagy, Anderson, & Herman, 1987; Nagy, Herman, & Anderson, 1985).

Direct instruction is also an important aspect of vocabulary acquisition. Studies have shown that direct instruction informs reading comprehension when children can integrate new words with other conceptual knowledge, are exposed to multiple encounters with the new word in natural print environments, and can process the new word in a meaningful manner (Beck & McKeown, 1991; Beck, McKeown, & Omanson, 1987; Nagy, 1988; Stahl & Fairbanks, 1986).

Because many curricular frameworks emphasize a literature-based approach for language instruction, questions arise as to how such programs facilitate vocabulary development. What components in a literature-based program foster vocabulary growth? How are these components implemented? How do teacher beliefs and perspectives about vocabulary influence the word learning opportunities in this type of reading program?

As a way to answer these questions, I studied the literature-based program of one seventh-grade teacher, with a focus on vocabulary teaching and learning. In this article, I will explain the shared components of vocabulary development and literature-based programs and then describe different word learning opportunities that emerged in this program.

Shared components of vocabulary development and literature-based programs

Literature-based programs use trade books as major instructional materials for enhancing reading development (Hiebert & Colt, 1989; Scharer, 1992; Zarrillo, 1989). Differing interpretations have created some "diversity among teachers' philosophical stances" (Zarrillo, 1989, p. 23) as well as variation in the degree to which specific components and patterns of literature-based instruction are emphasized (Hiebert & Colt, 1989). Nevertheless, the following characteristics consistently appear in different studies as descriptors for literature-based classrooms (Eeds & Wells, 1989; Hiebert & Colt, 1989; Huck, 1992; Huck, Hepler, & Hickman, 1993; McGee, 1992; Peterson & Eeds, 1990):

➤ Use of trade books as the primary material source

➤ Student response to literature in diversified ways

➤ Individualized reading time with self-pacing and self-selection of literature

➤ In-depth discussion groups

➤ Read-alouds

➤ Group projects

➤ Informal assessment/conferences

➤ Teacher-student interaction—whole class, group, and individual

➤ Direct instruction of strategies

➤ Literacy for authentic reasons

Important overlapping issues indicate how well these literature-based reading programs can inform vocabulary development. Three major components are described as (a) instruction or learning episodes that expand knowledge schemas, (b) social interactions and interventions, and (c) wide reading (see Table 1).

Learning episodes include those activities involving direct instruction of reading strategies, specifically independent word learning strategies for vocabulary development. Other situations arise in authentic, purposeful reading that call for direct instruction of specific word meanings. As students respond to literature in diverse ways, they should also develop awareness and appreciation for learning new words and for eventually using them in oral and written discourse across a variety of learning tasks. In this way we enhance procedural knowledge by teaching independent word learning strategies, declarative knowledge by emphasizing specific word meanings, and conditional knowledge by cultivating an awareness of and appreciation for learning new words (Paris, Lipson, & Wixson, 1994).

The second component stresses the importance of social interactions and interventions in the classroom community. Grand conversations (Peterson & Eeds, 1990) about shared readings of literature can include rich discussions about new words that students select themselves. Group projects enable students to work collaboratively in exploring their responses to the literature and in satisfying their curiosity about unfamiliar words. Furthermore, informal assessment procedures can also facilitate teacher interventions in helping individual students learn about new words.

Wide reading is repeatedly included as one important quality of effective vocabulary instruction (Blachowicz & Lee, 1991; Nagy, 1988) and is discussed in reports on literature-based programs (Galda, 1988). We know that time spent engaged in independent reading can have positive effects upon children's reading proficiency. It promotes inciden-

Table 1
Parallel and shared components of vocabulary development and literature-based reading programs

Vocabulary development	Literature-based programs
Learning episodes/instruction	
expanding knowledge schemas	
Direct instruction of independent word learning strategies	Direct instruction of strategies
Direct instruction of specific word meanings	Literacy for authentic reasons
Cultivation of an awareness, appreciation, and understanding for learning new words and using them in oral and written discourse	Student response to literature in diverse ways
Social interactions and interventions	
Rich discussions about new words	In-depth discussion groups (Grand Conversations)
Informal assessment and teacher intervention	Informal assessment
Teacher-student interactions fostering responses about important words	Teacher-student interactions—whole class, group, individual
Group projects	Group projects
Wide reading	
Promotion of incidental learning of words	Use of trade books as the primary material source
Practice for acquiring higher levels of word mastery in diverse settings (active engagement with words)	Independent reading time with self-pacing and self-selection
Promotion of lexical access (automaticity)	Read-alouds

tal learning of words through written contexts and provides meaningful practice for acquiring higher levels of word mastery in diverse settings. This active engagement with words also enhances lexical access and automaticity.

What we know about word meaning acquisition through direct instruction and incidental learning from context can inform the types of reading programs we offer middle school learners. It appears that these overlapping issues of learning episodes, the social climate of the classroom, and wide reading of literature hold important implications for how literature-based reading programs are fruitful grounds for promoting vocabulary development.

Purpose and description of the study

This article describes a study that explored vocabulary learning opportunities in a seventh-grade literature-based reading program. The purpose of the study was to closely examine the explicit and im-

plicit actions of the teacher as well as student responses to vocabulary teaching and learning events. This report provides information concerning word learning engagements embedded within a literature-based framework and how these opportunities paralleled the shared components.

I conducted the study at Katherine Stinson Middle School in San Antonio, Texas, USA. The principal, Debbie Sonnen, recommended one teacher, Denise Staton, because of her talent and excellent reputation in teaching reading. After Denise agreed to participate, I observed her and her students during every class meeting for approximately 6 months, from August until the end of February. My role as an investigator can be described as passive participant or complete observer, as I maintained an unobtrusive stance during my visits (Bogdan & Biklen, 1992). This stance was important because I wanted to observe explicit as well as implicit messages about vocabulary that may have been part of the classroom discourse. As this was a qualitative study, data collection occurred across multiple sources. Through interviews, prolonged observations, and taped transcriptions of classroom interactions, guiding questions and responses produced important information concerning vocabulary teaching and learning (Bogdan & Biklen, 1992; Patton, 1990).

Teacher beliefs about reading and vocabulary

Denise described her reading program as literature-based because trade books were the "textbooks of the program." She believed in allowing students time to read self-selected books at their own pace and for their own enjoyment. Her program emphasized the pleasure and satisfaction gained from reading. Denise's major focus for her program was critical thinking and problem solving, with little emphasis on segmented skills-based activities. She expressed her view about reading and the use of literature in the following manner:

> All of our work comes out of the literature—the vocabulary, the study skills, the research—everything has its origin in whatever books the students are reading. To me that's what a literature-based approach means. We don't use a basal reader and we don't do drills and study sheets. Our approach is broad where we are looking more at the thinking skills of the students. We really want them to look at what happens when they are reading; we want them to think about their own thinking. We want to find out what is going on in their minds, and we cannot do that with true-false statements and multiple-choice questions.

Denise's beliefs about vocabulary teaching and learning were situated within the broader purpose of promoting critical reading and reasoning. She felt that vocabulary was important even though it was not a major aspect of her reading program. She believed that students could not increase their vocabulary effectively from contrived lists of unrelated words. Rather, she asserted that words are more readily learned when students make connections to related ideas and other words. She also advocated the use of an individualized approach where students find words to study from their personal readings.

The reading program

Major components of Denise's program were Sustained Silent Reading (SSR) in which students

Table 2
Reading program

Components of the program	Word learning opportunities
Whole-class activities Teacher-directed lessons Teacher-selected short stories, excerpts, and poems related to a common theme Integrated instructional episodes addressing literary elements and related writing events	**Whole-class activities** Social interactions between teacher and students to promote word knowledge acquisition Text clarification Exposure to implicit modeling of ways to define words Opportunities to use words in speaking and writing events
Group activities Student-directed group sessions Self-selected books from a required list	**Group activities** Mobilization of independent word learning strategies Self-generated meaning constructions Shared meaning constructions Exposure to peer-selected words in expressive and receptive language Active word learning opportunities
Independent reading Sustained Silent Reading Self-selected readings	**Independent reading** Mobilization of independent word learning strategies Self-generated meaning constructions Active word learning opportunities

read self-selected trade books, specific activities with teacher-selected readings and discussions that focused on critical thinking, book discussion groups, and integrated instructional episodes addressing literary elements and related writing events. Classes met three times a week for 75 minutes per session. SSR lasted for approximately 20–30 minutes during each class meeting. The rest of the class time was devoted to the other literacy activities. Embedded within each program component were word learning opportunities as illustrated in Table 2.

These levels included whole-class teacher-directed lessons, student-directed group sessions in which one group member served as a "vocabulary enricher" (Daniels, 1994), and opportunities for word learning during independent reading with self-selected books. During whole-class sessions, Denise selected words from short stories to discuss as a prereading activity. With the book discussion groups, learners who served as "vocabulary enrichers" were responsible for selecting words to discuss in their groups. These reflections about new words were springboards for critical discussions about important concepts and literary elements in the readings.

Outcomes of vocabulary learning during teacher-directed instructional episodes focused on text clarification and exposure to teacher-selected words that were central to the story. When students engaged in more learner-centered activities, such as book discussion groups and independent reading, learning behaviors and outcomes shifted. In group sessions where students participated as vocabulary enrichers and group members, learning outcomes resulted in the mobilization of independent word learning strategies, self-generated and shared meaning constructions, and exposure to peer-selected words. Students had a vested interest in their own learning and that of the group, because they were responsible for creating specific opportunities to learn new concepts and ideas. Independent reading during Sustained Silent Reading provided another word learning opportunity for them. Learning outcomes during this time included the mobilization of independent word learning strategies and opportunities for active word learning through incidental encounters with unfamiliar words.

Whole-class instructional episodes

Teacher actions. Vocabulary instructional episodes were embedded within class discussions about stories. Denise's actions became major components in the process of vocabulary teaching and learning. During teacher-directed discussions, she related, explained, and questioned students about specific terminology. Students, in turn, reacted by activating their prior knowledge and past experiences, by making connections, and by asking questions about targeted words and related concepts. Outcomes in terms of vocabulary learning and meaning construction pivoted around the teacher's personal store of words, her beliefs about vocabulary instruction and acquisition, and her responses to students' inherent curiosity about words. She was a major vocabulary source and stimulus for students.

During these instructional episodes with vocabulary, Denise consistently tried to establish common references and links to what students knew. She sometimes generalized actions on a personal level to help students identify with new ideas. She also guided students back to the context in which the words were used. She would even tell students when context was not helpful in figuring out meanings, such as with the word *restitution* used in this sentence: "He specializes in requiring public acts of contrition and *restitution*." Denise related the word to something students would understand by stating, "*Restitution* is repayment. For example, if you steal something from someone and you have to make *restitution*, what would you have to do?" Such statements blended the use of synonyms and familiar scenarios to help learners understand the meaning of the word.

Denise used a variety of techniques to clarify word meanings through explanation. These techniques included the use of synonyms, brief descriptions, examples and nonexamples, rephrasing, repetition, associations, and unique expressions. Similar to direct questioning, these loosely woven categories represented Denise's way of clarifying terms that were central to the targeted readings.

Because Denise preferred to let students fashion their own definitions of words instead of using what they found in dictionaries, she frequently modeled definitions by using synonyms. Every vocabulary instructional episode contained examples of synonyms. Some included "compete" for *contend*, "winding and twisting" for *sinuous*, and "urges" for *exhorts*. She also explained word meanings with short, descriptive phrases, such as "army camp supplies" for *commissary stores* and "a machine in human form" for *android*. With each short definition, however, Denise elaborated, extended, and clarified meanings to make sure students had ample opportunity to make connections with the words. When words confused students, Denise offered important examples to describe meanings, as in the following excerpt:

> Have you ever seen an elderly person who has arthritis and their hands are all twisted? That's *gnarled*. Or have you ever seen a tree trunk that the trunk itself is twisted? That's *gnarled*.

When Denise used a certain word in her explanations, she often followed with an elaboration for the benefit of those who were uncertain of the word's meaning. Because of the frequent use of this technique, rephrasing was an intrinsic component of Denise's perceptions of how to explain concepts to students. The following decontextualized excerpts illustrate Denise's use of rephrasing.

> Let's start *recounting* the events of the story. *We will tell about the beginning, middle, and end.*
> This is an *excerpt—one tiny piece.*

In extended class discussions, Denise repeated general utility words frequently. Whether done purposefully or incidentally, such repetitions served to help students internalize word meanings. Denise also clarified word meanings through associations instead of definitions. In reference to the word *contend*, she asked students if they ever *contended in athletic events, academic events, and even poker games.* For the word *humble*, she asked the question: "If you have a *humble* home, is it like a castle?"

These teacher-directed discussions about words were a natural part of the classroom dialogue about the selected readings and occurred frequently as pre-reading activities. Apparently, Denise's beliefs concerning the importance of word knowledge in enhancing comprehension informed her decision to pursue these discussions. The ways in which she framed her questions and used familiar situations to help learners make connections proved essential in making this a worthwhile learning engagement. While focusing on specific word meanings, she also inadvertently modeled specific ways to define words. Students, in turn, used these methods to explain word meanings during other classroom episodes.

Student engagement. Because learners took their cues from the teacher, their responses were directly influenced by class discussions of required readings and specific writing assignments. A close examination of student responses during these episodes revealed several cognitive processes in use. Overall, they demonstrated engagement in activating prior knowledge when they used words recently discussed in class. They made connections by defining terms in their own words, using examples to define words, relating words to other languages, and engaging in word play. Furthermore, students asked questions about certain words when they were confused about the meaning. They used words mentioned in previous class events, unsolicited words described as general utility words used by mature language users, domain-specific words, and school-related words.

One segment of the program was a unit on heroes that lasted for 12 weeks. The six short stories selected by Denise depicted heroes from different cultures. Denise deliberately chose these stories so that students could reflect upon different perspectives about heroism. The focal point of this unit was a hero characteristics chart, which emerged from class discussions about each hero. Descriptive words listed on the chart were continually referred to in discussions across all six required readings. Furthermore, each successive reading of a story brought forth more words. Table 3 illustrates a segment of this chart.

As a result, students frequently used these words in both their talking and writing. Words such as *confidence, determination, self-reliance, achievement, loyalty,* and related derivations were used freely by students because they had been highlighted repeatedly across all hero stories. This repetition and

Table 3
Hero characteristics chart

Traits	Yudhisthir	Siegfried	Scarface	Luke Skywalker	Harriet Tubman	Judge
Skillful	x	x	x		x	
Intelligent	x	x			x	x
Physically strong	x	x	x	x	x	
Mentally strong	x	x			x	
Brave					x	
Loyal			x	x		
Confident				x		
Determined	x	x	x	x	x	x
Respectful		x	x		x	x
Persistent					x	
Honorable						x
Responsible						x
Patient						x
Good judgment						x
Positive						x
Open mind						x

continual referral to all descriptors on the heroes chart offered students rich opportunities through multiple exposures to use the terms in meaningful and functional ways. In addition, students had to think critically about what these words meant in different situations. For example, in a discussion about Harriet Tubman, one student rationalized that she was intelligent but not in the sense of "like school," but rather that she "was intelligent because she knew which way to go."

The use of these terms extended into their writing. At the end of the unit, they wrote an essay describing a personal hero. The following excerpts are representative samples of how students used descriptive words previously discussed in class.

> I think a hero is someone who's caring and also shows leadership in whatever he or she tries to conquer. A hero is also *persistent* in his or her task. Some of the characteristics that I value in a hero is the leadership and skill that a hero shows. I also value the *persistency* or the refusing to give up until he or she conquers the task. (David)

> Harriet Tubman was a very smart person. She was very skillful. She was not always *obedient* to others. What makes her so *admirable* is that she led so many people out of slavery. She is strong, loyal, and *confident*. (Amy)

> My hero is my dad. Both his parents were dead when he was 17 so he had to learn *self-reliance* and *responsibility* at a very young age. My dad and the heroes share other character traits such as *honesty, confidence,* and *dedication* and the ability to stay cool under pressure. There would be no *inspirations* and no dreams without heroes. (Mary Ann)

Students experienced multiple exposures of words describing heroes. The use of these terms in their writing appeared to be a natural progression from previous opportunities to listen, speak, and read about words that described different people from different cultures. This integrated approach enhanced and reinforced students' word knowledge.

During an instructional episode with "The Pledge of Allegiance," a discussion about the meaning of the word *justice* enabled students to make interesting connections.

Teacher:	All right, boys and girls. Steven wants to talk about *justice*.
Steven:	It's laws.
Heath:	*Justice* is like what you deserve. If somebody kills another person, then they deserve to pay the penalty for it. If like somebody hurts you, then you know they should pay the consequences.
Joanie:	It's like fairness for everybody. So everybody will have equal rights.
Teacher:	Fairness for everybody. At school through all the years I've been teaching, I've had students say that some teachers are not fair. I try to be fair but what does *fair* mean? Steven?

Steven:	Like equal, the same thing.
Teacher:	Can you treat every person exactly the same?
Whole class:	No.
Chad:	I think *justice* is in the eye of the beholder.
Teacher:	I know what you're saying. The person who is making the judgment and saying whether it's fair or unfair, it's in their eyes. Janine?
Janine:	I was going to say what you were saying about fair and equal being the same thing. But it wouldn't be really fair if like somebody who murders somebody got the exact same punishment as somebody who stole a piece of gum.
Teacher:	Okay. So should the punishment fit the crime?
Whole Class:	Yes.
Teacher:	Someone this morning said that in some countries the penalty for theft is to cut your hand off. They used to do that a long time ago.
Heath:	They still do in Iran and Iraq.
Teacher:	Where did you hear that?
Heath:	Because my uncle was in Desert Storm and he went to Saudi Arabia and he told us that's true.
Teacher:	That's pretty severe punishment, but will it keep them from stealing again? In our country that's cruel and unusual punishment. Jill?
Jill:	In social studies last year, like in the early years...[pause]
Teacher:	Medieval times?
Jill:	Yes. The punishment would be exactly what you did to them. Like if you killed a person, then you get killed.

This excerpt illustrates how students made important connections about the concept of *justice* in terms of what they already knew about fairness and equality for all. They tapped into schemas about universal sayings ("eye for an eye"), stories from relatives, and lessons from past history classes. They used their knowledge to contribute to the group effort of exploring the meaning of *justice*. Resulting social interactions among the teacher and students provided fertile ground for the enhancement of word learning through relevant and meaningful connections with prior knowledge and past experiences.

When students mobilized their conceptual knowledge and accompanying vocabulary about certain topics, they sometimes made inaccurate connections. For instance, Michael always thought that the Underground Railroad was the forerunner of today's *subway*. Quite often, however, their connections showed originality and insights. For example, Stephanie made connections to another language when she stated that *Negro* meant black in Spanish.

As they activated, connected, and questioned vocabulary during the course of class discussions, students also experienced those serendipitous moments when they played with words. One student caught the attention of others when he used the word *wiseness* instead of wisdom. Subsequent chuckles and smiles indicated that students appreciated and liked this word. These episodes heightened their attention and promoted inquiry about new words.

Book discussion groups

As part of a 12-week multicultural unit, students became participants in specific book discussion groups with books including *Bearstone* by Will Hobbs (1989), *Children of the River* by Linda Crew (1991), *Dragonwings* by Lawrence Yep (1993), *Jemmy* by Jon Hassler (1988), and *Roll of Thunder, Hear My Cry* by Mildred D. Taylor (1976). Table 4 outlines student engagement in these book discussion groups.

Denise used the idea of literature circles as described by Daniels (1994). She defined and discussed the roles of discussion director, literary luminary, connector, summarizer, vocabulary enricher, and process checker. The vocabulary enricher was responsible for selecting interesting or unfamiliar words in the readings and for conducting group discussions about these words. Once again, vocabulary was only one aspect of this activity, as learners engaged in discussing literary elements, making personal connections, and summarizing important events.

The following actions represent a variety of tactics students employed based upon their own interpretation of the role of vocabulary enricher:

➤ Some vocabulary enrichers defined words before the group sessions by using their own knowledge or by referring to the dictionary.

➤ Some vocabulary enrichers relied on the group to provide the definitions.

➤ Several vocabulary enrichers read their definitions to the group.

Table 4
Student engagement during book discussion groups

Student actions

Selected	Activated	Related
general utility words	background knowledge	sentence context
foreign words	prior knowledge	passage context
proper names		real-life experiences
domain-specific words		multiple sources
		multiple attempts

Modeled	Explained	Questioned
teacher actions	dictionary definitions	themselves
independent word-	synonyms	other students
learning strategies	brief phrases	

➤ A few vocabulary enrichers explained the words to the group.

➤ Some vocabulary enrichers either read aloud the passage containing the targeted words or asked other group members to read.

Students equated this role of vocabulary enricher in ways that parallel teacher actions. They targeted, defined, read, and explained words to the group. They even questioned the group's background knowledge about the words. For example, one student prepared herself for the group session by consulting a dictionary for meanings of her targeted words. During group discussion time, she presented each word by reading the sentence. Then she asked if anyone wanted to comment about the word. After listening to these comments, she read her definition. These actions were evident when the group discussed the word *expounding* in the following passage from *Roll of Thunder, Hear My Cry*:

> "See, fellows, there's a system to getting out of work," T.J. was *expounding* as I sat down.
>
> "Jus' don't be 'round when it's got to be done. See, you should do like me." (p. 72)

Lynette, the vocabulary enricher, pronounced the word *expounding* and then read the sentence to the group. This discussion followed:

Lynette: Okay. Do y'all like have any guesses to what it means?
Sam: Wait. Where is it again?
Janelle: I'll guess what it means.
Jill: Well, what is it?
Janelle: His ego is boasting and he knows exactly how to get out of working.

Lynette: Well, the definition I found was he did it with explaining. That's the definition I found. It says "state, interpret, or explain." So I thought explain was like the best one.

Discussions about other words followed this same pattern. Lynette was prepared with definitions and took the time to clarify these meanings in reference to the text. Members of this group were willing to take risks in constructing word meanings and sharing these constructions with the group. The ways in which words were described were similar to the way Denise defined words. Students used synonyms and brief phrases based upon dictionary definitions.

In other sessions, vocabulary enrichers found words but did not search for meanings. Rather, they chose to rely on group members to generate word meanings. In these episodes, some definitions remained at a general level of description. Examples include the word *Ute* defined as "an Indian group" and the word *irrigate* as "water your crops." Group members were satisfied with these general meanings and did not engage in any further discussion.

In general, vocabulary enrichers relied on the dictionary as well as their peers as sources of word knowledge. Some students adopted a "teacher" stance as they provided information to their groups. Others simply provided words and depended upon group members for definitions. As group members, students followed the lead of the vocabulary enricher in terms of the amount of discussion that emerged. When the vocabulary enricher asked for comments, students offered their ideas about targeted words as they interpreted and clarified points for others. When they interacted with one another, students generated word meanings in the form of synonyms, brief phrases, and examples. Again, these definitions were similar to the teacher's way of explaining words.

When Marian was vocabulary enricher, she initially shared her meaning of a word and then asked others to share their interpretations. For example, for the word *housemother* from *Bearstone* by Will Hobbs, the group members elicited descriptions, such as "a director like the main person in orphanages," "a matron," "a foster mother," and "a person in charge of a group home." As sources of knowledge, students used their own background knowledge about *housemother* to express these meanings. As a result, the various configurations for the word reinforced and expanded their own schemas. Furthermore, the social interaction among group members stimulated discussions that produced these variations in the meaning of the word.

On several occasions, students defined words in a syntactically correct fashion. For example, when Heath looked up *precipice* in the dictionary, he was quick to use a phrase from the definition as a substitute for the word. He told group members that the word meant "a very steep or overhanging place; a hazardous situation." Then he read the sentence containing *precipice* in the following manner:

> Cloyd put the smooth stone in his pocket and started back across the very steep overhanging place. (Hobbs, 1989, p. 16)

Group members agreed that the meaning fit the context of the sentence. This pattern of word meaning construction occurred across several book discussion groups.

On other occasions students used multiple sources and multiple attempts to construct word meanings that satisfied the group. For example, when Katherine served as vocabulary enricher, she targeted the word *erratically* in this passage:

> The saw didn't want to start. After dozens of attempts Cloyd made it idle *erratically*, but it cut out as soon as he tried the throttle. (Hobbs, 1989, p. 55)

Because the word was challenging to the group, students elicited several meaning attempts simul-

taneously. After David read the sentence, he used arm motions to demonstrate what he thought *erratically* meant, while Terry commented that it could mean "faster." Tom thought that it could mean "odd." Katherine then offered her dictionary definition of "deviating from what is ordinary or standard." With these four attempts, group members were satisfied that they understood what the word meant. They also talked about how some words, like *erratically*, were difficult to define, because it was hard to articulate a clear meaning without using examples or physical motions.

Overall, students worked collaboratively in these group sessions to construct word meanings when the vocabulary enricher assumed a role of group facilitator rather than "teacher director." They shared their opinions and interpretations of words and listened to the ideas of others. By focusing on these student-targeted words, they had the opportunity to engage in authentic word learning experiences where they modeled their own personal strategies for their peers. Denise's role during these book discussion groups was that of facilitator. She visited each group, offering clarification when needed, informally assessing student actions, and monitoring group progress.

Independent reading

Sustained Silent Reading presented opportunities for students to learn new words. This context enabled them to self-select texts and to engage in personal reading for at least 20–30 minutes during each class session. As an avenue for word learning, independent reading time allowed learners to actively use their strategies as they encountered unfamiliar words. It also offered opportunities for multiple exposures to new words. Students also kept personal logs where they recorded information about new words they encountered during reading.

Insights about vocabulary teaching and learning

As participants in a literature-based reading program, these students engaged in a variety of literacy tasks with a focus on critical reading and problem solving. Word learning opportunities were situated within this broad context and provided different engagements for the students. Denise emphasized knowledge of specific words in prereading discussions about stories. Students in turn used these words in subsequent writing assignments. Learners also benefited from activities where individual word learning strategies were highlighted. Specifically, students practiced these strategies in book discussion groups and in personal reading during Sustained Silent Reading.

Learners openly displayed their independent word learning strategies as they participated in book discussion groups. The roles of vocabulary enricher as well as group members served as ways for learners to use their word learning strategies to construct meaning and to contribute to group discussions. These social events enabled learners to actively engage in specific word learning and to observe the word learning strategies of their peers. The impact of Denise's instructional patterns was evident in how learners interpreted their role as vocabulary enricher. They emulated teacher approaches as they highlighted and defined new words for their groups. Members in the groups became actively involved in word meaning construction when the vocabulary enricher assumed a facilitative stance similar to Denise's actions during the multicultural unit.

Another aspect of vocabulary development in this literature-based reading program occurred in whole-class events, where students listened while the teacher talked about targeted words related to a required reading. Outcomes of these teacher-directed instructional episodes were attainment of specific word knowledge as well as exposure to implicit modeling of ways to define words. Conversely, the outcome of book discussion groups and independent reading, where students took a more active stance, was the enhancement of independent word learning strategies. These events resulted in opportunities where learners mobilized word learning strategies and constructed self-generated and shared meanings of unfamiliar words. In addition, they received exposure to the ideas and strategies of their peers, and, above all, a chance to develop a deeper awareness of individual word learning

strategies. Related research (cited in Baumann & Kameenui, 1991; Beck et al., 1987) also indicates the value of active student engagement in word learning opportunities and the need to help learners develop a stronger awareness and appreciation of words. Thus, word learning episodes in this literature-based program promoted acquisition of word knowledge and activation of independent word learning strategies.

Although literature-based programs are defined and implemented in different ways by different teachers, the configuration of this program supported vocabulary teaching and learning both explicitly and implicitly. The program resembled Burke and Short's description of "curriculum as activity" (cited in Heald-Taylor, 1996). Within this paradigm, the teacher made decisions about selections and activities, students read the same texts during a large portion of the time, discussions promoted higher level thinking, and the teacher guided meaning construction. She pulled stories from anthologies for the whole class to read and also presented a list of novels from which students could select a book. Thus, students read self-selected books during Sustained Silent Reading, teacher-selected short stories for whole-class activities, and self-selected books from a required list for small book discussion groups.

In sum, the reading program and observed student engagement paralleled and supported current research in regard to vocabulary learning. Like many other middle school teachers, this teacher wrestled with formulating a program that bridged different paradigms of teaching and learning. Her actions vacillated between objectivist and constructivist stances as she conscientiously sought to provide an effective reading program for students. As a result, the program encompassed a variety of important teaching and learning events where the teacher offered clarification about new words and learners practiced their existing repertoire of independent word learning strategies. The teacher demonstrated how a literature-based program could inform vocabulary through overlapping components of instructional learning episodes, wide reading of student-selected and teacher-selected books, and social interaction in peer groups and whole-class settings. A balance in varying classroom configurations provided learning opportunities that promoted vocabulary development in different ways. These engagements both expanded word knowledge and enhanced word learning abilities, as learners engaged in meaningful literacy events.

Literature-based reading programs can be fruitful grounds for vocabulary teaching and learning at the middle school level. Although vocabulary was not a major focus in this program, students still engaged in activities that supported word learning while enhancing overall reading proficiency. For example, through rich discussions and responses about words describing heroes, this teacher actually highlighted critical reading and reasoning as learners analyzed character traits. Her major goal of promoting critical reading and problem solving was embedded within these contextualized encounters with words as learners used their knowledge to make sense of text. Thus, vocabulary teaching and learning was an important aspect of the literacy experiences in this literature-based program.

Harmon teaches at the University of Texas at San Antonio (Division of Education, 6900 North Loop 1604 West, San Antonio, TX 78249-0654, USA). Staton may be contacted at Katherine Stinson Middle School, 13200 Skyhawk Drive, San Antonio, TX 78249, USA.

References

Baumann, J.F., & Kameenui, E.J. (1991). Research on vocabulary instruction: Ode to Voltaire. In J. Flood, J.M. Jensen, D. Lapp, & J.R. Squire (Eds.), *Handbook on teaching the English language arts* (pp. 602–632). New York: Macmillan.

Beck, I., & McKeown, M.G. (1991). Conditions of vocabulary acquisition. In R. Barr, M. Kamil, P. Mosenthal, & P.D. Pearson (Eds.), *Handbook of reading research: Vol. II* (pp. 789–814). White Plains, NY: Longman.

Beck, I., McKeown, M.G., & Omanson, R.C. (1987). The effects and uses of diverse vocabulary instructional techniques. In M.G. McKeown & M.E. Curtis (Eds.), *The nature of vocabulary acquisition* (pp. 147–163). Hillsdale, NJ: Erlbaum.

Blachowicz, C., & Lee, J. (1991). Vocabulary development in the whole literacy classroom. *The Reading Teacher, 45*, 188–195.

Bogdan, R.C., & Biklen, S.K. (1992). *Qualitative research for education: An introduction to theory and methods* (2nd ed.). Boston: Allyn & Bacon.

Chall, J. (1987). Two vocabularies for reading: Recognition and meaning. In M.G. McKeown & M.E. Curtis (Eds.), *The nature of vocabulary acquisition* (pp. 7–17). Hillsdale, NJ: Erlbaum.

Crew, L. (1991). *Children of the river.* New York: Dell.

Daniels, H. (1994). *Literature circles: Voice and choice in the student-centered classroom.* York, ME: Stenhouse.

Eeds, M., & Wells, D. (1989). Grand conversations: An exploration of meaning construction in literature study groups. *Research in the Teaching of English, 23*(1), 4–29.

Galda, L. (1988). Readers, texts, contexts: A response-based view of literature in the classroom. *The New Advocate, 1*, 92–102.

Hassler, J. (1988). *Jemmy.* Westminster, MD: Fawcett.

Heald-Taylor, B.G. (1996). Three paradigms for literature instruction in Grades 3 to 6. *The Reading Teacher, 49*, 456–466.

Hiebert, E.H., & Colt, J. (1989). Patterns of literature-based reading instruction. *The Reading Teacher, 43*, 14–20.

Hobbs, W. (1989). *Bearstone.* New York: Atheneum.

Huck, C. (1992). Literacy and literature. *Language Arts, 69*, 520–526.

Huck, C., Hepler, S., & Hickman, J. (1993). *Children's literature in the elementary school* (5th ed.). Fort Worth, TX: Harcourt Brace.

Jenkins, J.R., Stein, M., & Wysocki, K. (1984). Learning vocabulary through reading. *Educational Research Journal, 21*, 767–787.

McGee, L.M. (1992). Focus on research: Exploring the literature-based reading revolution. *Language Arts, 69*, 529–537.

Nagy, W. (1988). *Teaching vocabulary to improve reading comprehension.* Urbana, IL: National Council of Teachers of English.

Nagy, W., & Anderson, R. (1984). How many words are there in printed school English? *Reading Research Quarterly, 19*, 303–330.

Nagy, W., Anderson, R., & Herman, P. (1987). Learning word meanings from context during normal reading. *American Educational Research Journal, 24*, 237–270.

Nagy, W., Herman, P., & Anderson, R. (1985). Learning words from context. *Reading Research Quarterly, 20*, 233–253.

Paris S., Lipson, M., & Wixson, K. (1994). Becoming a strategic reader. In R. Ruddell, M. Ruddell, & H. Singer (Eds.), *Theoretical models and processes of reading* (4th ed., pp. 788–810). Newark, DE: International Reading Association.

Patton, M.Q. (1990). *Qualitative evaluation and research methods* (2nd ed.). Newbury Park, CA: Sage.

Peterson, R., & Eeds, M. (1990). *Grand conversations: Literature groups in action.* New York: Scholastic.

Scharer, P. (1992). Teachers in transition: An exploration of changes in teachers and classrooms during implementation of literature-based reading instruction. *Research in the Teaching of English, 26*, 408–445.

Stahl, S., & Fairbanks, M. (1986). The effects of vocabulary instruction: A model-based meta-analysis. *Review of Educational Research, 56*, 721–810.

Taylor, M. (1976). *Roll of thunder, hear my cry.* New York: Dial.

Yep, L. (1993). *Dragonwings.* New York: HarperCollins.

Zarrillo, J. (1989). Teachers' interpretations of literature-based reading. *The Reading Teacher, 43*, 22–28.

From *Journal of Adolescent & Adult Literacy,*
Vol. 41, No. 7, April 1998

SECTION VII

Comprehension

Preventing Reading Difficulties in Young Children

Catherine E. Snow, M. Susan Burns,
and Peg Griffin, *Editors*

Comprehension and Word Knowledge

Mature readers construct meaning at two levels. One level works with the words of the text for a literal understanding of what the author has written. However, superior word recognition abilities do not necessarily translate into superior levels of reading achievement (Chall, Jacobs, and Baldwin, 1990). Productive reading involves, in addition to literal comprehension, being able to answer questions like: Why am I reading this and how does this information relate to my reasons for so doing? What is the author's point of view, what are her or his underlying assumptions? Do I understand what the author is saying and why? Do I know where the author is headed? Is the text internally consistent? Is it consistent with what I already know or believe? If not, where does it depart and what can I think about the discrepancy? This sort of reflective, purposive understanding goes beyond the literal to the underlying meaning of the text. For purposes of discussion, the development of productive reading comprehension can be considered in terms of three factors:

(1) concept and vocabulary development, (2) command of the linguistic structures of the text, and (3) metacognitive or reflective control of comprehension.

Written text places high demands on vocabulary knowledge. Even the words used in children's books are more rare than those used in adult conversations and prime time television (Hayes and Ahrens, 1988). Learning new concepts and the words that encode them is essential for comprehension development. People's ability to infer or retain new words in general is strongly dependent on their background knowledge of other words and concepts. Even at the youngest ages, the ability to understand and remember the meanings of new words depends quite strongly on how well developed one's vocabulary is already (Robbins and Ehri, 1994)

Can children's word knowledge and reading comprehension be measurably improved through instruction? The answer is yes, according to a meta-analysis of relevant research studies by Stahl and Fairbanks (1986). First, vocabulary instruction generally does result in measurable increase in students' specific word knowledge. Sometimes and to some degree, it also results in better performance on global vocabulary measures, such as standardized tests, indicating that the instruction has evidently enhanced the learning of words beyond those directly taught. Second, pooling across studies, vocabulary instruction also appears to produce increases in children's reading comprehension. Again, although these gains are largest where passages contain explicitly taught words, they are also significant given general, standardized measures.

Looking across studies, Stahl and Fairbanks (1986) noted differences in the effectiveness of vocabulary instruction as well. Methods providing repeated drill and practice on word definitions resulted in significant improvement with the particular words that had been taught but no reliable effect on reading comprehension scores. In contrast, methods in which children were given both information about the words' definitions and examples of the words' usages in a variety of contexts resulted in the largest gains in both vocabulary and reading comprehension.

An important source of word knowledge is exposure to print and independent reading. As noted above, books introduce children to more rare words than conversation or television does. So educational approaches that encourage children to read more both in school and out should increase their word knowledge (Nagy and Anderson, 1984) and reading comprehension (Anderson, Wilson and Fielding, 1988). However, several efforts to increase the breadth of children's reading have produced little measurable effect on their reading ability (Carver and Liebert, 1995; see review in Taylor, Frye, and Maruyama, 1990), perhaps because books selected for free reading tend to be at too easy a level for most children (Carver, 1994). Alternately, perhaps children who are doing poorly are less likely to profit from extensive exposure to print than children who are already progressing quite well.

One group of researchers reviewed interactions among print exposure, word knowledge, and comprehension, teasing apart the relations among prior ability and increased reading (Stanovich et al., 1996). They concluded (p. 29): "In short, exposure to print is efficacious regardless of the level of the child's cognitive and comprehension abilities. Even children with limited comprehension skills will build vocabulary and cognitive structures through immersion in literacy activities. An encouraging message for teachers of low-achieving children is implicit here. We often despair of changing 'abilities,' but there is at least one partially malleable habit that will itself develop 'abilities'—reading."

The relation between print exposure and comprehension need not be limited to the child's own reading in school. Cain (1994) studied the home literacy activities of 7- and 8-year-olds whose word reading accuracy was appropriate for their chronological age but who differed in their comprehension ability. She reports the following contrasts: "The children who were skilled comprehenders reported reading books at home more frequently than the less skilled children, and their parents reported that they were more likely to read story books. The skilled comprehenders also reported that they were read to more frequently at home by their parents than the less skilled group and this was confirmed by their parents' responses. . . . The skilled children were significantly more likely to read books with their parents than were the less skilled children and also tended to talk about books and stories more frequently than did the less skilled comprehenders." (Cain, 1994:189)

It might be assumed that reading aloud with a child loses its value once children have attained independent accuracy in reading words, but Cain's findings raise the possibility that being read to promotes skilled comprehension at ages 7 and 8, although she points out that no causal link has yet been demonstrated.

Comprehension and Background Knowledge

The breadth and depth of a child's literacy experiences determine not only how many and what kinds of words she or he will encounter but also the background knowledge with which a child can conceptualize the meaning of any new word and to the orthographic knowledge that frees that meaning from the printed page. Every opportunity should be taken to extend and enrich the children's background knowledge and understanding in every way possible, for the ultimate significance and memorability of any word or text depends on whether children possess the background knowledge and conceptual sophistication to understand its meaning.

A program designed to enhance background knowledge and conceptual sophistication among third graders is Concept Oriented Reading Instruction (CORI). The emphasis of the program is on the comprehension of interesting texts. The program is designed around broad interdisciplinary themes, exploiting real-world experience, a range of cognitive strategies, and social groupings to promote self direction. Designed for third graders in high-poverty schools with a history of low achievement, it has been successfully used at both the classroom and the whole school level. The third grade students have ranged in reading levels from first to fourth grade, and students with limited English proficiency are mainstreamed and included in the classroom. The program has effectively increased narrative text comprehension, expository text comprehension, and other language arts skills on standardized tests, as well as increasing students' performance on the Maryland School Performance Assessment Program (MSPAP) (Guthrie, Van Meter, et al., 1994; Guthrie et al., 1996). Compared to control students, students in the program improved significantly on reading, writing, science, social studies, and language use but not in math, which was not taught in the program. CORI has also been shown to increase the amount and breadth of independent reading and volitional strategies for maintaining engagement in reading activities.

Structures, Processes and Meta-Processes in Comprehension Instruction

Research on comprehension among young readers has not resolved questions about the nature and separate identity of the difficulties they encounter as they attempt to understand texts. It is difficult to tease apart the effect of stores of word knowledge and background knowledge from the effect of processes (e.g., identifying words quickly and accurately, constructing mental representations to integrate information from the text) and meta-processes (making inferences, monitoring for inconsistencies) (Cornoldi and Oakhill, 1996). Instruction for comprehension, however, generally focuses on understanding complete connected text in situations in which many of the possible difficulties appear bound together and often can be treated as a bundle to good effect.

Many comprehension instruction techniques used in schools today are described as meta-cognitive. A meta-analysis of 20 meta-cognition instruction programs found a substantial mean effect size of .71 (Haller, Child, and Walberg, 1988). Instructional programs focusing on self-questioning and identifying text consistencies were found to be most effective. A meta-analysis of 10 studies related to a technique called reciprocal teaching found a median effect size of .88 (Rosenshine and Meister, 1994).

For most active comprehension instruction, whether considered meta-cognitive or not, two pedagogic processes are intermingled: traditional instruction in basic stores of knowledge (the background for the text and for particular words) and instruction in particular comprehension strategies complemented by the active skilled reading of the text by an expert (the teacher) done in such a way that the ordinarily hidden processes of comprehension are displayed (see Kucan and Beck, 1997; Beck and McKeown, 1996, 1997). The children have an opportunity to learn from the joint participation (a form of cognitive apprenticeship) as well as from the particulars in the instructional agenda. As Baker (1996) notes, it is an open question whether direct instruction or observational learning provides the greater contribution to student progress.

Reciprocal teaching is a particularly interesting approach to consider in detail both because of its apparent effectiveness and because it illustrates the mixed instructional agenda and pedagogical strategies. Reciprocal teaching provides guided practice in the use of four strategies (predicting, question generating, summarizing, and clarifying) that are designed to enhance children's ability to construct the meaning of text (Palincsar, Brown and Campione, 1993). To engage in reciprocal teaching dialogues, the children and the teacher read a piece of common text. This reading may be done as a read-along, a silent reading, or an oral reading, depending on the decoding abilities of the children and the level of the text. The children and the teacher take turns leading the discussion of segments of the text, using strategies to support their discussion. The ultimate purpose of the discussion, however, is not practice with the strategies but the application of the strategies for the purpose of coming to a shared sense of the meaning of the text at hand. The tenets of reciprocal teaching include: (a) meaningful use of comprehension-monitoring and comprehension-fostering strategies, (b) discussion for the purpose of building the meaning of text, (c) the expectation that, when children are first beginning these dialogues, they will need considerable support provided by the teacher's modeling of the use of the strategies and guiding students' participation in the dialogues, (d) the use of text that offers appropriate challenge to the children (i.e., there is content worth discussing in the text and the text is sufficiently accessible to the children), and finally, (e) the use of text that is thematically related so that children have the opportunity to build their knowledge of a topic or area over time.

Reciprocal teaching was designed as both an intervention to be used with youngsters who were experiencing language-related difficulties and as a means of prevention given the hypothesis that young children should experience reading as a meaningful activity even before they are reading conventionally. It has been investigated principally with children who come from high-poverty areas, children being served in developmental and remedial reading programs, and children identified as having a language or learning disability. Research on reciprocal teaching with young children in first and second grades indicates statistically significant improvement in listening comprehension (which assessed ability to recall information, summarize information, draw inferences from text, and use information to solve a novel problem) and fewer referrals to special education or remedial reading programs. In addition, teachers reported that, as a result of their experiences in reciprocal teaching dialogues, their expectations regarding these children were raised. In other words, children who appeared to have a disability on the basis of their participation in the conventional classroom dynamic appeared quite able in the context of reciprocal teaching dialogues.

Training studies on inferences and comprehension monitoring with 7- and 8-year-olds show that children identified specifically as poor comprehenders profit differentially from certain kinds of instruction. Yuill and Oakhill (1988) compared the effect on skilled and less skilled comprehenders (matched for age and reading accuracy) of a program that lasted for seven 30-minute sessions spread over about two months. The treatment group worked on lexical inferences, question generation, and prediction. One control group read the same texts and answered questions about them in a group discussion format. A second control group read the same texts and practiced rapid word decoding. There appears to have been an interaction between aptitude and treatment. Analyses of post-test results showed that the less skilled comprehenders benefited more from the experimental treatment than did the more skilled, that the less skilled comprehenders derived more benefit from the comprehension training than they did from the rapid decoding condition, but that the more skilled benefited more from the decoding training than from the comprehension training.

Yuill (1996) worked with a similar set of subjects (matched for age and reading accuracy, differing on comprehension ability) to train for the ability to recognize that texts could have more than a single obvious interpretation by using the genre of riddles, which depends on ambiguity and its resolution. The treatment condition focused the children on alternative interpretations in texts by training them to explain the ambiguity in riddles; the control group children also read amusing texts but focused on sublexical awareness activities rather than on meta-comprehension activities. At the end of the two month period, the experimental treatment group performed significantly better on the post-test in comprehension than the control group did but there was no significant interaction between skill group and training.

Excerpted from *Preventing Reading Difficulties in Young Children, 1998*

REFERENCES

Anderson, R.C., P.T. Wilson, and L. G. Fielding
1988 Growth in reading and how children spend their time outside of school. *Reading Research Quarterly* 23(3): 285-303.

Baker, L.
1996 Social influences on metacognitive development in reading. Pp. 331-352 in *Reading Comprehension Difficulties: Processes and Intervention*, C. Cornoldi and J. Oakhill, eds. Mahwah, NJ: Lawrence Earlbaum Associates.

Beck, I.L., M.G. McKeown, C. Sandora, I. Kucan, et al.
1996 Questioning the author: A yearlong classroom implementation to engage students with text. *Elementary School Journal* 96: 385-414.

Cain, K.
1996 Story knowledge and comprehension skills. Pp. 167-192 in *Reading Comprehension Difficulties: Processes and Intervention*, C. Cornoldi and J. Oakhill, eds. Mahwah, NJ: Lawrence Earlbaum Associates.

Carver, R.
1994 Percentage of unknown vocabulary words in text as a function of the relative difficulty of the text: Implications for instruction. *Journal of Reading Behavior: A Journal of Literacy* 26: 413-438.

Chall, J.S., V. Jacobs, and L. Baldwin
1990 *The Reading Crisis: Why Poor Children Fall Behind.* Cambridge MA: Harvard University Press.

Cornoldi, C. and J. Oakhill, eds.
1996 *Reading Comprehension Difficulties: Processes and Intervention.* Mahwah, NJ: Lawrence Earlbaum Associates.

Guthrie, J.T., K. McGough, I. Bennet, and M.E. Rice
1996 Concept-oriented reading instruction: An integrated curriculum to develop motivations and strategies for reading. Pp. 165-190 in *Developing Engaged Readers in School and Home Communities*, I. Baker, P. Afflerbach, and D. Reinking, eds. Mahwah, NJ: Lawrence Earlbaum Associates.

Haller, E.P., D. A. Child, and H.J. Walberg
1988 Can comprehension be taught? *Educational Researcher* 17: 5-8.

Hayes, D.P., and M.G. Ahrens
1988 Vocabulary simplification for children: A special case of "motherese?" *Journal of Child Language* 15(2): 395-410.

Kucan, L. and I. Beck
1997 Thinking aloud and reading comprehension research: Inquiry, instruction, and social interaction. *Review of Educational Research* 67: 271-99.

Nagy, W.E., and R.C. Anderson
1984 How many words are there in printed school English? *Reading Research Quarterly* 19: 304-330.

Palinscar, A.S., A.L. Brown, and J.C. Campione
1993 First-grade dialogues for knowledge acquisition and use. *Contexts for Learning: Sociocultural Dynamics in Children's Development.* E. Forman, N. Minick, and C.A. Stone, eds. New York: Oxford University Press.

Robbins, C., and L.C. Ehri
1994 Reading storybooks to kindergartners helps them learn new vocabulary words. *Journal of Educational Psychology* 86(1): 54-64.

Rosenshine, B., and C. Meister
1994 Reciprocal teaching: A review of the research. *Review of Educational Research* 64(4): 479-530.

Stahl, S.A., and M.M. Fairbanks
1986 The effects of vocabulary instruction: A model-based meta-analysis. *Review of Educational Research* 56(1): 72-110.

Stanovich, K.E., R.F. West, A.E. Cunningham, J. Cipielewski, and S. Siddiqui
1996 The role of inadequate print exposure as a determinant of reading comprehension problems. Pp. 15-32 in *Reading Comprehension Disabilities*, C. Conoldi and J. Oakhill, eds. Hillsdale, NJ: Erlbaum.

Taylor, B.M., B.J. Frye, and G.M. Maruyama
1990 Time spent reading and reading growth. *American Educational Research Journal* 27(2): 351-362.

Yuill, N.
1996 A funny thing happened on the way to the classroom: Jokes, riddles, and metalinguistic awareness in understanding and improving poor comprehension in children. Pp. 193-220 in *Reading Comprehension Disabilities*, C. Conoldi and J. Oakhill, eds. Hillsdale, NJ: Erlbaum.

Questioning the Author:
An Approach to Developing
Meaningful Classroom Discourse

MARGARET G. McKEOWN
ISABEL L. BECK
CHERYL A. SANDORA
University of Pittsburgh

A study that we conducted in 1991 on students' history learning included interviewing eighth graders as they finished their study of early American history. A question about what happened in the Revolutionary War prompted the following response from Jennifer, one of the students:

> I don't really remember this too well; I don't know why. We always learn about this and I always forget. It's so important, too. Something like one of the colonies was too strong and something happened and they got into a war over it, and it was going on for a while and that's just one of the things. I don't know why I don't remember this. It's pretty embarrassing. (Beck & McKeown, 1994, p. 249)

Jennifer's remarks illustrate two themes that have pervaded the program of research in which we have been involved over the past decade. The first is that textbooks, which are customarily the basis of students' history knowledge at this level, are not serving students well. The second is that students often react to inadequate text presentations by developing a view of themselves as inadequate readers.

In this chapter, we begin with a brief chronology of our research on students and texts and how it has moved from a focus on the qualities of textbooks to a focus on developing students' abilities to deal with text. In the second section of the chapter, we present a detailed look at how Questioning the Author, the approach we designed to help students deal with texts, influenced their thinking about what they read. In the final section, we describe a new shift in our research focus, this time toward developing ways to support teachers in helping students interact productively with the texts they read.

OUR WORK IN EXAMINING TEXTBOOKS AND HOW STUDENTS UNDERSTAND THEM

In the mid-1980s we initiated our program of research on students' understanding and learning from textbooks, with an analysis of the extent to which learning and understanding were promoted by the content as presented in four elementary social studies programs (Beck, McKeown, & Gromoll, 1989). Our approach to analyzing text was based on theory and research from a cognitive perspective. The cognitive orientation to reading research had brought much progress in understanding the ways that readers interact with texts. In investigations of the reading process, emphasis turned to trying to understand the mental activities involved in reading, that is, what the reader does while reading, rather than being confined to the products of reading, that is, what the reader remembers from reading. Insights gained from the cognitive perspective also yielded understanding of how the reader's execution and coordination of the processes involved during reading affect the products of reading (Just & Carpenter, 1987; Perfetti, 1985; Trabasso & Magliano, Chapter 7, this volume).

We saw the understandings gained from cognitive reading research as having much to offer textbook analysis work. Particularly fruitful is the inherent focus on learning, which could open the way for understanding how characteristics of texts affect the way textbooks function in a learning environment. Two specific areas of research particularly influenced our text analysis work: understandings about the nature of the reading process, with emphasis on the interaction of a reader's background knowledge and a text's content (Chiesi, Spilich, & Voss, 1979; Pearson, Hansen, & Gordon, 1979), and characteristics of texts that promote or impede comprehension (Black & Bern, 1981; Frederiksen, 1981; Trabasso, Secco, & van den Broek, 1984).

Drawing from cognitive theory and research, we developed an approach to analysis of text in which we examined extensive topic sequences.

Examination of sequences of text content enabled us to consider the learning that might develop as students move through a sequence and to communicate a sense of the raw material from which young students are expected to build understanding of a topic. In our analyses we gave particular attention to the explanatory material used to develop specific concepts within general topics and themes.

A major focus of our analyses was content about the American Revolutionary period, specifically the time frame from colonial development through the events at Lexington and Concord, from the fifth-grade texts in each of the four programs we examined. It was our judgment that the presentation of content in the programs was not likely to promote the development of understanding of the chain of events that led to the Revolution. We saw two major problems. The first was that the texts seemed to assume an unrealistic variety and depth of background knowledge on the part of young students. For example, although the issue of "no taxation without representation" is a critical element for understanding the causes of the Revolution, the texts, in presenting that issue, merely stated that the colonists had no representation in Parliament. None of the texts we analyzed attempted to explain the basic issue of what it means to be represented in a governmental body or how strong the motivation to acquire or protect that form of government can be. Rather, the text presentations seemed to assume that students already had a full grasp of the concept of representative government.

The second major problem identified in our text analyses was that the presentations lacked the coherence needed to enable students to draw connections between events and ideas. For example, the actions involved in the Boston Tea Party were portrayed quite clearly. But the cause of the event, which was rooted in the colonists' ongoing protest over Britain's taxes, was not explained. Thus, the event was not linked to the causal chain of events leading to the Revolution.

Following the analyses of textbook sequences, we engaged in a study to examine the kind of understandings that students were able to develop from reading these texts (McKeown & Beck, 1990). In this work we presented fifth graders with a sequence of passages about events leading to the Revolution from one of the textbooks that we had analyzed. The sequence covered the French and Indian War, the dispute over taxation without representation, the Boston Tea Party, and the Intolerable Acts. We asked students to read each passage and then recall what they had read and respond to some open-ended questions. The study occurred just before the students were slated to read the same material in their regular classrooms, and so they had already covered all the background material.

Examination of the students' recalls and answers to questions showed that the understanding that students were able to develop was rather shallow, suggesting that their interactions with the text were on a very surface level. As an illustration of why that might have been the case, consider a paragraph from the text that is meant to convey the harshness of the regulations that the British imposed on the colonists after the Boston Tea Party.

> The British were very angry! Within a few months, they passed what the colonists called the Intolerable Acts. Intolerable means "unbearable." These acts were meant to punish the people of Boston. The port of Boston was closed. No self-government was allowed in Massachusetts. British troops had to be housed by the Massachusetts colonists. (Silver Burdett, 1984, p. 109)

Many students' recalls of this terse text suggested that they did not engage with the material, but only picked up some isolated pieces of information. Matthew's response is an example. When asked to tell what the passage was about, Matthew simply said:

> It's about people from Great Britain [who] were very angry. . . . There was this new thing called the intolerable act, and they didn't like it. Then people from Massachusetts put them in houses for something.

Based on students' accounts of what they read, we concluded that the problems we had identified in our text analyses did indeed create obstacles to comprehension. Students did lack assumed background knowledge and often were unable to draw appropriate inferences.

Our research next turned to examining the extent to which more coherent text presentations would facilitate students' understanding. In this work we created revised versions of the four textbook passages about events leading to the Revolutionary War (Beck et al., 1989). Our revisions were intended to establish textual coherence by clarifying, elaborating, explaining, and motivating important information and by making relationships explicit.

The goal of our revisions was to create a text based on a causal sequence of events, with the information presented in a way that explained the connections from a cause to an event and from an event to a consequence. The basis for the revisions was our mental simulation of how a typical target-aged reader would respond to the information in the text. Thus, the original texts were evaluated by considering how each new piece of text information might be handled, what kind of knowledge the reader would need to bring to bear, and how the developing text representation would be influenced. Points where the process might break down, such as where an explanation seemed inadequate, were hypothesized, and ways in which an ideal reader might repair such breaks were generated. These potential repairs were used as the basis for the revised version of the text. As we considered what might happen as a young reader processed the text, we switched back and forth among hypothesizing what the student might be thinking, inducing what seemed to be intended by the text, and constructing text statements that might promote a coherent representation.

When the revised passages were presented to the students, they recalled significantly more of the text and answered more questions correctly (Beck, McKeown, Sinatra, & Loxterman, 1991). Even more important, the additional recall produced by the students reading the revised text represented exactly the concepts needed to explain the actions and connect them with the major chain of events. For example, in the "no taxation without representation" segment, the students reading revised text were more likely to understand that the colonists' objection to the taxes arose from their desire for representation in government rather than a squabble over money.

Despite the advantages shown for readers of the revised passages, the results of our study indicated that readers in both groups still had considerable difficulty understanding the texts. The recalls of many students from both groups pointed to surface-level treatments of text information. Reading the recalls gave us the impression that students took what they could get in one swift pass through the words on a page, and then formed that into a shallow representation of the text. This kind of cursory use of the text suggests that students resist digging in and grappling with unfamiliar or difficult content.

PROMOTING YOUNG READERS' ENGAGEMENT WITH TEXT: QUESTIONING THE AUTHOR

At this point, our research interests shifted to exploring ways to get readers to engage with texts and to consider ideas deeply. In cognitive terms, engagement with text means active processing of what is read, and research suggests that little meaningful interaction with text can take place unless a reader is active. Considering what it means for a reader to be active made us realize that the kind of processing we did in revising textbook passages was the kind of experience we wanted to create for students. One must become actively engaged with the content of a text in order to transform it into a comprehensible form. We reasoned that giving students a "reviser's eye" might create a subtle but important shift in their goal when interacting with a text—from trying to understand it to making it understandable.

The shift to trying to make a text understandable also embodies a change in attitude toward the status of the text. Textbooks carry weighty authority in the classroom. This authority arises both from the traditional role of the text as the center of the classroom curriculum and from the impersonal, objective tone of textbook language (Luke, DeCastell, & Luke, 1983; Olson, 1980). Having difficulty with a text, then, can give students the notion that they are to blame, as illustrated in Jennifer's interview excerpt at the beginning of the chapter. Students often respond by applying the principle of least effort; they seem to resist digging in and dealing with difficult text, because "not to try is not to fail."

As we developed our ideas into an approach to use with students—an approach that we have come to call Questioning the Author—three principles became key.

- Depose the authority of the text by letting students know that texts are just someone's ideas written down, and they need to be worked on if understanding is to develop.
- Focus attention directly on grappling with the meaning of what is written in the text.
- Have students take part in meaning-getting interactions on-line as text is read initially.

Based on these principles, we began pilot work with individual students, introducing our ideas to the students by telling them that "different people write things in different ways, and sometimes what someone has in their mind to say just doesn't come through clearly in their writing of it."

The purpose of this introduction was to create the expectation that figuring out the ideas behind an author's words requires work, and thus needing to work to understand was not an indication that their abilities were inadequate. We then modeled for students how a reader might think through a text in order to build understanding. The modeling involved our reading a brief text aloud and commenting on and evaluating text statements. For example, the text we used states, "Russia has used rockets to put a new moon in the sky," to which we responded, "Hmmm, I don't know what the author means. How can you put up another moon?"

Following the introduction, we worked with students by having them think aloud as they read a text, sometimes prompting them with questions such as, "What's that all about?" or "What's the author trying to say there?". We used these general probes in order to focus students on constructing meaning rather than on locating and retrieving specific information. Based on those questions that seemed most effectively to encourage students' construction of meaning, we developed a set of "Engagement Queries." The queries include questions to initiate meaning-building such as, "What is the author trying to say?" or "What is the author talking about?" and follow-ups such as, "What could the author mean by that?" and "Why is the author telling us that?" to prompt students to go beyond words to the ideas being communicated.

BRINGING QUESTIONING THE AUTHOR TO THE CLASSROOM

Our next step, after work with individual students, was to take our approach to the classroom. After testing the classroom dynamics of Questioning the Author by working with groups of about a dozen students, we were able to set up a collaborative relationship with two teachers and work toward implementing Questioning the Author in their fourth-grade classrooms.

From observations of the collaborating teachers, we learned that they both taught in a traditional manner, with lessons that focused on a text section or story, which was read in round robin style, followed by a teacher-led question and answer session directed toward retrieving text information. Students provided brief responses, and the teachers evaluated the correctness of each response and moved to the next question.

Questioning the Author was introduced to teachers during the summer. When the school year began, the teachers implemented the new approach, conducting their lessons with text by reading or asking students to read a portion of text, and then posing Engagement Queries from the set we developed to initiate and focus discussion. As the teachers worked with Questioning the Author, it was clear that the approach "upset the apple cart" of the traditional lesson in the way text was handled and in the way teachers needed to interact with students. In terms of the text, the Questioning the Author framework meant that lessons no longer consisted of reading straight through a text, followed by questions aimed at literal text information and direct student responses. Rather, the teachers needed to develop techniques for probing ideas as they were encountered in text, monitoring students' understanding, and prompting students to grapple with text ideas.

Questioning the Author required the teachers to deal with students in new ways. Teachers no longer got brief, predictable responses from students, but rather longer, elaborated accounts of what students understood or did not understand from the text, and student-initiated questions that could take the discussion in unpredictable directions. Also, teachers no longer were dealing with an individual student's isolated response; rather, students were reacting to each other's contributions by challenging each other's ideas, elaborating on comments, agreeing, disagreeing, and competing for opportunities to comment on issues that arose. Frequent and extensive interactions with the teachers over the year were directed toward supporting them in handling the changes that Questioning the Author required and using the changes to bring about a more productive learning environment.

OUTCOMES FROM TWO YEAR—LONG IMPLEMENTATIONS

As the implementation progressed, we began to observe changes in the discourse environments in the classrooms. We noticed that the pattern of questions requiring students to locate information followed by brief responses seemed to be giving way to a focus on meaning and a more collaborative atmosphere. We then developed indices to examine these changes systematically. These indices examine four aspects of the discourse environment: (1) types of questions teachers ask, (2) ways teachers respond to student comments, (3) proportion of teacher talk to student talk, and (4) frequency of student-initiated comments and questions.

We used these indices to analyze lessons of our two initial collaborating teachers (Beck, McKeown, Worthy, Sandora, & Kucan, 1996) and from two additional teachers who implemented Questioning the Author in their fourth-grade classrooms the following year. The set of lessons that was analyzed included at least one baseline lesson of each teacher and a sample of Questioning the Author lessons. The sample was selected to include lessons from across the school year and to represent both language arts and social studies classes. A total of 29 lessons was analyzed. The following brief description of the findings from our analyses highlights the changes that occurred in the four classrooms as a result of Questioning the Author.

Our examination of the discourse environment in the collaborating classrooms began with the kinds of questions teachers ask of students as they read, because teacher questions are a driving force behind the lesson. We identified four types of questions based on the type of information the teacher was seeking from students. Teachers appeared to ask students questions in order to:

(1) retrieve information from the text, such as, "Who are the characters in this story?"
(2) construct the message of the text, such as, "What is the author trying to tell us about these characters?"
(3) extend the construction of meaning, such as, "How did the author give you the idea that the characters weren't getting along?"
(4) check students' knowledge of a particular piece of information, such as, "Who remembers what *conceited* means?"

Examination of the questions according to these four categories showed that the types of questions teachers asked students as a result of Questioning the Author represented a shift from retrieving information to constructing meaning, particularly in extending the construction of meaning. The analysis showed that when teachers used Questioning the Author they no longer focused on factual questions, asking students to take information directly from the text, but rather on questions that asked students to think about and build ideas from what they were reading.

The changing nature of teachers' questions set in motion a change in classroom discourse patterns. In the Questioning the Author environment, rather than a student's response to a teacher's question being followed by a simple evaluation and then another teacher question, connections were drawn from the content of a student's response to the teacher's next move. Thus, our second analysis examined teachers' rejoinders to students' responses.

In a preliminary examination of lesson transcripts, we noted that teachers seemed to respond to student comments using one of three moves:

(1) repeating the comment;
(2) paraphrasing the comment, sometimes substantially changing the wording but leaving the meaning intact;
(3) refining the comment, shaping the ideas by clarifying or focusing them, or lifting them to more general language.

Analysis of the sample transcripts revealed differences between baseline and Questioning the Author lesson transcripts with regard to teacher rejoinders. In the baseline lessons, the most common way of making students' comments public was repetition; paraphrases and refinements of students' contributions were relatively rare. In Questioning the Author lessons, however, teachers increased their tendency to refine students' comments, indicating that teachers no longer were simply repeating students' comments, but were using students' comments as a means to move the discussion in a productive manner.

The two indices described so far suggest that Questioning the Author promotes constructive discourse, which begs the question of who is doing the constructing. Typically, one consequence of the traditional lesson pattern of teacher question, student response, and teacher evaluation is that teachers dominate the talk that occurs in a lesson and students are given very few opportunities to respond at any length (Alvermann, O'Brien, & Dillon, 1990; Cazden, 1986; Goodlad, 1984).

The changing pattern of discourse observed within Questioning the Author lessons included a shift away from teachers' domination of discussion. In order to examine the extent to which this shift occurred, we computed the amount of teacher talk and the amount of student talk in the sample set of transcripts. Results showed that the amount of student talk during Questioning the Author lessons increased significantly; student talk more than doubled in a typical lesson. This analysis of the proportion of talk in the classroom makes it evident that, in addition to affecting teacher behavior, Questioning the Author also influenced students' behavior.

The fourth analysis examined the extent to which students initiated their own questions and comments in addition to responding to teacher questions. In baseline lessons students rarely asked questions, but a substantial increase in student-initiated comments and questions in Questioning the Author lessons indicated that such contributions were an important part of those lessons.

The results of the four indices indicated that the discourse pattern had changed substantially under Questioning the Author. However, these indices shed somewhat more light on changes in teachers' actions in the classroom than on what students were doing. Although we knew that students were talking more and initiating more comments, the nature of their contributions had not been examined. In the next section of this chapter, we turn the focus to the students, to explore the kinds of thinking about and responding to text that were prompted by Questioning the Author.

CHANGES IN STUDENTS' THINKING ABOUT AND RESPONDING TO TEXT

Our observations of students' contributions during Questioning the Author lessons indicated that not only were students' comments longer than those in traditional lessons but the ideas expressed were more complex and the focus was more on meaning than on literal wording.

THE NATURE OF STUDENTS' RESPONSES

To examine these changes systematically, we developed a categorization scheme describing the responses students gave during discussions. Four categories were developed that encompassed the kinds of student responses found in the lessons. One category included responses that were verbatim or near verbatim repetitions of text. Both the concepts and the language of these responses stayed close to the text.

A second category included responses in which students constructed local meaning. These responses represented students' attempts to manipulate text ideas, explaining them and recasting them in their own language and sometimes adding simple elaborations. These responses stayed fairly close to the text in concept, although the language was transformed and movement toward meaning was evident. An example would be responding to the text sentence, "Reindeer herders depended on reindeer to fill all their needs," by saying, "They're hunters that go out and that depend on reindeer for their food and their fur and places to live." Some transformation and elaboration of the wording occurs; for example, the instantiation of *needs* as "food, fur, places to live."

A third category included responses in which students integrated information. These responses indicated dealing with text ideas or ideas in the discussion by integrating prior knowledge or previously learned text information, hypothesizing solutions to conflicts or problems that arose from the reading, or extrapolating consequences of text events and ideas. An example would be responding to the concept of reindeer herders by comparing their lifestyle with that of a group of people that the class had read about earlier: "The people who we learned about, Eskimos, they do like that, but they make their houses and clothes and stuff out of, well, caribou."

A fourth category included responses in which students introduced their own questions or comments into the discussion, and responses in which peers directly addressed those comments, either by answering a question, expressing agreement or disagreement, or adding to a comment made by a peer. For example, a student responded to the discussion of reindeer herders by adding: "Like Shanelle said, I think they get their food and stuff out of the reindeer, but they don't go out and hunt them, because they raise them and just herd them together."

The same set of sample transcripts analyzed for the four indices described earlier—teacher questions, teacher rejoinders, proportion of student/teacher talk, and student-initiated comments—was used for the analysis of student responses. A separate analysis was done for each teacher by subject area taught. Although we examined four teachers' classrooms, this resulted in five analyses because one collaborating teacher used Questioning the Author in both language arts and social studies, while two teachers taught only language arts, and one taught only social studies.

RESULTS OF THE ANALYSES

Because the same pattern emerged for the two analyses of social studies and for the three analyses of language arts, we present the results according to content area. Table 5.1 shows the patterns for both the language arts classes and the social studies classes.

Although the patterns for the two subject areas differed slightly, the table indicates that a similar shift occurred for both areas in the kinds of student responses. That is, in Questioning the Author, student responses were much more likely than in the baseline lessons to focus on meaning and

TABLE 5.1. Mean percent (and frequency per lesson) of student responses across four categories in baseline and questioning the author language arts and social studies lessons.

	Verbatim	Local meaning	Integration	Student comments
Baseline language arts	40(11)	49(14)	9(3)	2(1)
Q & A language arts	10(6)	49(28)	26(15)	15(10)
Baseline social studies	88(19)	12(2)	0(0)	0(0)
Q & A social studies	17(6)	51(21)	23(9)	9(4)

integration. The table also shows the increase in number of student responses during Questioning the Author lessons. Of note is that although the overall number of student responses increased substantially compared with baseline lessons, the number of verbatim responses dropped. Thus, the change in student response pattern was not simply an increase in more sophisticated responses, but also a decrease in verbatim responses.

Table 5.1 suggests that in the baseline language arts lessons, the majority of student comments fell into the first two levels, with 40% of the comments staying very close to the text, and 49% moving to construction of local meaning. There were very few comments in which students integrated outside information or interacted with their peers. During Questioning the Author lessons, the proportion of comments that were considered to be construction of local meaning remained the same. However, the proportion of verbatim responses dropped to 10%, with concomitant increases in the integration and student comments categories.

The table indicates that in the social studies baseline lessons, 88% of student comments were verbatim accounts of the information in the text, with 12% representing construction of local meaning. There were no responses that involved integration of information or student-initiated comments. The analysis of the Questioning the Author lessons reveals a different picture: The proportion of verbatim responses decreased to 17%, with a significant increase in comments in the other three levels.

SAMPLING THE QUESTIONING THE AUTHOR ENVIRONMENT

The analysis of the categories of student responses characterizes the nature of children's thinking about text ideas within Questioning the Author. In this section, we present excerpts from classroom lessons that illustrate the nature of the discourse environments that the student responses helped to create.

A context for contrast. To set up a context in which to consider the discourse environment, we first present an excerpt from a baseline lesson taught by one of our collaborating teachers prior to implementation of Questioning the Author. The class in this excerpt has been reading Beverly Cleary's *Ralph S. Mouse* (1982). In the part of the text that the class has just read, Ralph, the motorcycle riding mouse, had a spat with Ryan, the boy who keeps him. Ryan had taken away his motorcycle, so Ralph decided to stay at school alone over the weekend, and now he's been contemplating that decision, feeling lonely and thinking about his home. The teacher tried to engage students in a discussion of Ralph's feelings, but she did so by focusing on individual words to describe those feelings. The students responded in kind, offering individual words; little attempt was made to connect the words to create a picture of the scene or what it means in terms of the story.

TEACHER: Okay, I want some words now from you that would describe Ralph. All right? How does Ralph feel right now? Eric?

ERIC: He feels lonely.

TEACHER: Lonely. All right, we have a lot of adjectives to describe his feelings.

NICOLE: Cold.

TEACHER: Cold. How else?

LUKE: A little scared.

TEACHER: Scared.

STACEY: Disappointed.

TEACHER: Disappointed.

STACEY: That his motorcycle is broken.

TEACHER: All right, he's disappointed.

JUSTIN: He misses the hotel.

TEACHER: All right, he misses the hotel. Anything else he misses besides the hotel?

CHAD: His motorcycle.

TEACHER: His motorcycle.

MELISSA: His relatives.

At this point, the teacher did ask students to make a connection, but the student who responded simply hooked together two words with "and," making no further elaboration.

TEACHER: Okay. Can we put "misses" with something else? Can we connect some of these? Are there two words that we can connect here? Anthony?

ANTHONY: Misses and lonely.

This list-like treatment of the story continued, and little was done to explore ideas; the focus was on naming feelings and states. This excerpt very much typified what we saw in baseline lessons, both in language arts and in social studies.

Working to understand ideas. A very different kind of interaction characterized Questioning the Author lessons. Discussions focused much more on exploring and building meaning, with the students and teacher connecting and reacting to each other's responses. In the excerpt below from a Questioning the Author lesson, the class was reading the story *Ben and Me* (Lawson, 1939), which is about Benjamin Franklin and his mouse companion, whom he sends up in a kite to examine lightning. At the point in the lesson at which the excerpt begins, the class just read a portion of text early in the story and was grappling with this sentence: "This question of the nature of lightning so preyed upon his mind that he was finally driven to an act of deceit that caused the first and only rift in our long friendship." The teacher asked, "What's the author trying to tell us about Ben and Amos?"

TEMIKA: That their friendship was breaking up.

TEACHER: Their friendship was breaking up? OK, let's hang on to that. What do you think, April?

APRIL: I agree with the part that their friendship did break up, but um, I think that they got back together because when you were reading um, further, it said that he was enjoying the mouse.

TEACHER: OK, so let me make sure. You say that he knows that they're friends, and something happened that made them almost not be friends? But they're still friends?

ALVIS: I think that um, Amos is just, I think Amos is just lying because in the story it said if they weren't good friends, why would um, um, Ben build a um, kite for, build a kite for him so he could have fun?

TEACHER: OK, so Alvis is telling us that, why would Ben go to all that trouble and build that beautiful kite if they weren't friends? A lot of people agreed that their friendship was broken up. Alvis doesn't think their friendship is broken up. Can somebody help me out? What's the author want us to figure out here?

In their responses, April and Alvis were working to make sense of the text sentence by bringing in support from other parts of the text. The teacher responded by rephrasing their ideas in a way that defined the issue of whether the two story characters remained friends.

As the dialogue below shows, the discussion continued with two more students grappling with the meaning of the sentence. First, Tammy worked with the words of the text, manipulating them in an effort to make the ideas understandable to herself.

TAMMY: Um, um, deceit was an act of lying so that means, that means um, sometimes a lie broke up a friendship and, because it made a rift and um, so, and deceit was an act of lying, so their friendship must've broke up because of somebody told um, some kind of lie.

TEACHER: Oh, that's interesting. Tammy said that if there were some lying going on, something to break up their friendship, because that's what Amos said, "the first and only rift in our friendship," something must've happened. How many of you agree that something had to happen?

Next, Jamal's comments suggested a distinction between "a break" in the friendship and dissolving the friendship, which the teacher then acknowledged before reading resumed.

JAMAL: I disagree, 'cause a break in their friendship don't mean they gotta break their friendship.

TEACHER: OK, so Jamal thinks that they might still be friends, even though something happened. OK? We're gonna continue 'cause the only way we're gonna find out is if we read some more.

This excerpt showed students trying to come to terms with the meaning of one key sentence. In trying to figure out its meaning, the students spontaneously applied strategies such as rephrasing it, explaining parts of it, and bringing in other text information to interpret it. The teacher guided this process by rephrasing or clarifying comments, by keeping the focus on the issue being discussed, and by trying to draw other students into the discussion.

Developing ownership of ideas. An excerpt that provides a somewhat different flavor of the kinds of dialogue patterns that emerged during Questioning the Author discussions is presented below. In this example, students played off each other's comments to an even greater extent than in the foregoing discussion. The conversation focused on one idea, which the students seemed to have grasped from the beginning. Here, they worked to take ownership of the idea, creating an interpretation of it and expressing it in their own ways.

The excerpt is from a social studies class about Pennsylvania history. The class just read a text segment about the presidency of James Buchanan, a Pennsylvania native, which stated that many people believed that Buchanan liked the South better than the North because he held that it was a person's choice whether to have slaves. As an example of the problems that this position caused the President, the text states that settlers from Kansas wrote a proslavery constitution, which Buchanan supported but Congress rejected.

The teacher began the discussion by posing a general query about the paragraph. A student responded with a paraphrase of the main issue of Buchanan's position, and the teacher then asked a follow-up question that prompted the interpretation that the students then worked with.

TEACHER: All right. This paragraph that Tracy just read is really full of important information. What has the author told us in this important paragraph?

LAURA: Um, they um, think that Buchanan liked the South better because they, he said that it is a person's choice if they want to have slaves or not, so they thought um, that he liked the South better than the North.

TEACHER: Okay. And what kind of problem then did this cause President Buchanan when they thought that he liked the South better? What kind of problem did that cause?

In the next exchange, Janet generated an interpretation of how Buchanan's developing position on slavery might have affected the voters in his home state:

JANET: Well, maybe um, like less people would vote for him because like if he ran for President again, maybe less people would vote for him because like in Pennsylvania we were against slavery and we might have voted for him because he was in Pennsylvania, because he was from Pennsylvania. That may be why they voted for him, but now since we knew that he was for the South, we might not vote for him again.

The teacher and another student then took up and elaborated Janet's comment in their own ways. First, the teacher offered a capsulization of the idea:

TEACHER: Okay, a little bit of knowledge, then, might change people's minds.

Then another student, Jamie, acknowledged her peer's idea. She then went on to make explicit Janet's implication that Pennsylvania voters originally might have thought that Buchanan was himself against slavery because he was from Pennsylvania:

JAMIE: I have something to add on to Janet's 'cause I completely agree with her, but I just want to add something on. Um, we might have voted for him because he was from Pennsylvania so we might have thought that since he was from Pennsylvania and Pennsylvania was an antislavery state, that he was also against slavery. But it turns out he wasn't.

A third student, Angelica, weighed in with her spin on the developing interpretation. She turned the focus to another part of Janet's earlier comment, that Buchanan was "for the South":

ANGELICA: I agree with the rest of them, except for one that um, like all of a sudden, like someone who would be in Pennsylvania you want to vote for them but then they wouldn't, they be going for the South and then you wouldn't want to vote for them after that.

The teacher followed with another capsulization of the developing ideas:

TEACHER: Yeah. Just like, someone whom you think is your best friend, and then all of a sudden you find out, ooh, they're not.

Then, seemingly sensing that the notion under consideration had run its course, Rachel turned the discussion to a new part of the paragraph:

RACHEL: Um, as you said um, this paragraph is full of like a lot of stuff, well, the settlers wrote a constitution that the Wizard of Oz state would be a slave state and then they jump to 4 years later, and it's a free state.

The example suggests that the students have taken charge, even to moving on to a new topic. The degree to which students attended to and reacted to each other's comments was far beyond what typically is reported about traditional discussions of text in classrooms.

The analyses of student responses and excerpts from lessons presented in this chapter show students engaging in complex, meaning-focused, interactive thinking. The work that we have done with Questioning the Author suggests that this kind of thinking can emerge, given an environment in which the text is addressed as a product of a fallible author and discussions are based on general probes for the meaning of what has been written.

Teachers' roles in discussion. The kind of thinking and responding that students were doing in Questioning the Author lessons had much to do with the teachers' shaping of the environment. Teachers asked questions that encouraged students to focus on meaning rather than on locating text information; for example, asking, "What did Tony mean when he said that to his brother?" rather than simply, "What did Tony say to his brother?" The rejoinders that teachers gave to students' responses showed attention to the content of student responses and consideration of how they could fit into the discussion, as in this example: "Shanelle said that the reindeer herders moved to follow the reindeer. How does that fit in with what the author has already told us about these people?"

Teachers also encouraged student contributions to discussion by making it clear that students' responses were valued and that a range of responses was appropriate. Teacher comments such as the following were typical: "That's an interesting way to look at it, Amy, I never thought of it that way." Additionally, teachers shared their own reactions to the texts being read, with comments such as, "When I read this I was really confused," or "How can the author say it's cold when he just told us the sun shines 24 hours a day?" Such comments may have played a role in exposing the kinds of thinking that mature readers undertake when reading, also helping to reinforce the notion that reading takes effort and a "figuring it out" attitude.

LOOKING TO THE FUTURE

Developing and sustaining an environment that encourages students to share their thinking about text ideas and to work toward building meaning is a highly complex task. Discourse that leads to meaning-building needs direction, focus, and movement toward a goal. To foster such discourse effectively, a teacher must not only attend to the content of what is being read and the ideas important for building meaning from that content, but must also monitor where students are in that construction process and then pull from that combination of factors ways of directing the dialogue to promote understanding. As Cazden (1988) says, "It is easy to imagine talk in which ideas are explored rather than answers to teachers' test questions provided and evaluated. . . . Easy to imagine, but not easy to do" (p. 54).

We addressed the difficulties our collaborating teachers had in developing discourse environments in which ideas are constructed by providing extensive, ongoing, firsthand support. We observed and videotaped lessons and met with the teachers weekly. At those meetings we provided teachers with feedback about their lessons, and together we analyzed transcripts, identifying successful and less successful aspects, and worked to develop solutions to problematic issues. We also held collaborative planning sessions with the teachers to map out ways of dealing with specific texts or topics, and provided occasional demonstration lessons for the teachers to observe and critique.

Thus, our face-to-face interactions with the teachers were the major agent for the change that took place in the classroom discourse environment. This is a situation common to current research that is aimed at revamping instructional practices toward guiding students to build their own knowledge and understanding rather than transmitting information to them. This trend in pedagogical practice is referred to as "teaching for understanding" (Cohen, McLaughlin, & Talbert, 1993). In the current zeitgeist, researchers work closely with teachers, collaborating on developing and refining approaches to instruction and even taking turns in the classroom.

The current collaborative orientation arises from researchers' cognizance of the failure of older ways of working toward instructional change in which teachers were given an innovation to perform. Rather, the collaborative interactive approach recognizes that enacting new instructional strategies is a learning process, and that change needs to include teachers' understanding of the rationale for the change as well as their ownership of the new practices (see Au & Asam, Chapter 8, this volume, for a discussion of related issues). This research focus has produced some broad outlines of what seems to be needed for teachers to develop teaching-for-understanding orientations: fundamental change in teachers' beliefs about what learning is (Prawat, 1992; Richardson, 1990), development of practices that put those beliefs into action (Blumenfeld, Krajcik, Marx, & Soloway, 1994; Wood & Cobb, 1991), and ability to reflect on how classroom actions match beliefs (Colton & Sparks-Langer, 1993; Russell, 1993).

The details of how to produce changes in beliefs, practices, and reflection are quite sketchy, however. For example, in the area of pedagogical practices, constructs such as modeling, scaffolding, assisted performance, and coaching are pervasive (Duffy & Roehler, 1987; Duffy et al., 1989; Palincsar & Brown, 1984; Tharp & Gallimore, 1991). Yet, it is difficult to move from general constructs such as modeling and coaching to the kind of details that would bring those constructs to life, because the details are embedded in anecdotal accounts of face-to-face collaborations between researchers and teachers.

With the predominance of collaborative interactions, the focus in current instructional research has been on making change occur. Less attention has gone into what gives changed practice a life of its own after the research intervention is over, in particular when researchers can no longer sit face-to-face with teachers. Even when teacher–researcher interactions are carefully documented, the knowledge gained cannot be transported readily to new environments. In our work with Questioning the Author, we are confronted with the situation that is emblematic of current collaborative research on instruction; that is, the knowledge gained from 2 years of work with teachers and their classrooms produced a rich, extensive, anecdotal database, but that knowledge needs to be transformed in order to be applicable to new settings.

Various approaches exist to addressing the problem of transforming knowledge. Most commonly, they involve support personnel, either in the form of special implementors or teacher consultants who are more experienced with the innovative approach than their peers. Having access to "live" support and assistance can be very advantageous for teachers trying out a new instructional approach. There are drawbacks as well, however, to transforming knowledge through support staff. One issue is the quality of the personnel—their understanding of the approach and their ability to transform their understanding into productive assistance for others may exhibit wide individual differences. Another drawback is that support personnel may not be present when a problem arises and needs to be addressed. These potential drawbacks can be mitigated by extensive training of personnel and by having adequate numbers of support staff available. However, these solutions make this approach cost-intensive.

An alternative approach to supporting teachers in instructional innovation involves resources that teachers can use on their own. Probably the major issue with this approach is having the information, usually in the form of print materials, come to life in a powerful way. In the next phase of our work, we plan to design ways to transform the detailed and exquisite content of our face-to-face interactions with teachers into forms that are available and accessible to teachers broadly.

Our approach to transforming the knowledge will be to develop tangible resources that teachers can access in the course of acquiring a teaching-for-understanding orientation. The resources, in the form of printed materials and videotape segments, will be based on actual classroom interactions and issues that concerned teachers during our Questioning the Author implementations. We view the resources to be developed as vehicles for fostering principled understanding of the rationale underlying Questioning the Author and how the approach functions. Although developing principled understanding is key, providing teachers only with principles is insufficient. Principles and guidelines are merely abstract statements of what should be done. Experiences with instantiations of principles that clearly portray how the principles are put into action are called for if deep understanding is to develop.

The resources we develop will present a classroom problem or instructional issue accompanied by explanatory annotations addressed to teachers. The purpose of the annotations will be to set up the problem or issue, draw attention to how it was manifested, and show how it was dealt with in the classroom or in teachers' preparations for lessons. In our view, the interaction of textual and videotape examples and annotations has strong communicative potential because it operates at the intersection of understanding and actions. That is, it avoids both the Scylla of cookbook-type lesson plans that put words into teachers' mouths and connect only with actions, and the Charybdis of general principles that have only vague connections to useful pedagogical actions. We believe that the interaction of authentic examples from classrooms and explanatory annotations will encourage principled understanding by giving life to the principle that meaning is constructed through actively grappling with information.

The current focus of instructional research on collaborative classroom efforts between researchers and teachers has yielded rich and detailed information about what it takes to get new instructional approaches working in classrooms. The information provides great opportunity for enhancing classroom instruction. Attention now needs to be given to putting the richness and detail of what has been learned into generative forms.

ACKNOWLEDGMENT. The research described in this chapter was supported by the National Research Center on Student Learning of the Learning Research and Development Center, University of Pittsburgh, supported by funds from the Office of Educational Research and Improvement (OERI), United States Department of Education. The opinions expressed do not necessarily reflect the position or policy of OERI, and no official endorsement should be inferred.

REFERENCES

Alvermann, D. E., O'Brien, D. G., & Dillon, D. R. (1990). What teachers do when they say they're having discussions of content area reading assignments: A qualitative analysis. *Reading Research Quarterly, 24*(4), 296–322.

Beck, I. L., & McKeown, M. G. (1994). Outcomes of history instruction: Paste-up accounts. In J. F. Voss & M. Carretero (Eds.), *Cognitive and instructional processes in history and the social sciences* (pp. 237–256). Hillsdale, NJ: Erlbaum.

Beck, I. L., McKeown, M. G., & Gromoll, E. W. (1989). Learning from social studies texts. *Cognition and Instruction, 6*(2), 99–158.

Beck, I. L., McKeown, M. G., Sinatra, G. M., & Loxterman, J. A. (1991). Revising social studies text from a text-processing perspective: Evidence of improved comprehensibility. *Reading Research Quarterly, 26,* 251–276.

Beck, I. L., McKeown, M. G., Worthy, J., Sandora, C. A., & Kucan, L. (1996). Questioning the Author: A year-long implementation to engage students with text. *The Elementary School Journal, 94*(4), 358–414.

Black, J. B., & Bern, H. (1981). Causal coherence and memory for events in narratives. *Journal of Verbal Learning and Verbal Behavior, 20,* 267–275.

Blumenfeld, P. C., Krajcik, J. S., Marx, R. W., & Soloway, E. (1994). Lessons learned: How collaboration helped middle grade science teachers learn project-based instruction. *The Elementary School Journal, 94*(5), 539–551.

Cazden, C. (1986). Classroom discourse. In M. C. Wittrock (Ed.), *Handbook of research on teaching* (3rd ed.) (pp. 432–462). New York: Macmillan.

Cazden, C. (1988). *Classroom discourse: The language of teaching and learning.* Portsmouth, NH: Heinemann.

Chiesi, H. L., Spilich, G. J., & Voss, J. F. (1979). Acquisition of domain-related information in relation to high and low domain knowledge. *Journal of Verbal Learning and Verbal Behavior, 18,* 275–290.

Cleary, B. (1982). *Ralph S. Mouse.* New York: Dell.

Cohen, D. K., McLaughlin, M. W., & Talbert, J. E. (Eds.). (1993). *Teaching for understanding: Challenges for policy and practice.* San Francisco: Jossey-Bass.

Colton, A. M., & Sparks-Langer, G. M. (1993). A conceptual framework to guide the development of teacher reflection and decision making. *Journal of Teacher Education, 44*(1), 45–54.

Duffy, G. G., & Roehler, L. R. (1987). Teaching reading skills as strategies. *The Reading Teacher, 40*(4), 414–418.

Duffy, T. M., Higgins, L., Mehlenbacher, B., Cochran, C., Wallace, D., Hill, C., Haugen, D., McCaffrey, M., Burnett, R., Sloane, S., & Smith, S. (1989). Models for the design of instructional text. *Reading Research Quarterly, 24,* 434–457.

Frederiksen, J. R. (1981). Understanding anaphora: Rules used by readers in assigning pronominal referents. *Discourse Processes, 4,* 323–348.

Goodlad, J. L. (1984). *A place called school: Prospects for the future.* New York: McGraw-Hill.

Just, M. A., & Carpenter, P. A. (1987). *The psychology of reading and language comprehension.* Rockleigh, NJ: Allyn & Bacon.

Lawson, R. (1939). *Ben and me.* Boston: Little, Brown.

Luke, C., DeCastell, S., & Luke, A. (1983). Beyond criticism: The authority of the school text. *Curriculum Inquiry, 13*(2), 111–127.

McKeown, M. G., & Beck, I. L. (1990, April). What young students understand from their textbooks about the American Revolution. In *Subject specificity in social studies: How does the nature of the subject matter affect curriculum theory and practice?* Symposium conducted at the annual meeting of the American Educational Research Association, Boston.

Olson, D. R. (1980). On the language and authority of textbooks. *Journal of Communication, 30*(1), 186-196.

Palincsar, A. S., & Brown, A. L. (1984). Reciprocal teaching of comprehension-fostering and monitoring activities. *Cognition and Instruction, 1*(2), 117-175.

Pearson, P. D., Hansen, J., & Gordon, C. (1979). The effect of background knowledge on young children's comprehension of explicit and implicit information. *Journal of Reading Behavior, 11*, 201-209.

Perfetti, C. A. (1985). *Reading ability.* New York: Oxford University Press.

Prawat, R. S. (1992). Teachers' beliefs about teaching and learning: A constructivist perspective. *American Journal of Education, 100*, 354-395.

Richardson, V. (1990). Significant and worthwhile change in teaching practice. *Educational Researcher, 19*(7), 10-18.

Russell, T. (1993). Critical attributes of a reflective teacher. In J. Calderhead & P. Gates (Eds.), *Conceptualizing reflection in teacher development* (pp. 144-153). London: Falmer.

Silver Burdett. (1984). *The United States and its neighbors.* Morristown, NJ: Author.

Tharp, R. G., & Gallimore, R. (1991). *Rousing minds to life: Teaching, learning, and schooling in social context.* Cambridge: Cambridge University Press.

Trabasso, T., Secco, T., & van den Broek, P. (1984). Causal cohesion and story coherence. In H. Mandl, N. L. Stein, & T. Trabasso (Eds.), *Learning and comprehension of text* (pp. 83-111). Hillsdale, NJ: Erlbaum.

Wood, T. W., & Cobb, P. (1991). Change in teaching mathematics: A case study. *American Educational Research Journal, 28*(3), 587-616.

From *The First R: Every Child's Right to Read, 1996*

Andrea M. Guillaume

Learning with text in the primary grades

This article provides a rationale for learning-with-text experiences for primary-grade children, lists general approaches for these experiences, and gives a sample lesson that incorporates the approaches.

The day before yesterday, my 3-year-old son Zachary asked me, "What do our bodies look like on the inside?" As a science lover, I relish the opportunity to explore the natural world with children. In this instance, though, actual exploration was not feasible. Instead, Zachary and I talked some about our own ideas, then I suggested that we take out our book about human bodies. His enthusiastic response? "Yes! The giant book!" Together we turned the heavy cardboard pages of our human body big book and pored over the diagrams and descriptions to gain an answer to Zachary's question. I was struck by the power of text to help us find answers to personally relevant questions.

This article provides a rationale for providing learning-with-text experiences for primary-grade children, lists 10 general approaches to foster primary-grade content area reading, and gives a sample lesson that promotes comprehension of text and content matter.

A rationale

Five compelling propositions urge us to learn with text in the primary grades. First, knowledge is power. The more ways we have of gaining information to build knowledge, the more empowered we become. Literate people can use various resources to learn about the world and important ideas, can communicate with others, and can make informed decisions. Reading is one of the most efficient and flexible ways of learning. Through reading, we bring our prior experiences with the world and with the printed word to a text and use our knowledge and reading strategies to answer our questions. Classroom experiences in content area reading are of particular importance for dependent readers in that reading can occur with the structure and support that enable dependent readers to move toward independence. Reading is a powerful tool.

Second, content area reading is not the sole territory of those who are already proficient readers. Teachers of children of all ages have the important job of helping learners interact with text to produce meaning. Those who suggest that primary-grade teachers help children *learn to read* while upper-grade teachers help children *read to learn* deprive students at both levels of learning opportunities. Even young children can learn through text, and older readers should continue to refine their skills and find new ways to understand text. For this reason, content area reading should begin in the primary grades. As Olson and Gee (1991) suggest, learning to

Figure 1
A variety of texts for the primary-grade content area library

- **Textbooks**
  Assigned textbooks are a mainstay in classrooms across the grades, and they become increasingly prevalent through the grades. Because they *explain* rather than *tell a story* through narrative, textbooks can present comprehension challenges. Technical vocabulary and high concept load also make them slower going than storybooks.

- **Trade books**
  Trade books are often also expository. However, trade books typically include richer detail and more imaginative presentation than do textbooks. Their content tends also to be more focused and of greater depth (Ross, 1994).

- **Fiction with content information**
  Fictional literature across the curriculum is popular, in part because the narrative structure flows smoothly and is familiar to young children. Fiction often treats content area information fairly, but care must be taken to ensure that selections encourage better understanding of topics rather than perpetuating faulty content ideas.

- **Other kinds of print**
  Newspapers, interactive software, and magazines written for young children (e.g., *Zoobooks* and *Ranger Rick*) provide accurate information about topics of great interest to young children. Their format is also appealing.

learn from text takes many experiences with text. Rich experiences with primary-level texts build a foundation of skills and habits that will help readers as they face more—and more sophisticated—texts in later years.

Third, the content areas—science, social studies, mathematics, the arts—fuel questions. How did Egyptians make mummies? Are there volcanoes on Venus? What do our bodies look like on the inside? The content areas build motivation and purpose for reading: We read to know (Baghban, 1995).

Fourth, language, including reading and writing, permeates all of the content areas. Language can encourage careful thinking, support student participation, and motivate creative decision making. Reading and writing experiences thus belong from the very beginning across all subject areas (Dickson, 1995).

Finally, content areas provide a meaningful context for the reading/language arts goals teachers hold as dear. Content areas naturally embed skills like decoding into meaningful situations (Bristor, 1994; Romance & Vitale, 1992).

In sum, content area reading experiences help young children develop one of the critical attributes of a literate, responsible citizen: the ability to process and analyze information (Dickson, 1995). Given the strong rationale for primary-grade content area reading, how can teachers help young students learn to learn with text?

Ten big ideas

Teachers can provide potent content area reading experiences through the environments they create and through general approaches to content study. Fueled by the whole language movement, rich literacy programs have in recent years moved away from focusing solely upon textbooks to exploring texts of many kinds. (See Figure 1.)

Each kind of text can be a powerful resource for helping children learn to read and read to learn. How can text, no matter its kind, be incorporated in meaningful ways throughout the primary-grade program? Ten big ideas reflect the literature on content area reading and learning.

1. *Access and build prior knowledge.* One powerful determinant of what we will learn in a given situation is what we already know. In reading, the unique experiences that each child brings to the classroom affect transactions with the text. Limited background knowledge confounds comprehension. This is especially true in classrooms where students' background knowledge and literacy experiences are highly divergent, as is the case in classrooms where some or all students are learning English as a second language (Schifini, 1994) or where dependent readers are present (Tierney & Pearson, 1994). Schifini's (1994) five general strategies for accessing prior knowledge (see Figure 2) are helpful with diverse groups of children.

An additional technique particularly useful for accessing young children's knowledge is drawing. Primary-grade children are usually eager to draw, and their drawings can spark conversations that reveal what they know. Early drawings can later serve as helpful tools to reflect on what children have learned through hands-on activities and reading experiences. Figure 3 provides Zachary's interpretations of crickets as he studied them at home. Note that his drawings indicate scientific understandings (the head is separate from the body, the legs—6 in all—are jointed, both crickets have cerci on their back ends, but only the female has an ovipositor) as well as some concepts still under development (the body has only two segments, only two eyes appear, and the crickets carry eggs on their backs). Information from students' drawings can thus provide teachers with direction for the kinds of experiences that will help children build accurate conceptions of the content.

Classroom reading experiences also serve to build background knowledge for future reading experiences. The texts children read and create in the classroom can serve as resources for future learning experiences.

2. *Provide hands-on experiences prior to reading.* Perhaps because of the high vocabulary load of content areas, it is tempting to assign vocabulary activities before children have had sufficient opportunities to build concepts. Instead, interactive experiences like science activities, map making, cooperative discussions, and film viewing should be provided early in the lesson sequence so that children develop ideas and relationships among concepts and can use terms flexibly to express content-related ideas. Thus, building common experience before reading can help to remove one potential stumbling block for dependent readers: concept deficiencies. Hands-on experiences become part of the current knowledge store that children bring to bear on their readings, and subsequent reading experiences can help children attach labels to newly formed concepts.

For example, when a group of first graders and I studied the paper-making process, we began by making our own paper (American

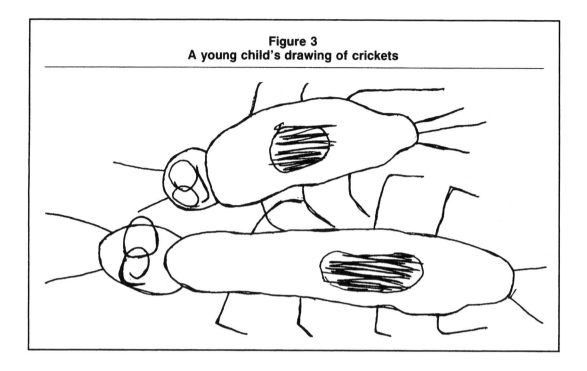

Figure 3
A young child's drawing of crickets

Forest Foundation, 1994). We blended soggy recycled paper in a blender, swished the pulp through screens in dishpans, pressed out extra water, then removed our damp new paper for drying. This messy and memorable activity allowed children to build a shared experience that they later recalled as we read a brief content area book on paper making. Instead of building rote recall of terms like *pulp, rollers,* and *metal screen*, students drew from their recent experience to connect vivid understandings to new vocabulary terms.

3. *Read aloud.* An adult's enthusiastic oral reading can have a mighty influence on children in developing a listening vocabulary, a recognition for the cadence of the language, and an appreciation for the powerful meanings that print can convey. This holds true for content area selections as well. In fact, for kindergartners, read-alouds may provide much of the content area reading experience. In addition to narrative text, teachers' read-alouds can include nonfiction and fiction with content information. Some specific suggestions for content area read-alouds are given in Figure 4.

4. *Read for a purpose.* School is a place where students often subsume their own purposes to those of the teacher (Jackson, 1968).

However, reading, like all tools, should be used to construct something useful or to enjoy or improve life in some way. When students set personally meaningful purposes for their reading, motivation and task persistence increase, and the idea that reading is a tool, not an end in itself, is reinforced.

In fact, when readers' purposes fail to match those of an author, breakdowns in comprehension are likely (Tierney & Pearson, 1994). Tierney and Pearson suggest that teachers can help dependent readers find reading purposeful by choosing highly motivating text or functional text that requires a reader response. Treasure maps and directions to science experiments are examples.

Strategies like the K-W-L chart (Ogle, 1986) and Manning and Manning's (1995) 3W2H strategy can also effectively support purposeful reading. In 3W2H, the reading experience begins with students' questions:

W1: What is your question?
W2: What do you already know about the topic?
W3: Where can you find the answers?
H1: How are you going to record your ideas?
H2: How are you going to share your findings?

I recently used an anticipation guide (Yopp & Yopp, 1996) to help set purposes for

---

Figure 4
Suggestions for reading aloud in the content areas

- For very young students, read science-based stories, then supply materials so students can experiment with the topics of the books. Keep the books on hand for reference (McMath & King, 1993).

- For all grade levels, choose read-alouds that show vivid examples of the content and that build appropriate attitudes related to that content (Richardson, 1994).

- Read a passage aloud as a fluent model, then allow children to read it alone or to a partner. This is especially helpful for building fluency for dependent readers.

- Use content area readings, including realistic fiction and biographical works, as your read-alouds in math, science, and social studies.

- Include content area texts of all kinds for your Sustained Silent Reading period.

Figure 5
A diamante poem composed by first graders after studying paper making

```
                    tree
              big       green
        standing    waving    falling
   shade    treehouse    pine    home
      crumbling    ironing    drying
            ripped    colorful
                   paper
```

---

reading as a class of second graders and I made fossils. The guide served to prompt students' existing ideas, encourage discussion, and spark student questions about fossils. In the anticipation guide, students checked "agree" or "disagree" for such statements as, "Fossils are made by people in a factory," and "We know all there is to know about dinosaurs." After we discussed students' responses, pairs of more and less dependent readers read an informational text on fossils. Before releasing partners to read, we studied the table of contents, and I suggested that they select portions of the text that addressed points of interest from our earlier discussion. Students with questions about how fossils are made, for instance, could read specific sections of text to meet that purpose. Our postreading conversation was enriched as children talked excitedly about the portions of the text they had selected.

5. *Provide access to content area materials.* Print-rich environments encourage the joy of pursuing one's own interests through the freedom of selecting what one reads (Smith & Johnson, 1994). Richardson and Morgan (1994) note that many young children choose nonfiction materials as often as they choose fiction, and young readers may even be more likely than older students to read for information. Thus, rooms stocked with varied nonfiction books and print materials allow learners to engage in purposeful communication that is contextually embedded. In addition to magazines and software, all three types of content area texts (textbooks, trade books, and realistic fiction) belong in the classroom (Manning & Manning, 1995). Helpful sources for locating content area materials include Kobrin's (1995) *Eye-Openers II: Children's Books to Answer Children's Questions About the World Around Them* and professional journals, which frequently recommend high-quality trade books. For instance, the National Science Teachers Association's journal, *Science and Children*, publishes an annual listing of outstanding science trade books for elementary students.

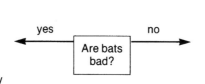

Figure 6
A completed discussion web graphic

- They have fangs and may bite you.
- They're scary.
- They can give diseases to cows, pigs, and other animals like people.
- Their claws can stick onto people or walls or anything.
- I had a bad dream that one bit me on the leg and I never saw my family again.
- When it comes to bats, Dracula's a pain in the neck.

yes ← → no

Are bats bad?

- They teach us about echolocation.
- They really don't bother people much.
- They keep bugs away from us by eating them.
- They're good parents. They hold their babies and feed them milk.

Additionally, the children's own content area writings serve an important role in the classroom library stacks: Children can reread their writings for continued practice and appreciation of their new knowledge.

Providing a variety of materials at different reading levels and across many topics allows students to read at their individual levels (Ross, 1994), make choices about what they read, and thus build their strengths and curiosities (Schifini, 1994), aspects of a literacy program considered essential for dependent readers (Manzo & Manzo, 1995).

6. *Encourage efferent and affective responses.* Although school life focuses primarily on the cognitive domain, the affective domain cannot be ignored. Affect captures attitudes inherent in the subject areas, like curiosity in science or the ability to view historical events from different perspectives in social studies, and reinforces them in reading. In social studies, affect is essential for bringing about change in preconceptions and prejudice (Lickteig & Danielson, 1995). Additionally, affect may motivate children to read in the content areas, where, as in science, reading may be devalued in favor of experimentation as a way of learning (Dickson, 1995). Affect, including the will to continue reading, can in part determine whether one will become an independent reader.

Because cognition and affect are essential in learning, reading experiences need to capture both domains by allowing learners to respond in both efferent (cognitive) and aesthetic (affective) ways (Rosenblatt, 1991; Ross, 1994). Too, children should be allowed at least occasionally to choose the type (efferent or aesthetic) of their response and the form of

their response. One example of an efferent response is a bookmaking activity wherein students write nonfiction books after studying content like the local community, geometry, earthquakes, or sharks. Gaylord (1994) provides a wealth of bookmaking strategies that can be used for content area writing across the curriculum.

As aesthetic responses, children can choreograph a dance; compose poetry; or write persuasive letters to appropriate legislators, companies, or individuals. Figure 5 contains a diamante poem that the first graders composed after their experiences studying the process of paper making. To aid the class in composing this poem, I put a diamante on a different topic (seeds) on the chalk board. We studied the structure of "Seeds" before writing our own diamante about trees. Children who were quick to discern patterns in text led us in the activity; others listened quietly, perhaps supplying single-word ideas. After reading and rereading our poem together aloud, I was ready to move on. However, students who listened silently as we initially analyzed "Seed" began, upon seeing the two similar poems side by side, blurting out important discoveries about the structure of the two works: "They both have no periods! Or capitals!" "They both have two lines of -*ing* words!" A whole-class activity intended to capture our aesthetic response to paper making also provided an unexpected opportunity to study text structure.

7. *Encourage discussion.* Discussion allows for finding main ideas, summarizing, and providing the redundancy (revisiting ideas and text) that may otherwise be neglected (Manzo, 1991). Participating in peer discussion can also

---

Figure 7
Contrasting examples of second-grade students' nonfiction writing (original spellings)

The Magnet Book
illustrated by Kay K.
words by Kay K.

by Randy A.
About Magnet.
How they Science

If you stick a magnet in your shert and put one on the top they stik to your shirt.

Magnets cen go throw metal.

Magnitism can travel throgh cardbourd. For example put the magnet on cardboard and hold on the cardbourd.

there are alu cins fo magnet
[There are all kinds of magnets.]

If you tack a nail and rub a magnet next to it the nail by itself can pike up metal.

Magnets cat go thero everytheing
[Magnets can't go through everything.]

And thats how you can use magnets.

---

build upon students' prior knowledge to enhance their reading experiences.

Some informal principles guide my use of discussion with primary-grade students. First, students must have opinions, ideas, or experiences related to the topic. Second, the discussion question or task must allow for multiple responses rather than for a single convergent or factual one. Third, the climate of the classroom must encourage the risk-taking necessary for children to share personal ideas. Finally, young children need structured opportunities and friendly teacher support to share their ideas in the classroom.

Manzo and Manzo (1995) share a discussion strategy that illustrates the use of each of these principles: the discussion web graphic developed by Alvermann (1991). The discussion web graphic has been used successfully with children as young as kindergarten (as a whole-class activity), and its use is supported by research. For the graphic, a central yes/no question related to the reading is posed in the middle of the responses. In partners, students respond in writing to the question, providing responses on both the left ("yes") side of the paper and on the right ("no") side. Figure 6 displays a web graphic two boys completed before studying Bash's (1993) *Shadows of Night: The Hidden World of the Little Brown Bat*. After pairs have completed their discussion webs, one partner group joins another so that, in teams of 4, students defend their positions and reach group consensus. One member of the team then reports to the class, sharing both the consensus and dissenting viewpoints. The teacher moni-

tors carefully throughout the writing and discussion phases in order to extend thinking and challenge students' misconceptions, especially those that may impair comprehension. The web in Figure 6 suggests that the authors hold many accurate concepts about bats and that the teacher's job may focus upon supplying readings and discussion to address misconceptions that arise from folklore and the media.

8. *Connect reading and writing.* For all students, content area writing can facilitate long-term memory of the content, can increase metacognitive skills and complex thinking, can foster recognition of text structure, can facilitate decoding and comprehension, and can increase learning in every content area (Armbruster, 1992; Richardson & Morgan, 1994). Informal classroom writing experiences can also serve affective purposes by fostering curiosity, alleviating anxiety, and promoting confidence.

Content area writing experiences may be most successful when they address varied audiences, are of consequence to the writer, and take a variety of forms. As a closure to our recent lesson on magnetism, second graders composed their own magnet books. Although the content (magnetism) was predetermined and the number of pages was dictated by the folded-page format I selected (Gaylord, 1994), all other decisions were left in the hands of the authors. The divergence of the results surprised me: One student wrote a comic book about Magnet Man, the Man of Steel, and another wrote a how-to book on induced magnetism. Also, Figure 7 shows the difference in

Figure 8
Sample strategies for pre-, during-, and postreading activities in the content areas

Prereading strategies:	During-reading strategies:	Postreading strategies:
Access and build prior knowledge. Prepare students to read.	Build conceptual understanding, reading fluency, and comprehension.	Synthesize and summarize content area information, build comprehension, and extend the reading experience.

• Brainstorm. • Factstorm (list all the facts we know about the content). • Brainwrite (individuals create their own brainstorming lists, then pass their papers to peers, who review and add to the lists). • Create graphic organizers. Use charts that match the text's structure (compare and contrast? description?). • Listen to one another's stories. • List student questions. • Provide concrete experiences. • Set a purpose for reading (What are we looking for?). • Preview the text: How is it organized? Does it have charts? An index? How can we find particular topics in it?	• Vary reading structures (Smith & Johnson, 1994): Paired reading, kaleidoscope reading, taped readings, literature circles, large-group discussion. • Find patterns in text structure. • Help children study text features. • Use simple notetaking strategies. • Expand on the charts used during prereading. • Use reading guides. • Pause to ask who, what, where, when, why, how. • Incorporate visual imagery and partner discussion. • Try guided reading/thinking activities. • Learn vocabulary in context. Include general terms with specific connotations in current usage and specific, technical terms. Connect to earlier hands-on experiences.	• Retell the passage. • Compose group or partner summaries. • Write structured expository paragraphs or journal paraphrases. • Try language experiences in whole groups for writing (for example, ABC books on the content). • Reflect on what text features were helpful and which ones seemed rude. • Use reading-to-learn experiences as a means to an end; in some way, use what is learned through reading. • Bridge back to real life to ensure that reading experiences have relevance. • Reflect on the answers found to children's earlier questions. • Ask for students' new questions.

the level of sophistication of text produced by two authors, Kay and Randy.

Although the amount of text and the usage of writing conventions vary widely between these two students' works, both authors produced accurate information about a scientific phenomenon, and both students' texts could be used for future individualized reading instruction.

9. *Use general strategies or heuristics.* Heuristics are effective in increasing comprehension and in moving students toward independent reading. Although some are too formal or complicated to be appropriate for primary-grade learners, others provide useful formats for guiding content area reading instruction, especially when the teacher leads students through the process. Two promising examples include the previously discussed 3W2H (Manning & Manning, 1995) and Manzo's (1991) Listen, Read, Discuss (LRD). During LRD, students:

*L*isten to the teacher discuss the content.

*R*ead content text aided by the background experience of the teacher's words.

*D*iscuss: What did you understand best? Least well? What questions or thoughts did this raise for you about the content or reading strategies?

LRD can be varied to meet students' interests and needs. Examples include varying the input for listening, providing a purpose for reading that requires critical or creative expression or application, and discussing which portions of the text struck readers as inconsiderate (poorly written or poorly organized). Teachers may hold postreading discussions on teaching and learning strategies or create research teams that allow students to delve into a topic in greater depth.

10. *Use pre-, during- and postreading activities.* Although proposed content area reading frameworks differ (e.g., Richardson & Morgan, 1994; Singer & Donlan, 1989), frameworks each suggest that teachers need to prepare students for readings, guide them through

---

Figure 9
A sample science content area reading lesson for primary grades: Crickets

---

Prereading activities
1. Teacher shares a personal story of wildly chasing noisy crickets that interrupted her sleep. She elicits cricket stories from students.
2. Children close their eyes and visualize a cricket. When they open their eyes, they compose a 30-second sketch of a cricket. Teacher circulates to check prior knowledge. (Did each child draw an insect? What notable features are apparent?)
3. The class constructs a semantic map on crickets: Cricket bodies, what they do, what they need, other information.
4. Teacher records questions and uncertainties in a different color.
5. Children fold a paper in fourths and record one cricket question related to each of the four sections of the semantic map in each fourth. Teacher models for students who need support.
6. Teacher distributes hand lenses and crickets (from tropical fish store), one per student pair. Students make observations to begin to answer their questions.
7. The class revises its map based upon observations (e.g., "crickets have four eyes; crickets have two pairs of wings; females and males look different"). They review their questions to determine which remain unanswered.
8. Teacher distributes text on crickets (one is available from the author in English or Spanish). The class studies text features (e.g., diagrams, headings, boldfaced terms) and notices that the organizational headings match the categories of their semantic map.

(Analysis: These activities allow children to respond affectively to the topic, connect the topic to their prior experiences, explore specific concepts related to the content, engage in hands-on activity to build background knowledge, set a purpose for reading, and examine text features and structure to gather information quickly.)

During-reading activities
1. Dependent readers listen to the text and follow along on their own copies as the teacher reads text aloud. A cross-age tutor may read the text, or students may listen to a taped reading by a fluent model.
2. Less dependent readers may meet in heterogeneous pairs to partner read the text. They may take responsibility for reading only a section of the text, then retell and summarize the information for the class.
3. Independent readers can silently read the material, focusing on sections that address their recorded questions.
4. The class takes simple notes, including words and drawings, upon their folded question papers.
5. Students attach vocabulary terms from the text to their observations. Examples of terms include *ovipositor, cerci, stridulation,* and *compound eye.*

(Analysis: These activities provide support for students as they read for a purpose.)

Postreading activities
1. Students examine their initial cricket drawings and compose new drawings to correct inaccuracies and add detail.
2. The class revises the semantic map.
3. Students analyze the text for its friendliness and make a list of the next set of cricket questions to be addressed.
4. Students select a writing activity to capture their knowledge and response to the cricket experience. Examples include pop-up cards with a single student-composed sentence, group paragraphs, and cinquain poems.

(Analysis: Students reflect on their knowledge gains, analyze the reading experience, and respond through writing to the experience. This aids comprehension and solidifies content knowledge. The purpose is set for future reading endeavors.)

---

readings, and then extend the reading experience. Use of pre-, during-, and postreading strategies offers dependent readers support to activate and maintain relevant schema (Tierney & Pearson, 1994). Explicit instruction about the framework helps children see that it can generalize to other texts and settings as well. Figure 8 presents a brief sampling of activities—many of which are particularly helpful for dependent readers—that can take children into, through, and beyond their content area readings while addressing vocabulary, content ideas, and text features and structures.

Figure 9 gives a sample primary-grade content area lesson that illustrates how the framework can be used to address vocabulary, concepts and relationships, text features, and text structure and to provoke efferent and affective responses. This lesson, used successfully with learners of many ages, embodies each of the 10 ideas related to content area reading.

Summary and conclusions

Trade books, textbooks, realistic fiction, and other print sources all have a place within the primary-grade classroom for content area reading. Exposure to abundant informational resources provides young students with the valuable opportunity to read for the purpose of learning about their worlds and to answer their questions. Primary-grade teachers can use content area reading experiences to help children learn, to build a foundation for getting meaning from text, to encourage the use of reading as a powerful tool to gain information, and to help children develop and respond to important ideas. Although time and effort are necessary to collect materials and develop content area learning experiences, teachers can draw on other resources to enrich their literacy programs. Students can bring materials from home, the librarian may provide assistance, and financial support may be available through sources like parent-teacher organizations or grant funds. Teachers can also work with colleagues to develop or implement meaningful content area reading experiences. They can listen to young students' questions about the world and work together with students to find answers to those questions and get meaning from the printed word. When primary teachers encourage content area reading, they

- provide a meaningful context for reading instruction.
- help children develop lifelong skills for gaining information.
- encourage comprehension, the exploration of big ideas, and connections among ideas.
- nurture students' quest to know and to seek answers to their important questions.

Guillaume began her career as an elementary teacher. She now teaches mathematics and science methods courses at California State University, Fullerton, where she may be contacted: Department of Elementary, Bilingual, and Reading Education, Fullerton, CA 92834, USA.

References

Alvermann, D.E. (1991). The discussion web: A graphic aid for learning across the curriculum. *The Reading Teacher, 45*, 92 – 99.

American Forest Foundation. (1994). *Project Learning Tree: Environmental education activity guide.* Washington, DC: Author.

Armbruster, B.B. (1992). Content reading in *RT*: The last 2 decades. *The Reading Teacher, 46*, 166 – 167.

Baghban, M. (1995, July). *Content reading: Is there any other kind?* Paper presented at the annual meeting of the National Council of Teachers of English International Conference, New York. (ERIC Document Reproduction Service No. ED 385 824)

Bash, B. (1993). *Shadows of night: The hidden world of the little brown bat.* San Francisco: Sierra Club.

Bristor, V.J. (1994). Combining reading and writing with science to enhance content area achievement and attitudes. *Reading Horizons, 35*, 30 – 43.

Dickson, B.L. (1995). Reading in the content-areas. *Reading Improvement, 32*, 191 – 192.

Gaylord, S.K. (1994). *Multicultural books to make and share.* New York: Scholastic.

Guillaume, A.M., Yopp, R.H., & Yopp, H.K. (1996). Accessible science. *Journal of Educational Issues for Language Minority Students, 17*, 67 – 85.

Jackson, P.W. (1968). *Life in classrooms.* New York: Holt, Rinehart & Winston.

Kobrin, B. (1995). *Eye-openers II: Children's books to answer children's questions about the world around them.* New York: Scholastic.

Lickteig, M.J., & Danielson, K.E. (1995). Use children's books to link the cultures of the world. *The Social Studies, 86*, 69 – 73.

Manning, M., & Manning, G. (1995). Reading and writing in the content areas. *Teaching K–8, 26*, 152 – 153.

Manzo, A.V. (1991). Training teachers to use content area reading strategies: Description and appraisal of four options. *Reading Research and Instruction, 30*, 67 – 73.

Manzo, A.V. & Manzo, U.C. (1995). *Teaching children to be literate: A reflective approach.* Fort Worth, TX: Harcourt Brace.

McMath, J., & King, M. (1993). Open books, open minds. *Science and Children, 30*, 33 – 36.

Ogle, D. (1986). K-W-L: A teaching model that develops active reading of expository text. *The Reading Teacher, 39*, 564 – 570.

Olson, M.W., & Gee, T.C. (1991). Content reading instruction in the primary grades: Perceptions and strategies. *The Reading Teacher, 45*, 298 – 307.

Richardson, J.S. (1994). A read-aloud for science classrooms. *Journal of Reading, 38*, 62 – 63.

Richardson, J.S., & Morgan, R.F. (1994). *Reading to learn in the content areas.* Belmont, CA.: Wadsworth.

Romance, N.R., & Vitale, M.R. (1992). A curriculum that expands time for in-depth elementary science instruction by using science-based reading strategies: Effects of a year-long study in grade four. *Journal of Research in Science Teaching, 29*, 545 – 554.

Rosenblatt, L. (1991). Literature—S.O.S.! *Language Arts, 68*, 441 – 448.

Ross, E.P. (1994). *Using children's literature across the curriculum* (Fastback 374). Bloomington, IN: Phi Delta Kappa Educational Foundation.

Schifini, A. (1994). Language, literacy, and content instruction: Strategies for teachers. In K. Spangenberg-Urbschat & R. Pritchard, (Eds.), *Kids come in all languages: Reading instruction for ESL students* (pp. 158 – 179). Newark, DE: International Reading Association.

Singer, H., & Donlan, D. (1989). *Reading and learning from text* (2nd ed.). Hillsdale, NJ: Erlbaum.

Smith, J.L., & Johnson, H. (1994). Models of implementing literature in content studies. *The Reading Teacher, 48*, 198 – 209.

Tierney, R.J., & Pearson, P.D. (1994). Learning to learn from text: A framework for improving classroom practice. In R.B. Ruddell, M.R. Ruddell, & H. Singer (Eds.), *Theoretical models and processes of reading* (4th ed., pp. 496 – 513). Newark, DE: International Reading Association.

Yopp, H.K., & Yopp, R.H. (1996). *Literature based reading activities* (2nd ed.). Boston: Allyn & Bacon.

From *The Reading Teacher, Vol. 51, No. 6, March 1998*

Shelby J. Barrentine

Engaging with reading through interactive read-alouds

Interactive read-alouds encourage children to verbally interact with the text, peers, and teacher. This approach to reading aloud provides a means of engaging students as they construct meaning and explore the reading process.

Primary teachers have long used reading aloud as a way to introduce students to the pleasures of reading and books. More recently, however, the purpose of reading aloud has expanded to include instructional purposes. For example, teachers read aloud to convey content in thematic units (Moss, 1995), to teach literature-based math lessons (Whitin & Wilde, 1992), and to demonstrate reading processes (Harste, Woodward, & Burke, 1984; Holdaway, 1979).

Many teachers are dissatisfied with straight-through storybook readings that relegate listeners to a passive role. They seek suggestions to help them increase student involvement during read-alouds. The purpose of this article is twofold: to shed light on read-aloud events as rich literacy demonstrations

that engage children through dialogue and to share planning considerations to assist implementing interactive read-aloud events.

Approaches to read-aloud events

Although teachers differ in their specific read-aloud styles (Martinez & Teale, 1993), many limit the amount of dialogue during reading and then conclude the event with in-depth class discussions about the story. These after-reading discussions create opportunities for students to connect the story to their personal lives and for teachers to explore the connections that the students have made (Peterson & Eeds, 1990). After-reading discussions provide opportunity to "trace" ideas that were significant but unclear (Smith, 1990), to explore layers of meaning, or to develop knowledge about the elements of literature. These after-reading discussions are reflective and aim to deepen, broaden, and personalize story meaning.

Other teachers prefer to handle discussion differently. They read stories interactively. These teachers encourage children to interact verbally with the text, peers, and the teacher during book reading (Barrentine, 1993; Mason, Peterman, & Kerr, 1988). During interactive read-alouds, teachers pose questions throughout the reading that enhance meaning construction and also show *how* one makes sense of text. Students offer spontaneous comments as the story unfolds. They are also engaged with reading process information—how stories work, how to monitor one's comprehen-

sion, what to think about as a story unfolds. Thus, interactions about process are elicited along with aesthetic, personal responses to text. These interactions aim to engage children with strategies for composing meaning and to facilitate their ability to respond to stories. Interactive read-aloud lessons have been less thoroughly documented in the literature than after-reading discussions, so their potential for facilitating discoveries about literature and literacy is largely unexplored. While both types of read-alouds are valuable approaches, the interactive read-aloud approach is explored in this article.

Conceptual foundations

Interactive read-alouds incorporate aspects of Cambourne's conditions of learning (1988) and of Goldenberg's instructional conversations (1992/1993). Observing how children interact and learn in everyday living situations, Cambourne developed a model that describes how children become proficient users of language. His theory of language learning asserts that certain conditions lie at the core of the effective teaching and learning in natural settings. These conditions are immersion, responsibility, use, approximations, demonstrations, feedback, expectations, and engagement. He argues that classroom teachers must simulate conditions available to learners in natural settings in order to achieve success in literacy teaching and learning (Mathie, 1995). Although each condition has implications for interactive storybook readings, demonstration and engagement especially support this approach to reading aloud.

A demonstration is a display of how something is done (Harste et al., 1984). For effective learning, Cambourne (1988) claims that a literacy demonstration for young children must emphasize how meaning is constructed, how language functions, and how language is used. He explains that demonstrations enable learners to select, interpret, and organize their developing literacy knowledge "into patterns and schemas that will eventually make them fully literate" (p. 47). Also emphasizing the role of demonstration in literacy learning, Harste et al. (1984) identify some of the information that is demonstrated to children during read-aloud events: how stories work, the relationship between page turning and moving through a story, how one reads, how one corrects (and monitors) reading/meaning, voice inflection and change, how language works, and what written language looks like.

During interactive storybook reading, listeners have opportunity to respond personally and interpersonally with the story.

They explain that the information available in a read-aloud is process and strategy information rather than just content information. Children can certainly gain new world knowledge from stories (e.g., canning is a special way of preserving food or butterflies experience metamorphosis), but relevant content knowledge is often gained in a single encounter. Unlike relevant content, process and strategy information is rarely acquired in a single encounter. As both Cambourne and Harste et al. point out, consistency and repeated demonstration are necessary to learn reading processes and strategies.

According to Cambourne, children do not learn from demonstrations by passively absorbing information. To learn, children must become engaged with the demonstration. During interactive storybook reading, engagement refers to the points at which the listeners have opportunity to respond personally and interpersonally with the story and with the process and strategy information used to make sense of the story. Engaged students interact with each other and the teacher in response to the text. With repeated engagement in demonstrations children internalize the ability to use process and strategy information.

Engagement cannot be forced, but it can be enticed. One way to entice learner engagement is to implement instructional conversations, which are a "particular kind of lesson [that is] geared toward creating richly textured opportunities for students' conceptual and linguistic development" (Goldenberg, 1992/1993, p. 317). These lessons focus on developing conceptual information, but the nature of the talk is conversational. Goldenberg states,

> On the one hand, they are instructional in intent, that is they are designed to promote learning.... On the other hand, [instructional conversations] are conversational in quality—they appear to be natural and spontaneous interactions, free from didactic characteristics normally associated with formal teaching. (p. 319)

Interactive storybook readings are similar to instructional conversations in that they aim to engage students in learning information—learning process and strategy information through seemingly unplanned, natural interactions with stories, peers, and the teacher. They differ from instructional conversations in that the conversation is ongoing during storybook reading rather than conducted after reading. The instruction and conversation are woven in with the reading aloud of the text. The following description of a first-grade read-aloud illustrates this concept.

An interactive read-aloud event

The first graders in Mrs. Herbert's classroom were engaged with the stories she read interactively. The interactions that follow are drawn from an event in which Mrs. Herbert read *Blueberries for Sal* (McCloskey, 1948).

In this classic picture storybook, a human mother and daughter and a bear mother and cub go picking berries on Blueberry Hill. Sal becomes separated from her mother, and she meets and follows mother bear. In parallel fashion, the cub separates from his mother and follows Sal's mother. Eventually youngsters and parents safely reunite.

Opening up the conversation. Mrs. Herbert gathered the children to sit comfortably on the carpet and encouraged them to sit so they could see the book. She held the book in a position that kept the print and illustrations in view of the students. She reminded them that over the past few days they had been talking, reading, and writing about bears. Next she explained that the new story, also about bears, was titled *Blueberries for Sal.* As she prepared students for listening to the story, Mrs. Herbert displayed the illustrated endpaper and asked them to identify the two main (human) characters, invited them to make predictions about the setting, and mentioned the name of the author/illustrator.

> T: Let's preview the pictures here. Who do you think this might be? [She displays the endpaper and points to Sal's mother who is in the kitchen pouring blueberries into a canning jar.]
> S1: They're gonna make berry pie!
> S2: The mama.
> T: And who might this be?
> S3: The—the—Sal!
> T: Very good. Do you think they live in the city or the country?
> Students: (overlapping comments): Country. City. They might be both.
> T: Country? What makes you think they live in the country?
> S: 'Cause there's a lot of trees.
> T: A lot of trees. Okay. Do you see any big, tall buildings and skyscrapers like we've talked about in our social studies book?
> Students: No.
> S: They live in the country.
> S: They live in the forest.
> T: Here's the title page, *Blueberries for Sal.* This is by Robert McCloskey. He's written some other stories that we have read. Raise your hand if you've heard *Make Way for Ducklings.*

Already important literacy demonstrations were taking place: Readers remembered other titles by the same author, readers examined various pages of a book before reading the story, readers used illustrations to make predictions. The kitchen window in the illustration looks out over a rural scene, and the teacher demonstrated to the students that they could use the illustration to make predictions about the story. The overlapping comments indicated that looking at the window scene did not establish the setting for some students. Mrs. Herbert focused on the "country" response and had a student justify it. Further, she engaged them by activating their common knowledge gained from their social studies lessons to help them confirm that the story would take place in the country rather than the city. It was important that Mrs. Herbert began the read-aloud with this comfortable exchange of information in which many children were verbally involved, setting the conversational atmosphere that lasted throughout the event.

Throughout the read aloud the teacher maintains a conversational tone by inviting brief interactions.

Ongoing interaction. Throughout the read-aloud the teacher can maintain a conversational tone by inviting brief interactions. Ongoing interactions help students notice aspects of the story that they might otherwise overlook, develop an informed perspective on a character, or consider each other's ideas. Note for example in the following interaction that Mrs. Herbert invited students to consider Sal's feelings as she sits in a patch of berries and eats them.

> T: How do you think Sal's feeling right now? Carley?
> Carley: Happy.
> T: You think she's feeling happy?
> Carley: Because there is a smile on her face.
> T: Do you think she likes blueberries?
> Students: Yes!
> T: What makes you think she likes blueberries?
> S: Because she is eating them right away.
> T: She's popping them right into her mouth, isn't she?

Through dialogue, an informed perspective on this character, Sal, was constructed by all participants in the setting. Students heard each other's ideas, and those who had not reflected on Sal's mood now had an opportunity to do so. Listeners had more to think about—

more to notice—as the story progressed. Rather than connecting with Sal's feelings only once, later the teacher engaged the class in articulating what they had noticed about Sal's feelings.

Response and balancing talk and text. Children have many responses to stories, and during interactive reading they have opportunity to bring their responses into the social realm. For example, during this story event when the students realized that Sal has separated from her mother, some students began to chatter among themselves, and several raised their hands to share. The teacher asked one student to relay a personal experience.

> S: One time we were in the market and my mom thought I was right behind her. So she went to another spot and then I couldn't see her. And I looked down on two aisles and started crying. Then I caught up with her.
> T: How do you feel when that happens?
> S: Sad.
> T: Everybody, how do you feel?
> Students: Sad.
> T: And scared, too?
> Students: Yeah.

One possible criticism of interactive read-alouds is that too much dialogue during reading could interfere with aesthetic aspects of good literature. Overanalysis of characters, too much informing, repeatedly activating background knowledge, and even lengthy sharing of personal experiences may disrupt the flow of the story and, thus, disrupt the pleasure of hearing the story read aloud. Harker (1988) found that when talk during read-alouds shifts away from the story itself, comprehension is reduced. But drawing upon students' personal experiences builds story relevance. In the above interaction, Mrs. Herbert used one student's experience to have all students connect their individual experiences and feelings with Sal's experience and feelings. Still, however, the teacher faced a decision: Do I have all of the children share their experiences or do I move ahead with the story?

Providing opportunity for individual response and maintaining the balance between talk and text during interactive read-alouds require good teacher judgment. As teachers gain experience with reading interactively, natural sensibilities develop and indicate when dialogue is becoming too extended and out of balance with generating pleasure from reading a story. Lengthy interactions have enlarged possibilities for sharing, promoting, and extending student response to text, but extended talk is usually most appropriately saved for after-reading discussion.

Engaging with strategy demonstrations. Because read-alouds are rich opportunities for literacy demonstrations, teachers can direct student responses when teachable moments arise. Teachable moments are opportunities for providing children with insights about process or content knowledge (McGee, 1995). During this read-aloud, Mrs. Herbert asked a timely question that engaged the class with creating an ongoing comparison between Sal and Little Bear. Collectively they constructed a sophisticated understanding of the parallels between the two characters. The construction was a demonstration of how to use the author's text structure to comprehend the story. Notice in the following interaction that, even though the teacher initiated the comparison, she provided meaning space for the students. For example, the statement, "They are both brown," was accepted even though there was no indication in the story or illustrations that Sal's skin color was brown. Also, the teacher did not clarify when there was lack of agreement among the students about whether or not both Sal and Little Bear were "girls."

> T: Can you think of a way that Little Sal and Little Bear are alike? Bart?
> Bart: They're both little.
> T: They're both little. Yes, they are. Matt, what do you think?
> Matt: They're both brown.
> T: Okay. Um, somebody in the back. Ben. Do you want to look at the picture, Ben? Here's Little Sal, and here's Little Bear.
> Ben: They're both girls.
> T: Okay. Maybe so.
> S: Uh, uh! It says *his* mother (referring to the text on page 18 where, indeed, the author refers to Little Bear with the masculine pronoun *his*).
> T: Bart?
> Bart: They both like blueberries.

As Mrs. Herbert continued to read, children interrupted the story to notice other parallels between Sal and Little Bear: They both stopped to pick berries, they both "had to hustle along to catch up" with their mothers, they both sat down in the middle of the bushes to eat berries. To sum up the parallels, a student commented, "It's the same, again!" And, another student chimed in saying, "They're doing the same thing. They're doing the same thing!"

To adults and some of the young listeners, the parallels may be obvious. To other young listeners, the parallels are an exciting discovery and subtle demonstration of how stories work. Using structure to make sense of a story is an important reading comprehension strategy (Dole, Duffy, Roehler, & Pearson, 1991). An advantage of weaving interactions into the read-aloud is that the discoveries are made along the way as a group. No one is left out of appreciating the clever way the story works. Moreover, everyone can make and confirm predictions since they are aware of the ongoing parallels.

Later, near the end of the story, a student raised his hand.

> Ben: There's a pattern.
> T: What pattern do you see?
> Ben (pausing for several seconds before stating his idea): The bear and the mom do the same thing.
> T: The bear mom and Sal's mom do the same thing. Yes. Good for you, Ben. There are a lot of good patterns in this story.

Ben carried his observation of the parallel pattern beyond the similarities between Sal and Little Bear. He observed that the mothers also "do the same thing." The discovery of these parallels assisted the students to develop a systematic rather than idiosyncratic understanding of the story. In interactive storybook readings, students are involved in an event that promotes involvement with stories and that demonstrates important reading process and strategy information. The teacher supports engagement by promoting conversational, nonartificial interactions that focus on the story and on process and strategy information—information that is naturally embedded in any good book. Through repeated demonstrations and engagement, children internalize their literacy knowledge (Cambourne, 1988; Harste et al., 1984).

Planning interactive read-alouds

Most students love to hear stories read aloud and look forward to storytime. They readily engage with good books read aloud by a teacher who enjoys books and the read-aloud experience. The teacher can enhance the read-aloud experience by leading children to engage with aspects of reading that contribute to the meaning-making process. Through on-going interaction during read-alouds teachers can target key literary and process information for the ultimate purpose of supporting richer individual response to stories. Surprisingly, however, the practice of using ongoing conversation to engage students with reading process information and to bring response into the social realm is more challenging than it may first appear. Eeds and Peterson (1991) found that teachers were unsure about conducting literary conversations with their students. Goldenberg (1992/1993) states that conversations between students and teachers that aim to instruct are intellectually demanding and do not come easily or naturally. Teachers who want to implement interactive read-alouds may find the following suggestions helpful in planning and conducting them.

Selecting books. High-interest picture books with rich language, absorbing plots, lively characters, and multiple layers of meaning will simultaneously promote pleasure and opportunity for learning. Very simple or highly familiar books may not successfully sustain meaningful interaction. Likewise, highly complex stories are unlikely to generate interactions that promote a pleasurable reading experience. For optimal engagement, review your favorite children's books and choose those that you love and that are suited to your students' interests.

Preparing for successful interactive read-alouds. Choosing an appropriate book does not ensure successful interactive read-alouds. Natural and meaningful engagement with stories is a result of thorough behind-the-scenes preparation.

1. *Read the book several times to yourself.* Take the time that is necessary to thoroughly understand and appreciate the book. Many children's books that appear simplistic on the surface are often quite complex. Think about the characters in the story; the structure of the text; the plot conflicts and resolutions; and the language the author has used to create the characters, the story, and the images. Articulate possible themes. Notice the point of view and setting. Ask yourself why these were chosen and how they are at work in the story. Examine the illustrations. Recognize where they enrich and add to the story. Notice where they clearly illustrate the events and characters in the text. It is time consuming but enjoyable to review the book from multiple dimensions.

Use this time to kindle your own intrigue with the literary and artistic nature of the book.

2. *Think about the reading goals you have for your students and identify the process and strategy information at work in the story.* Review some of the aims you have for your students as developing readers. What meaning-making strategies do you want the students to use? Do you want to emphasize utilizing text structure, identifying with a character's feelings and actions, summarizing the story, predicting, identifying and interpreting themes, critiquing and reflecting on the plot, or learning to ask questions when meaning breaks down? What goals are especially relevant to this particular text? When you pause to recall your instructional goals, you are compelled to think about storybook reading as a context for engaging students in reading demonstrations, students' current instructional needs, and what goals are appropriately taught in relation to the story you have selected.

In each event, idiosyncrasies of the students, the story, and the teacher lead to engaging with reading in fresh ways.

---

3. *Identify where students' predictions about the developing story should be sought and shared.* Having students make and share predictions at critical points in the story will create the opportunity for them to figure the story out for themselves. Anticipate, before you read to the class, moments when you can assist readers in constructing a "wise" interpretation of the story (Wolf, 1988). Predicting helps students recognize and think about how stories work—how they are put together—which helps them read like experts. Predicting activates students' background knowledge and experiences, which prepares them to compare their own feelings and experiences with those in the story. Comparing and contrasting feelings and experiences make the story relevant to students.

4. *Anticipate where you may need to build students' background knowledge.* Often stories will contain references to concepts or information with which some but not all of the students will have had experience. Consider at what points in the reading the information should be addressed (before or during the story) and consider to what extent it should be discussed.

5. *Think through how you will phrase your questions and predicting invitations, and anticipate student responses.* Surprisingly, even after all of the above preparation, as you first begin to implement interactive read-alouds, you may not automatically articulate well phrased questions. Initially, you might try writing clearly phrased questions onto the pages of the book. Then think about how your students might respond to the questions and predicting invitations. Realize that students will range in their ability to offer perceptive insights. Also realize that what is easily and accurately predicted by an adult is not necessarily easily or accurately predicted by young students. Value your student responses and use them as windows for peering into their thinking.

6. *After you have planned the read-aloud event, be prepared to relinquish your plans.* Above all, interactive read-aloud events should be responsive to the students. Be prepared to tailor your questions and comments to the dialogue that develops. In one interactive read-aloud that I observed, the teacher and I were both overwhelmed at the level of student interaction. They identified ideas that neither of us had discovered in the story. To the credit of the teacher, she was very responsive to their ideas and helped students explore them throughout the reading of the book, even though she spent extra minutes on storytime that day.

7. *After reading, devise opportunities for students to explore stories in personal and exciting ways.* Very often it is appropriate to follow interactive readings with discussion that further explores student response to the story. These discussions allow for greater personalization of stories, whereas interactive readings tend to focus on building a shared meaning. In addition to after-reading discussion, follow-up activities can lead to meaningful exploration. For instance, after the *Blueberries for Sal* reading, Mrs. Herbert arranged for the classroom paraprofessional to assist groups of 5–6 students in making blueberry pancakes. This extended the students' connection to Sal's feelings—now they could relate to the delight

of eating the berries! Writing, art, music, and drama also lead to literacy growth and meaningful exploration.

Other considerations. Classrooms are complex environments, and it is often the inconspicuous details that support successful lessons. Two inconspicuous but important details are at work in successful interactive readalouds: time and good judgment.

Set aside an adequate amount of class time to conduct interactive read-alouds. Reading a story interactively will approximately double the amount of time it would take to read the story in a straight-through format. If you plan adequate time for reading, you will resist the tendency to rush the event and limit student interaction. And use good judgment about the amount of interaction to include during reading. Excessive dialogue may disrupt the enjoyment of a story. Finding the appropriate amount of dialogue will evolve with your experience and with students' realization that storytime is also talk time.

Conclusion

Clearly, many elements contribute to successful interactive readings, but there is no formula for success. In each event, idiosyncrasies of the students, the story, and the teacher lead to engaging with reading in fresh ways. Dialogue during read-aloud events supports students as they construct meaning based on the story and their personal experiences. These meaning-centered interactions engage students with literacy information and demonstrate strategies that they can adopt for use when reading independently. Not every read-aloud event need be interactive, but this approach to reading aloud provides a way to expand teachers' techniques for engaging students with books and literacy information.

A former elementary teacher, Barrentine now teaches reading courses at the University of North Dakota (College of Education and Human Development, PO Box 7189, Grand Forks, ND 58202-7189, USA). She has written a chapter on this topic in IRA's new book, Lively Discussions! Fostering Engaged Reading, *edited by Linda B. Gambrell and Janice F. Almasi.*

References

Barrentine, S.J. (1993). *Teacher's comprehension building practices during storybook reading events.* Unpublished doctoral dissertation, University of California, Los Angeles.

Cambourne, B. (1988). *The whole story: Natural learning and the acquisition of literacy in the classroom.* Auckland, New Zealand: Ashton Scholastic.

Dole, J.A., Duffy, G.G., Roehler, L.R., & Pearson, P.D. (1991). Moving from the old to the new: Research on reading comprehension instruction. *Review of Educational Research, 61,* 239–264.

Eeds, M., & Peterson, R. (1991). Teacher as curator: Learning to talk about literature. *The Reading Teacher, 45,* 118–126.

Goldenberg, C. (1992/1993). Instructional conversations: Promoting comprehension through discussion. *The Reading Teacher, 46,* 316–326.

Harker, J.O. (1988). Contrasting the content of two story-reading lessons: A propositional analysis. In J.L. Green & J.O. Harker (Eds.), *Multiple perspective analyses of classroom discourse* (pp. 49–70). Norwood, NJ: Ablex.

Harste, J.C., Woodward, V.A., & Burke, C.L. (1984). *Language stories and literacy lessons.* Portsmouth, NH: Heinemann.

Holdaway, D. (1979). *The foundations of literacy.* Sydney, Australia: Ashton Scholastic.

Martinez, M.G., & Teale, W.H. (1993). Teacher storybook reading style: A comparison of six teachers. *Research in the Teaching of English, 27,* 175–199.

Mason, J.M., Peterman, C.L., & Kerr, B.M. (1988). Reading to kindergarten children. In D.S. Strickland & L.M. Morrow (Eds.), *Emerging literacy: Young children learn to read and write* (pp. 52–62). Newark, DE: International Reading Association.

Mathie, V. (1995). Making beliefs explicit: One teacher's journey. In B. Cambourne & J. Turbill (Eds.), *Responsive evaluation: Making valid judgments about student literacy* (pp. 28–37). Portsmouth, NH: Heinemann.

McCloskey, R. (1948). *Blueberries for Sal.* New York: Viking.

McGee, L.M. (1995). Talking about books. In N.L. Roser & M.G. Martinez (Eds.), *Book talk and beyond: Children and teachers respond to literature* (pp. 105–115). Newark, DE: International Reading Association.

Moss, J.F. (1995). Preparing focus units with literature: Crafty foxes and authors' craft. In N.L. Roser & M.G. Martinez (Eds.), *Book talk and beyond: Children and teachers respond to literature* (pp. 53–65). Newark, DE: International Reading Association.

Peterson, R., & Eeds, M. (1990). *Grand conversations: Literature groups in action.* New York: Scholastic.

Smith, K. (1990). Entertaining a text. In K.G. Short & K.M. Pierce (Eds.), *Talking about books: Creating literate communities* (pp. 17–31). Portsmouth, NH: Heinemann.

Whitin, D.J., & Wilde, S. (1992). *Read any good math lately? Children's books for mathematical learning, K–6.* Portsmouth, NH: Heinemann.

Wolf, D.P. (1988). *Reading reconsidered: Literature and literacy in high school.* New York: College Board Publications.

From *The Reading Teacher, Vol. 50, No. 1, September 1996*

Independent Reading

 Research Foundations to Support Wide Reading

Research Foundations to Support Wide Reading

Richard C. Anderson

Vocabulary Acquisition While Reading as Compared to Direct Vocabulary Instruction

Do children learn new words mostly from vocabulary instruction in school or from reading and other uses of language? This is a question that my colleagues William Nagy and Patricia Herman and I spent 10 years trying to answer. We believe we reached a conclusion which in its general outline is no longer open to dispute. Figure 1 presents a partial model of vocabulary acquisition; I will attempt to evaluate which of the paths in the model are most important for vocabulary acquisition.

Establishing Students' Vocabulary Size

The first questions that must be answered are how many words do students know and how many new words do they learn each year. If the average 12th grader knows 8,000 words, as some investigators have concluded (Dupuy, 1974), then it would seem that all a teacher would have to do is teach about 20 words a week for 12 years to cover all of the words. But if the average 12th grader knows 40,000 words, as other researchers have estimated (Anderson & Freebody, 1981), a teacher would have to teach 20 words a day to cover all 40,000 words—a much more daunting task. If 12th graders know 40,000 words, it should be apparent that they did not learn many of them in vocabulary lessons.

As these figures suggest, estimates of vocabulary size have varied dramatically (Anderson & Freebody, 1981). The variation occurs because of differences in the procedures used by vocabulary researchers.

Figure 1 Partial Model of Vocabulary Growth

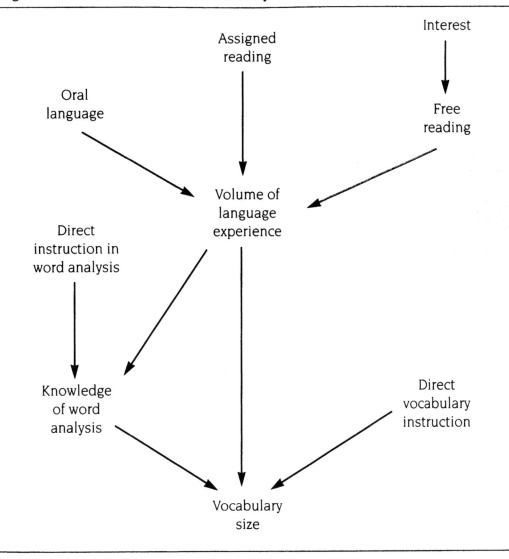

To estimate vocabulary size, researchers select a source of words, usually a dictionary, that is considered representative of English or some other language; define criteria for selecting a sample of words from this source; devise a test to assess knowledge of the sample of words; give the test to a representative sample of children; and extrapolate the results to all words and all children. Errors of estimation can arise at any of these steps. For example, the size of estimates depends on the word source: a researcher who selects words from a pocket dictionary will conclude that the size of the vocabulary learning task is smaller than that estimated by a researcher who selects words from an unabridged dictionary.

Another reason for inconsistencies in the size of estimates comes from the definition of what is considered a distinct word in English. Everyone agrees that, for instance, dog and dogs or look, looks, looked, and looking should not be counted as separate words. Beyond simple inflections such as these, however, there has been continuing controversy about the proper definition of a functionally distinct word. Researchers who, for instance, group carriage with carry and nevertheless with never arrive at smaller estimates of vocabulary size than researchers who count these as distinct words.

Nagy and I (1984) attempted to resolve questions about the size of the vocabulary learning task. First, instead of using either a large or a small dictionary, we employed the Carroll, Davies, and Richman (1971) corpus of more than 5 million running words from a thousand items of published materials in use in schools. The materials sampled included textbooks, workbooks, kits, novels, general nonfiction, encyclopedias, and magazines chosen to represent, as nearly as possible, the range of required and recommended school reading.

We analyzed relatedness among words, not in terms of their historical derivations, as many before us have done, but in terms of the similarity of their current meanings. We judged pairs of words, attempting to decide whether a student who knew the meaning of only one of the words would be able to infer the meaning of the other word upon encountering it in context while reading. We judged, for example, that most students who knew sweet would be able to understand sweetness, but that knowing busy usually would be insufficient to understand business. Compound words were judged in a similar fashion. For example, with some help from context, most students could infer foglights if they knew fog and light, but knowing fox and trot would be little help to them in inducing the meaning of foxtrot, assuming they did not already know that compound word.

Based on an in-depth analysis of a 7,000 word sample from the Carroll, Davies, and Richman (1971) corpus, we calculated that there are about 88,500 distinct words in printed school English. Next we recalibrated previous estimates of the number of words known by students in different grades, using bench marks from our analysis (Nagy & Herman, 1987). When we applied the same definition of a distinct word in English, the variability in estimates of students' vocabulary size was substantially smaller. We concluded that the average 12th grader probably does know about 40,000 words and that the average student in primary or secondary school probably learns 2,000 to 3,000 new words each year.

We have decided that our previous estimate of 88,500 distinct words in printed school English is too small (Anderson & Nagy, 1992). It does not include any proper words, although writers are likely to assume the meanings of proper words such as <u>Moslem</u>, <u>Pacific</u>, or <u>Republican</u>. Nor does our previous estimate include multiple meanings of words, although knowing one meaning of a word is more likely to be a hindrance than a help in recognizing another meaning. For instance, knowing <u>bear</u> to mean a large animal does not help a reader understand <u>to bear a child</u>.

The largest category omitted from our previous estimate was idioms—any expression made up of two or more words, whose meaning is not fully predictable from the meanings of its parts. This definition covers a broad range of expressions beyond just colloquial expressions such as <u>kick the bucket</u>. It also covers stock phrases such as <u>by and large</u>; technical terms such as <u>standard deviation</u>; and ubiquitous compound verbs such as <u>put out</u> (as in <u>put out the fire</u>), <u>put up</u> (as in <u>put up the money</u>), and <u>put up with</u> (as in <u>put up with the noisy teenagers</u>). Most native speakers use and understand idioms without being fully aware of their frequency or the fact that their meanings are more than, or different from, the sum of their parts. <u>Make yourself at home</u> may sound like a regular, literal phrase, but <u>make yourself at house</u>, although presumably similar in meaning, does not sound like normal English. Moreover, some idioms, such as <u>by and large</u>, are not analyzable, because it is almost impossible to see any relation between the meanings of the component words and the meaning of the expression.

Derivatives and compounds whose meanings are distant from their roots, unknown proper words, unknown alternate meanings, and unknown idioms complicate the task of reading in the same way as unknown basic words. Thus, a complete assessment of the size of the vocabulary learning task would have to take account of these categories. There is limited research on how many derivatives, compounds, multiple meanings of homonyms, and idioms students know, but they certainly know thousands of items in these categories (see Anglin, 1993). Therefore, estimates of how many vocabulary items students of different ages know will have to be increased. Just how much must await further empirical research. In the meantime, we have guessed that, if an inclusive definition is used, there may be 180,000 distinct vocabulary items in school English, that an average 12th grader may know 80,000 of them, and that students may learn 4,000 to 6,000 new items each year (Anderson & Nagy, 1992).

Vocabulary Learning While Reading

Now that we have some idea of the size of the vocabulary learning task for English-speaking children, we can address the question of where and how they acquire the words they know. The first source I will consider is natural learning while reading—acquiring word meanings from context as the incidental byproduct of reading.

The idea that reading could play a major role in vocabulary acquisition has been attractive to many reading educators, dating back to Huey (1908) and Thorndike (1917), although early research failed to produce convincing evidence in favor of the idea (Gray & Holmes, 1938). Nagy, Herman, and I (1985) theorized that learning from context while reading is a gradual, incremental process. We argued that previous research had been inconclusive because the measures employed were insensitive to small increments in word knowledge and because the research designs were not powerful enough to detect small increments. Improved measurement and design has led to a different conclusion. Beginning with Jenkins, Stein, and Wysocki (1984) and Nagy, Herman, and Anderson (1985), a number of studies have now found reliable learning of word meanings from context during more or less normal reading (Herman et al., 1987; Nagy, Anderson, & Herman, 1987; Shefelbine, 1990; Shu, Anderson, & Zhang, 1995).

One study in which I was involved (Nagy, Anderson, & Herman, 1987) examined the word learning of 352 U.S. students in the third, fifth, and seventh grades. At each grade, four texts were selected from grade-level books. A random half of the students in each class read two of the texts, and half read the other two texts. Several days later all the students were tested on knowledge of the meanings of difficult target words from all the texts. The logic was that, if reading leads naturally to word learning, students who had read a text would perform better on a test of difficult words from the text than students who had not read the text. This design controlled for variation due to classroom climate; story difficulty and interest; and differences among the children in ability, motivation, and prior knowledge of the words, factors that might otherwise have overwhelmed the expected small influence of reading.

To increase sensitivity to partial knowledge, the vocabulary test we employed contained an easy and a difficult multiple-choice question for each target word. Question difficulty was manipulated by varying the similarity of the distracters (the incorrect multiple-choice answers) to the correct answer. The correct answer to the easy question was a synonym or in the general category of the target word. The distracters were definitions of words distant in meaning from the target word. Thus, a child who knew anything about the meaning of the target word had a good chance of selecting the correct answer. In contrast, the correct answer for the difficult question consisted of the exact definition of the target word, and the distracters included the definitions of words close in meaning to the target word. So, selecting the correct answer was not likely unless a child had more complete and discriminating knowledge of the target word.

We found small but highly reliable increments in word knowledge attributable to reading at all grades and ability levels. The overall likelihood of learning an unfamiliar word while reading was about 1 in 20. The likelihood ranged from better than 1 in 10 when children were reading easy narratives to near zero when they were reading difficult expositions.

At first glance, the likelihood of incidental learning of word meanings while reading may seem too small to be of any practical value. However, further reflection will show that one must consider how much reading children do to assess properly the contribution of reading to vocabulary growth.

How much does the average child read? According to Anderson, Wilson, and Fielding (1988), the average U.S. fifth grader reads about

600,000 words a year from books, magazines, and newspapers outside of school. If a student reads 15 minutes a day in school, another 600,000 words of text could be covered. Thus, a conservative estimate of the total volume of reading of a typical U.S. fifth grader is 1 million or more words per year, although many children read two or three or even five times this amount.

How many new words do children acquire in a year simply from reading? We have estimated that a child who reads 1 million words a year will encounter at least 20,000 unfamiliar words. With a 5% chance of learning a word, it follows that the typical child may be learning about 1,000 words a year from reading. This is a low estimate: when reading self-selected material or assigned material that is not too difficult, the chances of learning an unfamiliar word rise to 10% or more, and the yearly yield may be 2,000 words or as many as 4,000 if proper names, alternate meanings of homonyms, and idioms are considered. These figures represent the expected yield for children who do an

average amount of reading; avid readers may be learning two or three times as many words simply from reading.

Vocabulary Learning from Direct Instruction

How many words do children learn from direct vocabulary instruction in school each year? Nagy and Herman (1987) counted the number of words listed to be taught by several basal reading programs for third through sixth grade. The number ranged from 290 to 460. These were words "new" to the basal reading program, but studies show that students already can read and understand as many as 70% of them (Roser & Juel, 1982). Moreover, classroom observation suggests that the typical teacher skips most of the recommended vocabulary instruction (Durkin, 1979; Roser & Juel, 1982). Classroom observation also suggests that not much vocabulary instruction occurs during content area reading instruction (Durkin, 1979). Nagy and Herman (1987) surmised that in the typical classroom 300 words a year, at most, are covered in instruction aimed specifically at word learning.

Of course, not every word that is "covered" is learned. Rich, varied, and intensive vocabulary instruction may lead to a rate of learning as high as 67% or more (Beck, McKeown, & McCaslin, 1983). In contrast, when all students do is study definitions and compose sentences using the words, the average rate of learning is much lower, maybe as low as 33% or less (McKeown, 1993; Miller & Gildea, 1987).

Assuming that the typical student receives instruction in about 300 unfamiliar words each year, and that the typical rate of learning is 33%, vocabulary instruction would result in the learning of 100 new words a year. With superior instruction, the rate of learning might rise to 67% and the annual gain to 200 words. The number could be considerably higher than 200 in classrooms where substantial time and effort are devoted to vocabulary instruction. Nonetheless, as Nagy and Herman (1987) have concluded, even in an ideal program of vocabulary instruction, the number of words actually learned in a year will still be in the hundreds. In contrast, the number of words learned in a year from independent reading is in the thousands for the typical child. So, regardless of whether conservative or liberal assumptions are made, independent reading appears to be a far more important source of vocabulary growth than direct vocabulary instruction.

Vocabulary Growth from Using Oral Language

Looking again at Figure 1, next I will consider the role of oral language in vocabulary growth. Oral language is primary for young children, and it continues to be important for all kinds of learning throughout life. However, there is good reason to doubt that oral language is the primary source for vocabulary growth when a child has become a fluent and frequent reader. This is because conversations and popular television shows do not contain a sufficiently rich vocabulary to allow for much growth. According to Hayes (1988, p. 584), a leading authority on vocabulary,

> Daily newspapers, most popular magazines, and even most comic books contain several times as many rare terms as conversation and television. While some sections of the newspaper are avoided by children, the comics, sports, Ann Landers–like columns, and the entertainment sections all provide at least twice as many rare words per thousand as natural conversation. Children's books such as *The Black Stallion* or the Nancy Drew series are on average three times richer in these terms than texts of comparable length from parent or teacher speech. Books designed to be read to preschool children have texts whose lexical pitch is 50% higher than average adult-child talk. Even Peter Rabbit and the Bugs Bunny cartoons are expressed at two or three times higher a lexical pitch than adult-child talk.

A special case of oral language is reading aloud to children. When there is discussion of a book, as in the shared book approach (Holdaway, 1979), there is direct evidence of increased word learning (Elley, 1991; Feitelson, Kita, & Goldstein, 1986). Captioning a television program is another enhancement of oral language that increases word learning (Neuman & Koskinen, 1992). Further, words that are partly known from oral language are more likely to be learned when encountered during independent reading (Nagy, Anderson, & Herman, 1987; Shu, Anderson, & Zhang, 1995).

In conclusion, the best available evidence suggests that at least one-third, and maybe as much as two-thirds, of the typical child's annual vocabulary growth comes as the natural consequence of reading books, magazines, and newspapers. It appears that reading may be about 10 times as important a source of vocabulary growth as direct vocabulary instruction. Although the exact contribution of oral language to vocabulary growth cannot be delimited at this time, there is reason to believe that, once a child has learned to read, reading is a more important direct source of word learning than oral language.

Amount of Reading and Growth in Reading Competence

How much does the average child read? How extensive is the variation among children in amount of reading? Is variation in amount of reading associated with rate of growth in reading proficiency? Numerous studies of children's reading habits have been completed, but there are serious faults with the majority of them. A characteristic fault has been overreliance on questionnaires to assess amount of reading. It is not easy to have confidence in an assessment that requires children to remember their activities over lengthy periods of time, to discriminate precisely between options such as "usually" and "often," or to refrain from circling the socially desirable larger number instead of the possibly more accurate smaller number.

Among the studies using sound methods is one conducted by Greaney (1980) in Ireland. Nearly 1,000 fifth-grade students from 31 Irish primary schools completed diaries of out-of-school activities for several days. Analysis of the diary entries revealed wide individual variation in amount of reading. Fully 44% of the students did not read books on any of the three days they completed diaries, whereas 6.4% devoted at least an hour a day of their leisure time to book reading. Greaney reported a positive correlation between book reading time and a standardized measure of reading achievement.

Colleagues and I (Anderson, Wilson, & Fielding, 1988) performed a study similar to Greaney's in the United States. A total of 155 fifth-grade students from two schools completed activity diaries recording out-of-school activities for periods ranging from 8 to 26 weeks. Every morning the students wrote on a form how many minutes they spent the previous day on each activity. Table 1 reproduces the principal findings of the study. The scale is percentile rank on each of several measures of amount of reading.

The table shows profound differences among children in amount of reading. Starting at the bottom of the table, notice that successive

Table 1 Variation in Amount of Independent Reading

Percentile Rank[a]	Minutes of Reading per Day		Words Read per Year	
	Books	Text[b]	Books	Text[b]
98	65.0	67.3	4,358,000	4,733,000
90	21.2	33.4	1,823,000	2,357,000
80	14.2	24.6	1,146,000	1,697,000
70	9.6	16.9	622,000	1,168,000
60	6.5	13.1	432,000	722,000
50	4.6	9.2	282,000	601,000
40	3.2	6.2	200,000	421,000
30	1.8	4.3	106,000	251,000
20	.7	2.4	21,000	134,000
10	.1	1.0	8,000	51,000
2	0	0	0	8,000

[a] Percentile rank on each measure separately.
[b] Books, magazines, and newspapers.
Adapted from "Growth in Reading and How Children Spend Their Time Outside of School," by R.C. Anderson, P.T. Wilson, and L.G. Fielding, 1988, *Reading Research Quarterly*, 23, p. 292.

groups of children read for increasingly long periods of time and covered increasingly large numbers of words. For example, the child who was at the 90th percentile in amount of book reading spent nearly 5 times as many minutes per day reading books as the child at the 50th percentile and more than 200 times as many minutes per day reading books as the child at the 10th percentile.

Notice, also, that the average fifth grader in this study was not reading very much. Table 1 shows that the median child read books for a little less than 5 minutes per day and only read 9 minutes a day when magazines and newspapers are considered in addition to books. Other research confirms that children in the United States do not read very much (Allen, Cipielewski, & Stanovich, 1992; Walberg & Tsai, 1984).

We (Anderson, Wilson, & Fielding, 1988) found significant, positive relation between the measures of amount of reading, particularly amount of book reading, and measures of reading comprehension, vocabulary, and reading speed. Perhaps most interesting and important was that the number of minutes a day reading books was a significant predictor of growth in reading proficiency between the second and the fifth grade, after statistically controlling for second-grade reading level. This suggests that reading books may be a *cause*, not merely a *reflection*, of children's level of reading proficiency.

A series of studies by Stanovich and his associates (Stanovich, 1993) has added substantially to knowledge about the relation between amount of reading and reading proficiency. These studies employ several measures of amount of reading. One is an author recognition test: students check the authors of children's books on a list of peoples' names; to catch the student who is just guessing, some of the names on the list are not authors of children's books. Another measure, the title recognition test, requires students to pick the titles of books from among a list of possible titles, some of which are not really book titles. Except for the fact they do not permit estimates of the absolute amount of reading, the two tests appear to measure amount of reading just as well as the activity diary method, but with much less time and trouble (Allen, Cipielewski, & Stanovich, 1992).

Using the author and title recognition tests, Stanovich and his collaborators have confirmed the results of Anderson, Wilson, and Fielding (1988), finding that amount of reading is significantly associated with growth in reading comprehension between third grade and fifth or sixth grade, after statistically controlling for third-grade reading level (Cipielewski & Stanovich, 1992). In other studies with adults as well as children, they have found that amount of reading is strongly associated with vocabulary knowledge, verbal fluency, spelling, general information, knowledge of history and literature, and cultural literacy, after statistically controlling for such factors as decoding skill, nonverbal intelligence, and age (Cunningham & Stanovich, 1991; Stanovich & Cunningham, 1992).

In a naturalistic study, West, Stanovich, and Mitchell (1993) unobtrusively observed travelers in departure lounges at National Airport in Washington, DC. A person under observation was classified as a "reader" if he or she read for 10 consecutive minutes and a "nonreader" if he or she read nothing during the 10-minute observation period. A total of 217 people classified in this manner were approached and agreed to take a battery of tests. The results are displayed in Table 2. Readers performed significantly better than nonreaders on all the measures, except the ones involving television. On each measure, the

Table 2 Mean Scores of Readers and Nonreaders at Washington, DC National Airport

Variable	Readers	Nonreaders	t Test
Author recognition test	.635	.401	7.75*
Magazine recognition test	.751	.598	5.21*
Newspaper recognition test	.529	.370	6.12*
Television programs checklist	.352	.366	−0.51
Television newsperson names	.650	.578	3.37*
Television characters and actors	.392	.363	1.06
Film recognition test	.320	.292	1.10
Vocabulary checklist	.731	.516	7.57*
Cultural literacy test	.770	.600	7.00*

*$p < .01$
Adapted from "Reading in the Real World and Its Correlates," by R.F. West, K.E. Stanovich, and H. Mitchell, 1993, *Reading Research Quarterly*, 28, p. 40.

advantage remained significant after statistically removing the influence due to age and years of education.

The conclusion from the studies reviewed in this section is that amount of reading is consistently associated with an array of indicators of reading proficiency and topical knowledge. Studies of natural variation in reading are necessarily correlational, so these studies fall short of proving that amount of reading causes these effects. Still, several of the studies have included controls for earlier reading level, basic decoding skill, nonverbal intelligence, age, or years of education. Therefore, it seems safe to conclude, at least, that amount of reading is strongly implicated as a major factor in growth in literacy.

References

Allen, L., Cipielewski, J., & Stanovich, K.E. (1992). Multiple indicators of children's reading habits and attitudes: Construct validity and cognitive correlates. *Journal of Educational Psychology, 84*, 489–503.

Anderson, R.C., & Freebody, P. (1981). Vocabulary knowledge. In J.T. Guthrie (Ed.), *Comprehension and teaching: Research reviews* (pp. 77–117). Newark, DE: International Reading Association.

Anderson, R.C., & Nagy, W.E. (1992, Winter). The vocabulary conundrum. *American Educator*, 14–18, 44–46.

Anderson, R.C., Wilson, P.T., & Fielding, L.G. (1988). Growth in reading and how children spend their time outside of school. *Reading Research Quarterly*, 23, 285–303.

Anglin, J.M. (1993). Vocabulary development: A morphological analysis. *Monographs of the Society for Research in Child Development*, 58 (10, Serial No. 238). Chicago, IL: The University of Chicago Press.

Beck, I., McKeown, M., & McCaslin, E. (1983). Vocabulary development: All contexts are not created equal. *Elementary School Journal*, 83, 177–181.

Carroll, J.B., Davies, P., & Richman, B. (1971). *Word frequency book*. Boston, MA: Houghton Mifflin.

Cipielewski, J., & Stanovich, K.E. (1992). Predicting growth in reading ability from children's exposure to print. *Journal of Experimental Child Psychology*, 54, 74–89.

Cunningham, A.E., & Stanovich, K.E. (1991). Tracking the unique effects of print exposure in children: Associations with vocabulary, general knowledge, and spelling. *Journal of Educational Psychology*, 83, 264–274.

Dupuy, H.P. (1974). *The rationale, development and standardization of a basic word vocabulary test* (DHEW Publication No. HRA 74–1334). Washington, DC: U.S. Government Printing Office.

Durkin, D. (1979). What classroom observations reveal about reading comprehension instruction. *Reading Research Quarterly*, 14, 481–533.

Edelsky, C. (1990, November). Whose agenda is this anyway? A response to McKenna, Robinson, and Miller. *Educational Researcher*, 19, 7–11.

Elley, W.B. (1991). Acquiring literacy in a second language: The effects of book-based programs. *Language Learning*, 41, 375–411.

Elley, W.B., Watson, J.E., & Cowie, C.R. (1976). *The impact of a book flood*. Wellington, New Zealand: New Zealand Council for Educational Research.

Feitelson, D., Goldstein, Z., Iraqi, J., & Share, D.L. (1993). Effects of listening to story reading on aspects of literacy acquisition in a diglossic situation. *Reading Research Quarterly*, 28, 70–79.

Feitelson, D., Kita, B., & Goldstein, Z. (1986). Effects of listening to series stories on first graders' comprehension and use of language. *Research in the Teaching of English*, 20, 339–356.

Goodman, K. (1989). Whole language research: Foundations and development. *Elementary School Journal*, 90, 207–221.

Gray, W., & Holmes, E. (1938). *The development of meaning vocabularies in reading*. Chicago, IL: The University of Chicago Press.

Greaney, V. (1980). Factors related to amount and type of leisure-time reading. *Reading Research Quarterly*, 15, 337–357.

Greaney, V. (1992). *Reading achievement levels and reading habits of Indonesian pupils*. Unpublished paper. Washington, DC: World Bank.

Guthrie, J.T., Schafer, W., Wang, Y.Y., & Afflerbach, P. (1995). Relationships of instruction to amount of reading: An exploration of social, cognitive, and instructional connections. *Reading Research Quarterly*, 30, 8–25.

Hayes, D.P. (1988). Speaking and writing: Distinct patterns of word choice. *Journal of Memory and Language*, 27, 572–585.

Herman, P.A., Anderson, R.C., Pearson, P.D., & Nagy, W.E. (1987). Incidental acquisition of word meanings from expositions with varied text features. *Reading Research Quarterly*, 22, 263–284.

Holdaway, D. (1979). *Foundations of literacy*. Sydney: Ashton Scholastic.

Huey, E.B. (1908). *The psychology and pedagogy of reading*. New York: Macmillan.

Ingham, J. (1982). *Books and reading development: The Bradford Book Flood Experiment*. London: Heinemann.

Jenkins, J., Stein, M., & Wysocki, K. (1984). Learning vocabulary through reading. *American Educational Research Journal*, 21, 767–788.

Krashen, S.D. (1989). We acquire vocabulary and spelling by reading: Additional evidence for the input hypothesis. *Modern Language Journal*, 73, 440–465.

Krashen, S.D. (1993). *The power of reading: Insights from the research*. Englewood, CO: Libraries Unlimited.

Manning, G.L., & Manning, M. (1984). What models of recreational reading make a difference? *Reading World*, 23, 375–380.

McKeown, M.G. (1993). Creating effective definitions for young word learners. *Reading Research Quarterly*, 28, 16–31.

Miller, G.A., & Gildea, P. (1987). How children learn words. *Scientific American*, 257(3), 94–99.

Nagy, W.E., & Anderson, R.C. (1984). How many words are there in printed school English? *Reading Research Quarterly*, 19, 304–330.

Nagy, W.E., Anderson, R.C., & Herman, P.A. (1987). Learning word meanings from context during normal reading. *American Educational Research Journal*, 24, 237–270.

Nagy, W.E., & Herman, P.A. (1987). Breadth and depth of vocabulary knowledge: Implications for acquisition and instruction. In M. McKeown & M. Curtis (Eds.), *The nature of vocabulary acquisition* (pp. 19–35). Hillsdale, NJ: Erlbaum.

Nagy, W.E., Herman, P.A., & Anderson, R.C. (1985). Learning words from context. *Reading Research Quarterly*, 20, 233–253.

Neuman, D.B., & Koskinen, P. (1992). Captioned television as comprehensible input: Effects of incidental word learning from context for language minority students. *Reading Research Quarterly*, 27, 95–109.

Roser, N., & Juel, C. (1982). Effects of vocabulary instruction on reading comprehension. In J. Niles & L. Harris (Eds.), *New inquiries in reading research and instruction* (Thirty-first Yearbook of the National Reading Conference, pp. 110–118). Rochester, NY: National Reading Conference.

Schon, I., Hopkins, K.D., & Davis, W.A. (1982). The effects of books in Spanish and free reading time on Hispanic students' reading abilities and attitudes. *National Association of Bilingual Education Journal*, 7, 13–20.

Shefelbine, J.L. (1990). Student factors related to variability in learning word meanings from context. *Journal of Reading Behavior, 22,* 71–97.

Shu, H., Anderson, R.C., & Zhang, H. (1995). Incidental learning of word meanings while reading: A Chinese and American cross-cultural study. *Reading Research Quarterly, 30,* 76–95.

Stahl, S.A., McKenna, M.C., & Pagnucco, J.R. (1993). *The effects of whole language instruction: An update and a reappraisal.* Paper presented at the National Reading Conference, Charleston, SC.

Stahl, S.A., & Miller, P.D. (1989). Whole language and language experience approaches for beginning reading: A quantitative research synthesis. *Review of Educational Research, 59,* 87–116.

Stanovich, K.E. (1993). Does reading make you smarter? Literacy and the development of verbal intelligence. In H. Reese (Ed.), *Advances in Child Development, 24,* 133–180.

Stanovich, K.E., & Cunningham, A.E. (1992). Studying the consequences of literacy within a literate society: The cognitive correlates of print exposure. *Memory and Cognition, 20,* 51–68.

Thorndike, E.L. (1917). Reading and reasoning. A study of mistakes in paragraph reading. *Journal of Educational Psychology, 8,* 323–332.

Walberg, H.J., & Tsai, S. (1984). Reading achievement and diminishing returns to time. *Journal of Educational Psychology, 76,* 442–451.

West, R.F., Stanovich, K.E., & Mitchell, H. (1993). Reading in the real world and its correlates. *Reading Research Quarterly, 28,* 34–51.

Excerpted from *Promoting Reading in Developing Countries, 1996*

Effective Reading Programs

 Diverse Learners and the Tyranny of Time:
Don't Fix Blame; Fix the Leaky Roof

Edward J. Kameenui

Diverse learners and the tyranny of time: Don't fix blame; fix the leaky roof

Kameenui is Associate Dean of the College of Education and Associate Director of the National Center to Improve the Tools of Educators at the University of Oregon, Eugene, Oregon. His research and writing have focused on instructional approaches for special education students and other diverse learners.

I n this commentary, I argue against a single "right" method or approach to literacy instruction. I assert that such a search for the "right" approach to literacy instruction is misguided and takes its greatest toll on students who have diverse learning and curricular needs. Instead, I suggest that diverse learners face on a daily basis the tyranny of time, in which the educational clock is ticking while they remain at risk of falling further and further behind in their schooling. I maintain that we should not spend any more time and effort determining or assigning fault for why diverse youngsters are failing, or which approach is the "right" approach to literacy instruction. Rather, we ought to move forward by designing, implementing, and validating instructional programs and interventions for children with diverse learning and curricular needs. These programs and interventions should not be wedded to any single, "right" instructional method, but instead simply work. To achieve this end, I offer six general pedagogical principles that provide a conceptual framework for guiding educators in the development of literacy programs for diverse learners.

The right method myth

As reading professionals, we have imposed upon ourselves an untenable standard of always searching for the single right best method, process, or approach to literacy development and instruction, especially for children in the formative years of schooling. The search for "rightness" is not unique to reading, nor is it unique to reading educators. It seems to be a peculiar and persistent artifact of human beings, no matter what craft we profess or practice. According to literary folklore, Mark Twain once observed, "The difference between the almost right word and the right word is really a large matter—'tis the difference between the lightning bug and the lightning." In another attempt to discern the rightness of something, the noted physicist Wolfgang Pauli responded to a highly specula-

tive proposal in physics by stating, "It's not even wrong" (Flanagan, 1988, p. 226).

Discerning what is *right*, what is *almost right*, and what's *not even wrong* is an especially troublesome task these days for educators, reading researchers, administrators, publishers, and the international reading community in general. The difficulty rests in part in responding to the unique and diverse needs of learners in the classroom. Evidence of this difficulty can be found in the current debates and discussions about definitions of literacy (Calfee, 1991; Goodman, 1990; McGill-Franzen & Allington, 1991; Rush, Moe, & Storlie, 1986; Venezky, 1990, 1992; Venezky, Wagner, & Ciliberti, 1990), literacy instruc-

tion (Fisher & Hiebert, 1990; Yatvin, 1991), whole language and direct instruction (Chall, 1992; Goodman, 1992; Kameenui, 1988; Liberman & Liberman, 1990; Mather, 1992), beginning reading (Adams, 1990, 1991; Bower, 1992; Chaney, 1991), and diverse learners (Garcia, Pearson, & Jimenez, 1990; Stein, Leinhardt, & Bickel, 1989).

Although such debates are intellectually stimulating, they are often based upon the premise that there is a right approach, philosophy, or method of literacy instruction, something that is unlikely to be empirically established anytime soon, and even less likely to be accepted by reading professionals who hold multiple perspectives and epistemologies. Further, the identification of children as diverse learners itself suggests that *multiple* perspectives and approaches will be necessary to accommodate the needs of children who possess differences in abilities and learning histories, and who will be schooled in various instructional contexts.

The realities of diversity

While many of these debates and discussions about the right approach to literacy development and instruction take place within the professional community of reading educators, they are often distant from the realities of the world outside the reading community.

The identification of children as diverse learners itself suggests that multiple *perspectives and approaches will be necessary to accommodate the needs of children who possess differences in abilities and learning histories, and who will be schooled in various instructional contexts.*

Some of these realities were made stark in a recent article by Hodgkinson (1991) entitled "Reform Versus Reality":

- Since 1987, one-fourth of all preschool children in the U.S. have been in poverty.

- Every year, about 350,000 children are born to mothers who are addicted to cocaine during pregnancy. Those who survive birth become children with strikingly short attention spans, poor coordination, and much worse. Of course, the schools will have to teach these children, and getting such children ready for kindergarten costs around $40,000 each—about the same as for children with fetal alcohol syndrome.
- On any given night, between 50,000 and 200,000 children have no home.
- The "Norman Rockwell" family—a working father, a housewife mother, and two children of school age—constitutes only 6% of U.S. households.
- About one-third of preschool children are destined for school failure because of poverty, neglect, sickness, handicapping conditions, and lack of adult protection and nurturance.

(Hodgkinson, 1991, p. 10)

These facts, according to Hodgkinson, are indicative of education's "leaky roof," a metaphor he uses "for the spectacular changes that have occurred in the nature of the children who come to school" (p. 10).

Hodgkinson's (1991) demographic analysis is reinforced by additional reports in the popular press documenting the plight of diverse learners. For example:

The child poverty rate rose by more than 11% during the 1980s, reaching 17.9% in 1989. Black children were the most likely to fall into this group. In 1989, a black child had a 39.8% chance of living in poverty, a Native American child a 38.8% chance and a Hispanic child a 32.2% chance. The figure for Asian children was 17.1% and for white children 12.5%. ("Poverty Rates Rise," 1992)

Similarly, an advertisement for the Children's Defense Fund reads:

Approximately 2.5 million American children were reported abused or neglected last year ....Fourteeen nations boast smarter 13-years-olds than the United States. ("Children's Defense Fund," 1992)

Hodgkinson (1991) concludes his analysis by offering a poignant soliloquy on the current slings and arrows of education's outrageous fortunes:

There is no point in trying to teach hungry or sick children. From this we can deduce one of the most important points in our attempts to deal with education: *educators can't fix the roof all by themselves.* It will require the efforts of many people and organizations—health and social welfare agencies, parents, business and political leaders—to even begin to repair this leaky roof. There is no time to waste in fixing blame; we need to act to fix the roof. And unless we start, the house will continue to deteriorate, and all Americans will pay the price. (p. 10)

The tyranny of time

Hodgkinson's assertion that *"there is no time to waste in fixing blame; we need to act to fix the roof"* is of particular significance to students who reside in the basement of the house with the leaky roof—children identified as poor readers, reading disabled, at-risk, low performers, mildly disabled, language delayed, and culturally disadvantaged, all of whom have diverse learning and curricular needs. Like literacy, the face of diversity is complex, and at this point, it defies a definition comprised of only the right words (Garcia et al., 1990).

Despite the differences that these children bring to school, what is profoundly and unequivocally the same about them is that they are behind in reading and language development. Moreover, they constantly face the tyranny of time in trying to catch up with their peers, who continue to advance in their literacy development. Simply keeping pace with their peers amounts to losing more and more ground for students who are behind. This predicament has been referred to as the "Matthew effect," a concept resurrected and insightfully applied to reading by Stanovich (1986). According to the Matthew effect, the literacy-rich get richer, and the literacy-poor get poorer in reading opportunities, vocabulary development, written language, general knowledge, and so on.

The pedagogical clock for students who are behind in reading and literacy development continues to tick mercilessly, and the opportunities for these students to advance or catch up diminish over time. Benjamin Bloom (1964) concurred with this general phenomenon almost 30 years ago when he observed that *"growth and development are not in equal units per unit of time"* (p. 204, emphasis added). In other words, not all human characteristics (e.g., height, intelligence, vocabulary) grow at the same rate over time; there are periods of rapid growth and periods of relatively slow growth. Bloom noted what we have now come to accept as a developmental and pedagogical truism: "Although it is not invariably true, the period of most rapid growth is likely to be in the early years and this is then followed by periods of less and less rapid growth" (p. 204).

Evidence of the critical importance of what Bloom (1964) referred to as "the early environment and experience" (p. 214) now appears overwhelming:

- According to a study by Juel (1988), the probability that a child who is a poor reader at the end of Grade 1 will remain a poor reader at the end of Grade 4 is .88. There is a near 90% chance of remaining a poor reader after 3 years of schooling. Juel noted, "Children who did not develop good word recognition skills in first grade began to dislike reading and read considerably less than good readers both in and out of school" (p. 27).

Hodgkinson's assertion that "there is no time to waste in fixing blame; we need to act to fix the roof" *is of particular significance to students who reside in the basement of the house with the leaky roof.*

- Allington's program of research (1980, 1983, 1984) on the opportunities children have to read reveals that the average skilled reader reads almost three times more words than the average less-skilled reader (Stanovich, 1986). Similarly, students identified as mildly handicapped appear to "spend significantly less time engaged in writing and silent reading, and more time passively attending, than do their nonhandicapped peers" (O'Sullivan, Ysseldyke, Christenson, & Thurlow, 1990, p. 143).
- Phonemic awareness and knowledge of letter names that prereaders have upon entering school appear to influence reading acquisition (Adams, 1990; Griffith & Olson, 1992; Stahl, 1992; Williams, 1984). As Adams (1990) states, "In the end, the great value of research on prereaders may lie in the clues it gives us toward determining what the less prepared prereaders need most to learn. For these children, we have not a classroom moment to waste. The evidence strongly suggests that we must help them develop their awareness of the phonemic composition of words" (p. 90).

- The amount of reading that children do outside of school appears to strongly influence reading proficiency (Anderson, Wilson, & Fielding, 1988). However, many children come from homes in which there is very little, if any, preschool language and literacy support (Heath, cited in Adams, 1990).
- Children in Grades 2 and 3 who lack decoding skills and a reasonable base of sight words "may be condemned to school careers marred by increasing distance between them and other children unless successful remediation occurs" (Byrne, Freebody, & Gates, 1992, p. 150).
- Matching classroom instruction with reading abilities appears to be difficult for teachers in general education kindergarten classrooms (Durkin, 1990). Durkin notes, "Use of whole class instruction was the practice even when differences in children's abilities were so great as to be obvious to anyone willing to take but a few minutes to observe. Such differences meant that some children kept hearing what they already knew; for others, the observed lesson was too difficult and proceeded too quickly" (p. 24).

Teacher uncertainty and experimentation in the face of diversity

When this evidence is considered in the context of education's leaky roof, it carries the potential for creating at least two serious problems for reading educators. The first is pedagogical paralysis, which is in part reflected in a teacher's lack of personal teaching efficacy (e.g., "What can I possibly do as one teacher to make a difference?") in the face of a "concentration of low-achieving students" in the classroom (Smylie, 1988, p. 23). In a study of teachers' teaching efficacy, Smylie observed, "The lower the achievement level of students in the class, the less likely teachers seem to be to believe that they can affect student learning, despite the level of confidence they may have in their knowledge and skills related to teaching" (p. 23). The characteristics of the classroom (e.g., class size) and heterogeneity of learners appear to affect teachers' beliefs about their ability to influence student learning (Chard & Kameenui, 1992).

Equally problematic, however, is the tendency for educators to engage in fashionable

experimentation—experimentation that often draws on fad and fashion (Kameenui, 1991; Slavin, 1989)—rather than well-established and documented practice. This kind of experimentation often occurs when teachers are unsure of what to do with children who are behind. As a result, they experiment with practices that leave some children at risk of falling even further behind in their reading and language development. The experimentation reflects teachers' genuine desire to do the best for their children who, they believe, despite their diverse learning and curricular needs, should benefit from the same "literacy events" and reading activities provided more able readers. However, children who are behind because of language, learning, or reading problems *do* require substantially different kinds of *reading experiences*—ones that go beyond those typically provided more able readers (Mather, 1992).

Some have argued that the current emphasis on "whole language" approaches to beginning reading exacts its harshest consequence on students with learning and language difficulties (Liberman & Liberman, 1990; Mather, 1992). Others have called for striking a reasonable balance between whole language and direct instruction (Chall, 1992; Cunningham, 1991). Still others have argued for whole language only (Edelsky, 1990; Goodman, 1992). While the debates about how best to teach beginning reading are age-old, reaching back more than 100 years to the "beginning of pedagogy" (Bower, 1992, p. 138), the current context of education's leaky roof requires that we consider the purpose and consequences of these debates.

Although educators alone cannot fix education's leaky roof, the plight of today's children in society (Garcia et al., 1990; Hodgkinson, 1991) places an unusual burden on schools, teachers, and even professional organizations such as the International Reading Association to get their houses in order. The water from the leaky roof is rising in the basement, and its cost is greatest to students with diverse curricular, learning, and literacy needs. There is not time to waste in fixing blame; we need to act *now* to fix the roof.

Principles for guiding action

The realities that poor readers remain poor readers, that insufficient opportunities to read seriously deter reading progress, and that particular instructional arrangements (e.g., whole-class instruction) fail to promote adequate reading growth set the stage for the reading community to reconsider the needs of students who face pedagogy's ticking clock. The reading experiences required for these students can be derived and constructed from at least six general pedagogical principles (Dixon, Carnine, & Kameenui, 1992). These principles do not prescribe a single method and by no means represent an exhaustive list. Rather, they offer a conceptual framework for informing our decisions about how to develop the early reading and literacy experiences of these students:

1. *Instructional time is a precious commodity; do not lose it.* If a reading strategy, concept, or problem solving analysis can be taught two different ways and one is more efficient, use the more efficient way.

2. *Intervene and remediate early, strategically, and frequently.* The magnitude of growth in the early years for students who are behind is influenced substantially by what we teach and how we teach. As Stanovich (1986) argues, "Educational interventions that represent a *more of the same* approach will probably not be successful....The remedy for the problem must be more of a *surgical strike*" (p. 393). The following applications should be considered:

- Provide children with more frequent opportunities to read.
- Promote instructional arrangements that allow children to actively participate in literacy activities, for example, small group story reading instead of one-to-one or whole-class instruction (Morrow & Smith, 1990).
- Help children develop phonemic awareness and knowledge of letter names early.

3. *Teach less more thoroughly.* The conventional wisdom in working with students who have diverse learning and curricular needs is to teach more in less time (Kameenui, 1990; Kameenui & Simmons, 1990). While the logic of this advice seems reasonable (i.e., children who are behind in conceptual knowledge and skills must be taught more in a shorter period of time in order to catch up), the actual practice of trying to teach more in less time simply ignores the constraints of

teaching. Instead, by selecting and teaching only those objectives that are essential, and by focusing instruction on the most important and most generalizable concepts or strategies (i.e., "big ideas," Calfee, Chambliss, & Beretz, 1991; Carnine & Kameenui, 1992), more can be learned more thoroughly in the limited time available.

4. *Communicate reading strategies in a clear and explicit manner, especially during initial phases of instruction.* For many students with learning problems, new concepts and strategies should be explained in clear, concise, and comprehensible language. Explicit instruction is still most effective for teaching concepts, principles, and strategies to at-risk students.

Children will not automatically bloom by being immersed in a literacy hothouse rich with literacy events and activities.

5. *Guide student learning through a strategic sequence of teacher-directed and student-centered activities.* Teacher-directed instruction is necessary if students are to catch up and advance with their able-reading peers. Children will not automatically bloom by being immersed in a literacy hothouse rich with literacy events and activities. While these activities enrich students' literacy development, they are not sufficient for children who are behind. Teacher-directed instruction need not preempt, minimize, or supplant child-directed activities to develop literacy (Yatvin, 1991). Both sets of activities have their place; however, reading instruction guided by an efficacious teacher is essential. The goal of reading and literacy instruction is to move from teacher-directed to student-centered activities.

6. *Examine the effectiveness of instruction and educational tools by formatively evaluating student progress.* In testimony given on March 18, 1992, to the Select Committee on Education, Kenneth Komoski, Director of the Education Products Information Exchange,

noted educational materials (e.g., print materials, computer software) are used during more than 90% of the 30 billion hours in which America's 40 million students are in school. In many cases, the efficacy of these materials is questionable, despite state laws (e.g., Florida statute 233.25) that require a learner verification and revision process to substantiate their "instructional effectiveness." Teachers must formatively evaluate the effectiveness of their instructional approaches and materials in order to adapt instruction to meet the needs of learners. As a guideline, current research suggests that measuring student performance twice per week provides an adequate basis for instructional decision making (Deno & Fuchs, 1987).

Conclusion

Human beings, like the words they use, are peculiar creatures, idosyncratically possessive of their thoughts and words (Bryson, 1990). Even under ideal circumstances, finding the *right* words is indeed difficult. Unless you are part of Wolfgang Pauli's professional community of physics, selecting the right word in the Twain tradition is risky business. Paradoxically, it seems as though words have gotten in the way of our real goal. The standard of always searching for the single right best method for literacy development may be misguided. The search instead should be for multiple perspectives of rightness guided by the diverse needs of learners and sound instructional principles, practices, and craft knowledge.

Hodgkinson (1991) concludes his analysis of the realities in educational reform by posing two "high-priority" questions—"What can educators do to reduce the number of children 'at risk' in America and to get them achieving well in school settings? And how can educators collaborate more closely with other service providers so that we can all work together toward the urgent goal of providing services to the same client?" (p. 16). Before reading educators can begin to collaborate with "other service providers," they must first collaborate with one another. Our charge is clear, and because the rain won't cease, there is no time to waste; we need to act to fix education's leaky roof. These are the right words; anything less is not even wrong.

This article is based in part on a Visiting Minority Scholar lecture at the University of Wisconsin-Madison, March 19, 1992. The preparation of this paper was supported in part by the National Center to Improve the Tools of Educators (NCITE), Grant H180M10006 from the U.S. Department of Education, Office of Special Education Programs.

References

Adams, M. (1990). *Beginning to read: Thinking and learning about print.* Cambridge, MA: MIT Press.

Adams, M. (1991). Beginning to read: A critique by literacy professionals. *The Reading Teacher, 44,* 371-372.

Allington, R.L. (1980). Poor readers don't get to read much in reading groups. *Language Arts, 57,* 872-876.

Allington, R.L. (1983). The reading instruction provided readers of differing reading abilities. *The Elementary School Journal, 83,* 548-559.

Allington, R.L. (1984). Content coverage and contextual reading in reading groups. *Journal of Reading Behavior, 16,* 85-96.

Anderson, R.C., Wilson, P.T., & Fielding, L.G. (1988). Growth in reading and how children spend their time outside of school. *Reading Research Quarterly, 23,* 285-303.

Bloom, B.S. (1964). *Stability and change in human characteristics.* New York: Wiley.

Bower, B. (1992). Reading the code, reading the whole: Researchers wrangle over the nature and teaching of reading. *Science News, 141*(9), 138-141.

Bryson, B. (1990). *The mother tongue: English and how it got that way.* New York: Morrow.

Byrne, B., Freebody, P., & Gates, A. (1992). Longitudinal data on the relations of word-reading strategies to comprehension, reading time, and phonemic awareness. *Reading Research Quarterly, 27,* 141-151.

Calfee, R. (1991). What schools can do to improve literacy instruction. In B. Means, C. Chelemer, & M.S. Knapp (Eds.), *Teaching advanced skills to at-risk students* (pp. 176-203). San Francisco: Jossey-Bass.

Calfee, R.C., Chambliss, M.J., & Beretz, M.M. (1991). Organizing for comprehension and composition. In W. Ellis (Ed.), *All language and the creation of literacy.* Baltimore, MD: Orton Dyslexia Society, Inc.

Carnine, D., & Kameenui, E.J. (1992). *Higher order thinking: Designing curriculum for mainstreamed students.* Austin, TX: Pro-Ed.

Chall, J. (1992, May). *Whole language and direct instruction models: Implications for teaching reading in the schools.* Paper presented at the meeting of the International Reading Association, Orlando, FL.

Chaney, J.H. (1991). Beginning to read: A critique by literacy professionals. *The Reading Teacher, 44,* 374-375.

Chard, D.J., & Kameenui, E.J. (1992). *Instructional efficacy: Toward a specification of efficacy research.* Monograph Number 3, Project PREPARE. Eugene, OR: University of Oregon.

Children's Defense Fund. (1992, July). *SV Entertainment,* p. 13.

Cunningham, P. (1991). *What kind of phonics instruction will we have?* Paper presented at the National Reading Conference, Palm Springs, CA.

Deno, S., & Fuchs, L. (1987). Developing curriculum-based measurement systems for data-based special education problem solving. *Focus on Exceptional Children, 19*(8), 1-16.

Dixon, R., Carnine, D.W., & Kameenui, E.J. (1992). *Curriculum guidelines for diverse learners.* Monograph for National Center to Improve the Tools of Educators. Eugene, OR: University of Oregon.

Durkin, D. (1990). Matching classroom instruction with reading abilities: An unmet need. *Remedial and Special Education, 11*(3), 23-28.

Edelsky, C. (1990). Whose agenda is this anyway? A response to McKenna, Robinson, and Miller. *Educational Researcher, 19*(8), 7-11.

Fisher, C.W., & Hiebert, E.H. (1990). Characteristics of tasks in two approaches to literacy instruction. *The Elementary School Journal, 91*, 3-18.

Flanagan, D. (1988). *Flanagan's version: A spectator's guide to science on the eve of the 21st century.* New York: Vintage.

Garcia, G.E., Pearson, P.D., & Jimenez, R.T. (1990). *The at risk dilemma: A synthesis of reading research.* Champaign, IL: University of Illinois, Reading Research and Education Center.

Goodman, K. (May, 1992). *Whole language and direct instruction models: Implications for teaching reading in the schools.* Paper presented at the meeting of the International Reading Association, Orlando, FL.

Goodman, Y.M. (Ed.). (1990). *How children construct literacy.* Newark, DE: International Reading Association.

Griffith, P.L., & Olson, M.W. (1992). Phonemic awareness helps beginning readers break the code. *The Reading Teacher, 45*, 516-523.

Hodgkinson, H. (1991). Reform versus reality. *Phi Delta Kappan, 73*, 9-16.

Juel, C. (1988, April). *Learning to read and write: A longitudinal study of fifty-four children from first through fourth grade.* Paper presented at the annual meeting of the American Educational Research Association, New Orleans, LA.

Kameenui, E.J. (1988). Direct instruction and the Great Twitch: Why DI or di is not the issue. In J.R. Readence & S. Baldwin (Eds.), *Dialogues in literacy research: Thirty-seventh yearbook of the National Reading Conference* (pp. 39-45). Chicago, IL: National Reading Conference.

Kameenui, E.J. (1990). The language of the REI—Why it's hard to put into words: A response to Durkin and Miller. *Remedial and Special Education, 11*(3), 57-59.

Kameenui, E.J. (1991). Guarding against the false and fashionable. In J.F. Baumann & D.D. Johnson (Eds.), *Writing for publication in reading and language arts* (pp. 17-28). Newark, DE: International Reading Association.

Kameenui, E.J., & Simmons, D.C. (1990). *Designing instructional strategies: The prevention of academic learning problems.* Columbus, OH: Merrill.

Liberman, A., & Liberman, I. (1990). Whole language vs. code emphasis: Underlying assumptions and their implications for reading instruction. *Annals of Dyslexia, 40*, 52-76.

Mather, N. (1992). Whole language reading instruction for students with learning disabilities: Caught in the cross fire. *Learning Disabilities Research & Practice, 7*, 87-95.

McGill-Franzen, A., & Allington, R.L. (1991). Every child's right: Literacy. *The Reading Teacher, 45*, 86-90.

Morrow, L.M., & Smith, J.K. (1990). The effect of group size on interactive storybook reading. *Reading Research Quarterly, 25*, 213-231.

O'Sullivan, P.J., Ysseldyke, J.E., Christenson, S.L., & Thurlow, M.L. (1990). Mildly handicapped elementary students' opportunity to learn during reading instruction in mainstream and special education settings. *Reading Research Quarterly, 25*, 131-146.

Poverty rates rise. (1992, July). *Time*, p. 15.

Rush, R.T., Moe, A.J., & Storlie, R.L. (1986). *Occupational literacy education.* Newark, DE: International Reading Association.

Slavin, R. (1989). PET and the pendulum: Faddism in education and how to stop it. *Phi Delta Kappan, 90*, 750-758.

Smylie, M.A. (1988). The enhancement function of staff development: Organizational and psychological antecedents to individual teacher change. *American Educational Research Journal, 25*, 1-30.

Stahl, S.A. (1992). Saying the "p" word: Nine guidelines for exemplary phonics instruction. *The Reading Teacher, 45*, 618-625.

Stanovich, K.E. (1986). Matthew effects in reading: Some consequences of individual differences in the acquisition of literacy. *Reading Research Quarterly, 21*, 360-407.

Stein, M.K., Leinhardt, G., & Bickel, W. (1989). Instructional issues for teaching students at risk. In R.E. Slavin, N.L. Kesweit, & N.A. Madden (Eds.), *Effective programs for students at risk* (pp. 145-194). Boston: Allyn & Bacon.

Venezky, R.L. (1990). Definitions of literacy. In R.L. Venezky, D.A. Wagner, & B.S. Ciliberti (Eds.), *Toward defining literacy* (pp. 2-16). Newark, DE: International Reading Association.

Venezky, R.L. (1992, Summer). Matching literacy testing with social policy: What are the alternatives? *Connections.* Philadelphia, PA: National Center on Adult Literacy, University of Pennsylvania.

Venezky, R.L., Wagner, D.A., & Ciliberti, B.S. (Eds.). (1990). *Toward defining literacy.* Newark, DE: International Reading Association.

Williams, J.P. (1984). Phonemic analysis and how it relates to reading. *Journal of Learning Disabilities, 17*, 240-245.

Yatvin, J. (1991). *Developing a whole language program for a whole school.* Richmond, VA: Virginia State Reading Association.

From *The Reading Teacher, Vol. 46, No. 5, February 1993*

(Acknowledgments, continued from page 2)

Stephen Krensky: The History of the English Language," by Stephen Krensky. Copyright ©1996 by Stephen Krensky. He is the author of over fifty books for children, including *The Iron Dragon Never Sleeps* (Delacorte Press), *Breaking Into Print* (Little, Brown and Company) and *Striking It Rich* (Simon & Schuster). No part of this material may be reproduced in whole or part without the express written permission of the author or his agent.

Dr. G. Reid Lyon: "Statement of Dr. G. Reid Lyon - Before the Committee on Labor and Human Resources (April 28, 1998)," by Dr. G. Reid Lyon, Chief of Child Development and Behavior Branch, National Institute of Child Health and Human Development, National Institutes of Health, Bethesda, MD. Reprinted by permission of the author.

National Academy Press: Excerpted from *Preventing Reading Difficulties in Young Children*, edited by Catherine E. Snow, M. Susan Burns and Peg Griffin. Copyright ©1998 by the National Academy of Sciences. Courtesy of the National Academy Press, Washington, D.C. Reprinted by permission of the publisher.

National Council of Teachers of English: "Why Do They Get It on Friday and Misspell It on Monday?" by Charlene Gill and Patricia L. Scharer, in *Language Arts*, Vol. 73, February 1996 issue. Copyright ©1996 by the National Council of Teachers of English. Reprinted with permission of the publisher.

The Ohio State University, College of Education: "Repeated Reading: A Strategy for Enhancing Fluency and Fostering Expertise," by Irene H. Blum and Patricia S. Koskinen from *Theory Into Practice*, Vol. 30, No. 3, Summer 1991. Copyright ©1991 by the College of Education, The Ohio State University. Reprinted by permission of the authors and The Ohio State University.

PRO-ED: "Developing Syntactic Sensitivity in Reading Through Phrase-cued Texts," by Timothy V. Rasinski from *Intervention in School and Clinic,* Vol. 29, no. 3, January 1994 issue. Copyright ©1994 by PRO-ED, Inc. Reprinted by permission of the publisher.

Scholastic Inc.: "Why Direct Spelling Instruction Is Important," by Barbara Foorman, in *Scholastic Spelling: Research Paper*, Vol. 2, 1997 issue. Copyright ©1997 by Scholastic Inc. Reprinted by permission of the publisher.

Teachers College Press: "Questioning the Author: An Approach to Developing Meaningful Classroom Discourse," by Margaret G. McKeown, Isabel L. Beck, and Cheryl A. Sandora. Reprinted by permission of the publisher from Graves, M. F., Taylor, B., & van den Broek, P. (Eds.), *The First R: Every Child's Right to Read* (New York: Teachers College Press, ©1996 by Teachers College, Columbia University. All rights reserved.), pp. 97-119.

Joseph K. Torgesen and Patricia Mathes: "What Every Teacher Should Know About Phonological Awareness," by Joseph K. Torgesen and Patricia Mathes, Florida State University. Reprinted by permission of the authors.

PHOTO CREDITS

B.A. Shaywitz, et al., p. 38, Yale Medical School; Kim Hairston: Sun Staff, p. 39; Richard Mei, p. 39